GLYPH 4

Vicki Souillet
New Haven 1979

GLYPH

JOHNS HOPKINS TEXTUAL STUDIES

4

THE JOHNS HOPKINS UNIVERSITY PRESS
Baltimore and London

This book has been brought to publication with the generous assistance of the Andrew W. Mellon Foundation.

The Johns Hopkins University Press, Baltimore, Maryland 21218
The Johns Hopkins Press Ltd., London
Library of Congress Catalog Card Number 76–47370
ISBN 0–8018–2143–6 (hardcover)   ISBN 0–8018–2151–7 (paperback)

STATEMENT TO CONTRIBUTORS

The Editors of *Glyph* welcome submissions concerned with the problems of representation and textuality, and contributing to the confrontation between American and Continental critical scenes. Contributors should send *two* copies of their manuscripts, accompanied by return postage, to Samuel Weber, Editor, *Glyph*, Humanities Center, The Johns Hopkins University, Baltimore, Maryland 21218. In preparing manuscripts, please refer to *A Manual of Style*, published by the University of Chicago Press, and *The Random House Dictionary*. The entire text, including extended citations and notes, should be double-spaced.

Copies of *Glyph*, both hardbound and paperback may be ordered from The Johns Hopkins University Press, Baltimore, Maryland 21218.

The illustration on the cover and title page, an Egyptian crocodile from the Ptolemaic period executed in black and red ink on papyrus, is reproduced through the courtesy of the Walters Art Gallery, Baltimore.

CONTENTS

GLYPH 4

ONE

IT
Samuel Weber

ANYONE having had the occasion of translating or otherwise transposing theoretical discussions from a foreign language into our own will sooner or later be struck by what appears to be a remarkable terminological deficiency of English with respect to other Indo-European languages. One, if not indeed *the* most fundamental, operation of theoretical thinking seems to lack a precise English equivalent. What in German is designated as "*erkennen,*" and in French as "*connaître,*" the act or process of "coming-to-know," has no precise corresponding verb in English. As a noun, of course, *connaissance* or *Erkenntnis* may be translated as cognition, or, less accurately, as knowledge (which is less accurate inasmuch as both French and German make a distinction between *Erkenntnis/ connaissance*, as the immediate effects of the cognitive process, and *Wissen/savoir*, as the more sedimented store of knowledge—a distinction that the English word tends to collapse). What seems to be missing, by contrast, is the ability of English to render the active process of cognition itself, as opposed to its substantive results. And the fact that the *OED* lists words such as "cognize" or "cognosce" is, in view of their restricted use, more a sign of the problem than of its solution.

Confronted with this situation, the translator will probably have to settle for a compromise, in particular if he wishes to retain the relatively familiar connotations of *erkennen* or *connaître*, which, apart from their

Samuel Weber

use in philosophical discourse, are entirely commonplace, household words. That compromise will doubtless be the word: *recognize*.

Like most compromises, this will not be an entirely satisfying solution, not at least for a scrupulous translator. For if *recognition* does have the virtue of rendering the cognitive process in familiar language, upon second thought that language may appear to be just a little *too* familiar. Instead of designating an act, the very essence of which seems to be a kind of discovery, the English word, by adding the prefix "re-," suggests that what is involved is not simply the discovery of something new, but rather the repetition of something already known and familiar. You do not "recognize" a person or a thing for the first time, but only after you have already come to know him or it. In other words, the English word tends to obscure the distinction between the original act and its subsequent repetition, between *Erkennen* and *connaître*, on the one hand, and *Wiedererkennen* and *reconnaître* on the other. And in philosophical or theoretical questions, where precision and accuracy are of the utmost importance, such an obfuscation or distortion is bound to be a cause for concern.

Is it merely making a virtue out of necessity to point out that such concern is as old as Western philosophy itself, a fact that tends to indicate that what is at stake here is perhaps not simply limited to a merely terminological deficiency of a particular "natural" language? From the Socratic doctrine of anamnesis to the Hegelian notion of *Er-Innerung*, the problematic relation of cognition to recognition has been one of the most powerful motifs of Western thought.

We can, however, if we prefer, rely upon the more immediate and narrower sphere of our individual experience in order to arrive at the problem. Any act of intellection, such as perception, conception, or interpretation, entailing the identification of an object, must include two distinct, if interdependent operations. There must be contact made with something new, different, something other than what has previously been presented to our minds. But at the same time, for the process of identification to take place, for us to apprehend anything as a determinate object, as a "this" and not a "that," that something new must be assimilated, compared, put into relation to things already known, to the familiar.

Once we have identified an object, determined it as a "such and such," it has ceased to be something entirely foreign, has lost a portion of its newness, its otherness, and has, to some extent, been integrated into our existing systems of thought and action. To come-to-know something, in short, is never a self-contained, singular occurrence: it necessarily entails and presupposes a process of repetition. There are thus good reasons for asserting that the English *recognition* is, in fact, the most accurate rendering of the process of coming-to-know.

All this is nothing new. As I have indicated, the problem and its implications have constituted one of the major occupations and preoccupations of Western thought from its inception. Why preoccupation? Because, thought out to its conclusion, this dependency of cognition upon recognition has some rather unsettling implications. Thus, it is not insignificant that the Socratic doctrine of anamnesis is generally considered to be more "mythological" or "allegorical" than properly philosophical. For once we have conceded that our knowledge, our coming-to-know presupposes a prior knowing, it is difficult to *know* where to stop. And yet, if we cannot know where to stop, then the very notion of knowledge itself becomes questionable. If the *re-* of recognition cannot be grounded in an original, self-contained cognition, then there are no reasonable grounds for asserting that cognition itself—that is, true knowing—is possible. Instead, we are faced with an intrinsically open-ended process of repetition: the cognitive act can only accede to its object by reproducing an earlier cognition, which itself is only related to *its* object through another repetition of an earlier cognitive act . . . and so on.

Much of Western philosophy, from the Platonic theory of ideas, to Kant's transcendental deduction of the categories, to the Hegelian speculative dialectic, can be seen as an effort to master the implications of what Hegel himself called this "schlechte Unendlichkeit"—this "bad infinitude."

Why bad? Does this evaluation merely reflect the problem of the professional philosopher, whose legitimation presupposes the possibility of more or less rigorous knowledge? One need only recur to our own everyday lives to become aware that what is at stake here involves much more than the authority of the philosopher. Every value-judgment, indeed every judgment itself, our very ability to act, to cope with the most ordinary, most trivial, but also with the more important problems that confront us daily, all depend upon our taking for granted what those philosophers, throughout a large part of their history, were endeavoring to demonstrate: the possibility of a perception, a cognition, an interpretation, that would be reliable, in the sense of its reproducing not simply another perception, cognition, interpretation—but the object itself.

Thus, the exasperation manifested by Aristotle, railing against the Sophists, against their sceptical denial of the possibility of objectively grounded judgments, is symptomatic of a problem, the consequences of which transcend by far the narrow bounds of philosophy itself:

Thus, then, it is in the highest degree evident that neither any one of those who maintain this view nor any one else is really in this position. For why does a man walk to Megara instead of staying at home when he thinks he ought to be walking there? Why does he not walk early some morning into a well or over a precipice, if one happens to be in his way? Why do we observe him guarding against this, if he really considers that falling in is both good and not good? Evidently, then, he judges one thing to be better and another worse. And if this is so, he must also judge one thing to be a man and another to be not-a-man, one thing to be sweet and another to be not-sweet. . . . Therefore, as it seems, all men make unqualified judgments, if not about all things, still about what is better and worse. And if this is not knowledge but opinion, they should be all the more anxious about the truth. . . . (*Metaphysics*, IV, 1008b)[1]

Confronted with this argument, however, the Sophists would hardly have been at a loss for an answer. "Of course," they might have replied, "we are continually choosing to do one thing and not another, preferring one thing to something else. But such *facts* can hardly be adduced as evidence or proof of the possibility of objective truth, or of its knowability. And if the argument of impending danger can be used to make us 'all the more anxious about the truth,' this only indicates that the belief in truth may well be an effort to cope with anxiety, not an objectively grounded cognition."

Protagoras, who is reported to have taught his pupils—his *paying* pupils—to perfect their mastery of language, argument, and of the manipulation of *opinion*, would not have denied the *force* of the arguments brought forward by Aristotle; he would only have questioned whether that force was grounded in objective knowledge. Which is perhaps why it was not so much truth that Protagoras is said to have treated in his writings, but rather such topics as contradiction, refutation, ambition, and struggle.

II

All this is familiar in philosophy and, mutatis mutandis, has been so ever since the *Sophist*; also ever since the Sophists, and no one will be astonished when I observe that they haunt our present debate, as more than one sign shall indicate.[1]

The writer is Jacques Derrida, and the "present debate,"[2] the one he and John Searle have recently engaged, apropos of Derrida's reading of Austin, the founder of speech act theory. For Searle, Derrida misreads Austin so crassly that a confrontation between the two in fact "never quite takes place." Derrida agrees—and there is little else that the two can agree on—but he does so for reasons very different from those of Searle.

But perhaps we should begin at the beginning, which in this case seems to be the central notion developed by Derrida in his reading of Austin, and which is termed "iterability." The term is introduced in order to call into question what Derrida considers the proton pseudos of speech act theory, namely, the assumption that language takes place in and through a series of individual, singular, self-contained events or acts. Before we elaborate Derrida's notion of iterability, however, let us first review Searle's use of it. He seems to accept the notion, while drawing from it conclusions very different from those of the French thinker. This is how Searle describes the function of iterability in language:

The performances of actual speech acts . . . are indeed events, datable singular events in particular historical contexts. But as events they have some very peculiar properties. They are capable of communicating from speakers to hearers an infinite number of different contents. . . . Furthermore, hearers are able to understand this infinite number of possible communications simply by recognizing the intentions of the speakers in the performances of the speech acts.[3]

Searle concludes that if speakers and hearers are able to understand each other, to "recognize" the intentions of the other—and such recognition comprises the essence of understanding for Searle—it is because they both are "masters of the sets of rules we call the rules of language, and these rules are recursive. They allow for the repeated application of the same rule."[4]

For Searle, then, the iterability of language consists in those "rules of language" which "allow" for their "repeated application" while at the same time remaining identical to themselves. It is this constant self-identity of the rules that renders the act of cognition both possible and, in essence, a *simple* process ("Hearers are able to understand . . . *simply* by recognizing . . ."), which can and must be realized, and hence observed, in "datable singular events."

If Searle can thus conceive of language in terms of a repetition that is ultimately understood to be repetition of the same (of the same rules, namely), it is because of an assumption that he makes without apparently being aware that he is assuming anything at all. Searle assumes that language functions, in *fact* but also in *principle*, as a means and medium of communication, through which meanings and intentions are conveyed from one subject to another according to (intuitively learned) rules of the language-game. This determination of language as a means of communication, something which Searle seems to regard as the simple (theoretical) reproduction of a state of affairs rather than as an interpretation, allows him to subordinate linguistic repetition to something that he claims to be logically anterior to that repetition, since it renders such repetition possible: the rules that constitute the language-game. What Searle never seems to question, however, is that the name of the game, its purpose and function, could be anything other than the conveyance of meaning in various forms and to various ends. Language *is*, in this view, speaking meaningfully; and if speakers and hearers follow the rules without being fully aware of them, speech act theory emerges here as the elevation of those rules to full self-consciousness.

No wonder, then, that Searle accuses Derrida of misunderstanding and of misstating Austin's position, and that this accusation is meant as a full disqualification. For Searle's conception of iterability as repetition of the same implies that understanding is both simply possible and simply opposed to misunderstanding. Need it be emphasized that such a conviction is by no means the exclusive property of the author of *Speech Acts*, who in this respect as in many others demonstrates himself to be representative not merely of a notable current of contemporary thought, but of the opinions of the majority of his contemporaries, independently of their professional affiliations.

If, however, this is how Searle understands the notion of iterability, it can justifiably be asked whether or not he has "understood" it *properly*, in the sense in which he himself understands "understanding": namely, as the adequate reproduction or recognition of the meaning intended by the term. Of course, Searle is free to reinterpret or redefine this term in any way he sees fit, but as a first step it would seem necessary for him to have accurately reproduced the meaning the term originally intended.

In order to determine the extent to which this has occurred, let us recall how iterability is described in "Signature Ev⌐nt Context" (a text to which I shall henceforth refer, for purposes of convenience, by the nickname given it in its sequel, "Limited Inc": *Sec*). This description takes place in two steps, the first of which being as follows:

Let us say that a certain self-identity of this element (mark, sign, etc.) is required to permit its recognition and repetition. Through empirical variations of tone, voice, etc., possibly of a certain accent, for example, we must be able to recognize the identity, roughly speaking, of a signifying form. . . .[5]

In order for a mark to function, it must be recognized—that is, repeated. It is only in and through such repetition, which includes "empirical variations" of all kinds, that the identity of the mark constitutes itself as that which stays the same and is recognized as such. This first step of the argument is phenomenological in character, and it indicates why no act of recognition, and no "identity" depending upon such an act, can ever be simply or essentially empirical: identification entails what Husserl calls "idealization," that is, a repetitive process of recognition. But if this first step is phenomenological, the second is it no longer:

The unity of the signifying form only constitutes itself by virtue of its iterability, by the possibility of its being repeated in the absence not only of its "referent," which is self-evident, but in the absence of a determinate signified or of the intention of actual signification.[6]

Derrida's inflection of repetition here can be situated with respect to our discussion of recognition: if identity is a product of recognition, and hence of repetition, there is no consistent possibility of recognizing an identity independent of and prior to such repetition. Repetition will always exceed, qua possibility, its determination in terms of an object that is unique and self-contained. Whether it is made explicit or not, acknowledged or not, such determination will always, necessarily, be constituted in this repetition. And this holds not simply for identification of an object, but for the structure of *consciousness* that such an object implies:

Intention or attention, directed towards something iterable [and, inasmuch as it seeks to identify, consciousness will always be directed towards something iterable] will strive or tend in vain to actualize or fulfill itself, for it cannot [be] totally present to its object and to itself. It is divided and deported in advance . . . from itself. This re-move makes its movement possible.[7]

Iterability, then, is what, for Derrida at least, precludes consciousness from ever becoming fully conscious of its object or of itself. If something must be iterable in order to become an object of consciousness, then it can never be entirely grasped, having already been split in and by its being-repeated (or more precisely: by its *repeated being*). To understand anything, or as Searle puts it, "simply to recognize" anything, becomes—despite its apparent simplicity, or rather precisely because of it—an impossible project: recognition can never be simple, nor understanding undivided. We can choose to ignore or to forget iterability, but never to comprehend it fully.

From this argument two highly interesting consequences may be deduced. First of all, if iterability makes recognition and understanding possible, it also makes them possible only as forms of misrecognition or misunderstanding, since the object recognized or understood will never be fully present to consciousness, nor entirely identical to itself. This, of course, endows the notion of "misunderstanding" with a status quite different from that traditionally ascribed to it, as long as it is considered to be simply the opposite or other of understanding. As an ineluctable aspect of iterability, misunderstanding no longer excludes understanding (an example of this might be glimpsed in those slips and errors studied by Freud in the *Psychopathology of Everyday Life,* about which Theodor Adorno once wrote that they are the means by which the incommunicable is communicated). We should not therefore precipitously condemn such a revaluation of misunderstanding as mere sophistry or as excessively abstract, however unfamiliar it may be to our ingrained habits of thought.

Samuel Weber

On the other hand—and this brings me to the *second* consequence—
the argument of iterability entails a peculiar and paradoxical difficulty,
even if it is granted that it effectively exposes certain inconsistencies in
theories of language and thought based upon what I have called the
simple notion of repetition as repetition of the same. This difficulty may
be formulated as follows: in order to speak about something called
iterability, we must name it, identify it, describe it, and thereby treat it
as though it were an object. In other words, we must conceive it in a way
that it itself seems to call into question. If it is to disrupt and to decenter
every effort to determine the mark, or to portray an utterance as an act
or individual occurrence, it can only produce those disruptive effects by
itself being made an object of thought. To the extent to which such an
object can never be simply identified with the empirical cases it makes
possible (and simultaneously disrupts), and yet must also be conceived,
it will ineluctably begin to resemble something like a transcendental
category. The severity of this problem can be sensed in the disclaimers
that recur with increasing frequency in the latter half of "Limited Inc."
For instance:

Iterability is . . . not a transcendental condition of possibility. . . . It is neither
an essence nor a substance to be distinguished from phenomena, attributes,
or accidents. . . .[8]

If such precautionary statements are necessary, it is because it is easier to
say what iterability is *not*, than what it *is*. For

the unique character of this structure of iterability . . . renders the project of
idealization possible without lending itself to any pure, simple, and idealizable
conceptualization.[9]

In other words, it must be made an *object of thought,* if we are to know
or to say anything concerning its effects, and yet at the same time it must
not be made—in any simple sense at least—an *object of comprehension.*
It must be *conceived* without being (fully) *conceptualized*: something
that is easier said than done.

The difficulty of this task suggests why the "defense" of iterability
against a certain kind of misunderstanding—construing it as repetition
of the same—cannot entail simply the elaboration and clarification of an
insight, the validity of which has been established, once and for all. To
defend iterability against a particular misunderstanding is also, and
above all, to assert the ineluctability of misunderstanding in general:

The *mis-* of those misunderstandings to which we have succumbed, or to
which each of us here accuses the other of having succumbed, must have its
essential condition of possibility in the structure of marks, of remarkable
marks. . . .[10]

—in the "structure of iterability," in short. And yet what distinguishes that "structure" is precisely what makes it both more and less than a structure in the conventional sense: "for it comports an internal and impure limit that prevents it from being identified, synthesized, or re-appropriated. . . ."[11] This "internal and impure limit" is what makes iterability not simply a *term* designating an object that is self-contained, structured in and of itself, but rather "itself" a mark, a divided and divisive part of a movement that no one term can decisively determine, i.e., *terminate*. This is why this particular term refers not so much to a "structure" as to a "chain, since iterability can be supplemented by a variety of terms. . . ."[12] And "can be supplemented" here should perhaps read: "Must be substituted," if it is to avoid the paradoxical fate of becoming, itself, another form of repetition of the same, even as it seeks to delineate "the logic that ties repetition to alterity."

This is perhaps the point, however, to interrupt the discussion for a moment in order to introduce a modification that may serve to simplify matters considerably. I propose to invoke a venerable and characteristically American custom in henceforth referring to iterability by what might be considered its nickname: *it*. Aside from the obvious advantages of brevity, convenience, and economy, this innovation is, in fact, nothing more than a consolidation of established procedure. For instance, that of calling "Signature Event Context" *Sec*; indeed, wherever it has been a question of describing or determining iterability at any length, the use of this nickname has inevitably imposed itself ("It is neither an essence nor a substance . . .," "it comports an internal and impure limit that prevents it from being identified," etc.). Here, then, as elsewhere, the use of a nickname can be taken as the sign of a certain *familiarity*, if not necessarily either of intimacy or of affection. And if such a shift, from what has resembled a noun to what seems more like a pronoun, may at times introduce an element of uncertainty as to what is *really meant*, the reader can doubtless be trusted to make the necessary discriminations and to draw the required conclusions.

Returning now to the problem at hand, perhaps one way of getting at it is by contrasting the manner in which Searle and Derrida conceive the *object* of their investigation in relation to what they both call *strategy*. Strategy, for Searle, designates precisely a means of *getting at*: at an *object*—the language-game—that is determined in and of itself. For instance, once he has summed up what he holds to be Derrida's arguments, Searle immediately poses the crucial question:

In order *to get at* what is wrong with these arguments let us begin by asking *what is it exactly that distinguishes written from spoken language. Is it*

Samuel Weber

iterability, the repeatability of the linguistic elements? Clearly not. . . .[13]
[italics mine]

Searle's matter-of-factness reflects his conviction that what is at stake, the object under discussion, is precisely *a matter-of-fact:* "spoken" vs. "written language." Such a conviction can be stated in matter-of-fact fashion because Searle can count on its being shared by many, if not most, of his readers. The *fact* to which Searle thus appeals is the *belief* of most persons that they know *when* they are speaking seriously and when not, even if they do not know just *how* they accomplish this. Most of us know—or in any case, want to think we know (for reasons that Aristotle may already have indicated)—*what* we are doing and *why,* and it is this that makes it tempting to take language, and things in general, *for granted.* What Searle appeals to, and at the same time reproduces, is a certain *consensus,* a certain consciousness about language, not merely about *what language is,* but more fundamentally, *that language is:* namely, a self-contained, identifiable object, something that can be *grasped* and comprehended. Terms like "standard," "normally," and the like serve to strengthen this appeal: they are invoked as though they were univocal, whereas in fact they function precisely equivocally, to merge consciousness with object, fact with essence. The "fact" that most persons think—or would like to think—that they know what they are doing when they use language, and that language is therefore in essence a means of communication, is what enables the assumption that language *is,* in *fact* and in *essence,* such a means, to pass for self-evident. The matter-of-fact alluded to, which in *fact* is evidence only of a *state-of-mind,* is held to pertain to language itself.

This explains why for Searle *strategy* can be regarded merely as a means for *getting at* an object that, itself, is deemed to be already constituted. Strategic decisions, such as Austin's to exclude "parasitic" forms of discourse from his investigation, which is nevertheless intended to lead to a theory of *language itself,* has consequently for Searle no wider ontological (or as he puts it, "metaphysical") implications: they merely follow the logic of the object itself.

It is precisely this conception of strategy as an essentially heuristic device that prevents Searle from understanding Derrida's "blinking quasi-concepts," and

the strategic reasons that have motivated the choice of this word [viz. grapheme] to designate "something" which is no longer tied to writing in the traditional sense any more than it is to speech or to any other type of mark.[14]

The strategic use of language—and can there be any other?—does not respond to a self-identical object that it seeks to designate, but rather to a *conflict,* a relation of forces, the stability of which is always more or less precarious. If the status of "writing" becomes—at a certain time, in a certain place—a privileged object of this strategy, what is involved is not simply an empirical phenomenon, "writing itself," but a *mode of interpretation* in which the *determination of writing* has played a significantly ambivalent role. The general or generic *name* of this strategy is, of course, "deconstruction," and it is no accident if its procedure is described, very schematically, towards the end of *Sec*:

> Very schematically: an opposition of metaphysical concepts . . . is never the confrontation of two terms, but a hierarchy and the order of a subordination. Deconstruction cannot be restricted or immediately pass to a neutralization: it must, through a double gesture, a double science, a double writing––put into practice a *reversal* of the classical opposition and a general *displacement* of the system. It is on that condition alone that deconstruction will provide the means of *intervening* in the field of oppositions it criticizes and that is also a field of non-discursive forces.[15]

Thus, in focussing upon writing, it was precisely not writing *itself* that comprised the object of the strategy of deconstruction, but rather the conceptual and axiological system of "Metaphysics," which endeavored to impose itself by arguing that things such as "writing itself" did in fact exist—i.e., by determining "Being" as "Presence," and its own operation as (merely) a Repetition of the Same. The strategy of deconstruction was to repeat this repetition as rigorously as possible, and in so doing to demonstrate how its Sameness necessarily entailed an element of alterity that could neither be entirely excluded from nor fully integrated into the system. If the latter sought to determine that Other within the structure of an opposition, and thus to put it in its place, the strategy of deconstruction pointed out the ambivalence of such an effort of determination.

In the case of Austin, for instance, the apparently neutral exclusion of non-serious and parasitic forms of discourse—admitted none the less to constitute a permanent possibility of language—from the object under consideration, is demonstrated to be the indispensable condition for construing language to be an *act* that can be situated in a "total context" (Austin), as a "singular, datable event" (Searle). For speech to be individualized and context totalized in this way, language must be considered as the actualization or fulfillment of consciousness; it is just such a process that the exclusion of non-serious discourse, in which such fulfillment is most obviously problematic, is designed to establish as the "normal," "standard," and above all *essential* case of language. In this perspective, the discussion of Condillac and Husserl with which *Sec* begins is concerned not so much with what writing *is*, as with what consciousness, with regard to language, is *not*—and why. If writing is traditionally characterized as the specific form of language able to function in the absence of the author or intended receivers, this purportedly *distinctive* feature is shown to be presupposed by the mark *in general*. The deconstructive strategy of repetition, here as elsewhere, proceeds by what might be called—paraphrasing *Sec*—the *disruptive, de-generative force of generalization:* the supposedly *distinctive* feature is demonstrated to be the *general* condition of that under which it was seemingly subsumed. The "radical absence of every empirically determined receiver in general"[16] becomes what characterizes not merely the written mark, but the mark in general as its structural condition of possibility. At the same time, what this "condition" designates is—first and foremost—a *certain* form of *impossibility*. Thus, when Searle takes that "radical absence" to mean the *actual* absence of the subject (of the author, readers, etc.), he substitutes an empirically determinable absence for what is meant to indicate that which inevitably *eludes* each and every determination. Far from designating the simple (physical or spiritual) absence of the subject, "radical absence" points to the fact that no act of understanding, no understanding *as* act, can ever exhaust the meaning of a mark nor account for the process that renders it (*it*) possible.

In this context, "Limited Inc" cites the phrase of Nietzsche, "I have forgotten my umbrella," in order to demonstrate that "a thousand possibilities will always remain open even if one understands something in this phrase that makes sense."[17] Understood strategically, as a response to Searle's notion of understanding both as the reproduction of authorial intention and as the essential function of the mark, the thrust of the assertion is to underscore that the function of language cannot be defined in terms of its intelligibility. "Strategy" here implies that no assertion can ever be taken simply at face-value, for it will have been determined not by a "total context," but by a *context of conflict*. Where there is strategy, then, there will also be polemics, even if they are not always as manifest as in the texts we are discussing.

And yet, if the strategic function of an utterance will always make it say something other than what it means to say, something that can never be entirely grasped by any act of understanding, that excess, remainder, left-over (*restance*), will in turn never be *simply in-determinate*. Of those "thousand possibilities" that "will *always* remain open," *some* will *always* remain *more open*, more pressing, more interesting than *others*. It is precisely this more-or-less, this *relative determination*, that makes strategy in a certain sense inevitable, and that it strives to take into account.

Such a strategy, however, will hardly be able to avoid a certain *ambivalence*. For it will—by virtue of *it*—always in part be *taken in* by what it *takes in* (to account). And if it is one thing to formulate this as a general rule—the "set-hypothesis" in "Limited Inc"[18]—it is quite another to submit to its effects. For these contaminate the rule itself, even if the latter states, in its most general form, the inevitability of such contamination:

It alters, contaminating parasitically what it identifies and enables to repeat "itself"; it leaves us no choice but to mean (to say) something that is (already, always, also) other than what we mean (to say). . . .[19]

But if "it alters" and contaminates what it identifies, can this alteration and contamination stop short of *it itself*? To assert the *general* law of such contamination is, therefore, to imply the contamination of the assertion "itself," in its very generality. Yet since the very *form* of the *assertion* belies such contamination, it is no wonder that this implication will tend towards articulations that are highly *ambivalent*. On the one hand, this may take the form of asserting an *ability* that is simply *opposed* to its other (the latter being inscribed only parenthetically, in passing, in order to be *denied*):

What must be included in the description . . . is not merely the factual reality of corruption and of alteration, but corrupt*ability* . . . and dissoci*ability*. . . . That can only be done if the "-bility" (and not the lability) is recognized from the inception on [dès l'entame] as broached and breached [entamée] in its "origin" by iter*ability*.[20]

If what is at stake in it is a "structural possibility"[21] to be rigorously distinguished from its empirical effects, then of course its operation must be described in terms of an *ability* that is not a lability nor a liability, even if that ability is also nicked (*entamée*), so to speak, in the nick of time (*dès l'entame*). However, if recognition surely presupposes some such object as -ability (and not lability), this is also why our nickname for it was obliged to nick that essential suffix, causing it to drop off even at the risk of rendering the rest less easily recognizable. For does not its ability entail, above all, precisely a certain lability, a certain ability to fall (albeit catlike, on its feet)? In any case, only its (l)ability can transform it from an object of recognition to what might, provisionally, be described as an *instance* of *ambivalence*.

In such ambivalent denials, for instance, it marks the spot where deconstruction *assumes* what *Sec* calls the "will-to-know," that "epistemic intention" that is invoked in order to be ascribed to *another*: to Husserl as a representative of the tradition of western metaphysics.[22] It is introduced in that text still as part of a strategy of deconstruction, which, however, strangely enough, had precisely at that time—1971 (a datable, if not entirely singular event)—reached what could be described as a certain *closure*. The fact that in *Sec*, but also in the interview published as "Positions," the strategy could be schematized in its overall generality,

Samuel Weber

was not and could not be without consequences for that strategy itself. Its own operation had, in a certain generality, become recognizable as more of the Same.

In a certain sense, it takes this closure into account: first, by formulating what is doubtless the most general law governing the strategy of deconstruction, as "the logic that ties repetition to alterity."[23] At the same time, what this "logic" fails to sufficiently remark—qua logic—is what in "Positions" was emphatically designated as "the conflictual character of difference and of alterity."[24] It is just this that may explain the fascination of Searle's polemical "Reply": it may have enabled the strategy of deconstruction to re-mark its own closure by doubling back upon itself, thus assuming a will-to-know that can never be exclusively that of others, even while it can never entirely be true to itself.

It, then, can be said to mark the spot where deconstruction, in defending itself against an attack from without, recognizes the effort to appropriate the other as both inevitable and impossible. Without the desire to *know it*, there could be *no it*. *K(no)w it*. Kwit . . . And yet, not quite: for to take it in is, ineluctably, to be taken in by it. In assuming its will-to-know, then, deconstruction becomes this ambivalent taking-in, it becomes *incorporation*.[25] It, taking in everything else, alters itself. For instance, precisely where its autonomy and its integrity are at stake:

I do not believe that it is necessarily tied to convention, and even less, that it is limited by it.[26]

As a *defense*—and incorporation is always a defense—against the traditional opposition of "nature" and "convention" (still operative and unquestioned in Speech Act theory), this assertion is strategically . . . understandable. But what it asserts is, simply, that it is not limited by convention. By what, then, is it limited? Or is it unlimited: unlimited inc?

Ink, however, dries in remarkable ways, and it is this that allows it to be read. And reread, for instance this passage in *Sec*:

Austin . . . appears to consider solely the conventionality constituting the *circumstance* of the utterance, its contextual surroundings, and not *a certain conventionality intrinsic to what constitutes the speech act* [locution] *itself*. . . .[27] (second emphasis mine)

The coming-together of a certain conventionality will, to be sure, never be simply identical with the conventions that Speech Act theory takes for granted, nor with the state-of-mind that it thereby presupposes. And yet the ineluctability of a certain state-of-mind, a certain matter-of-fact, is also what it serves to re-mark. The question, then, becomes: how to remark the peculiar *certainty*. One possibility, surely no worse than many others, might be as *reading*. On the condition, however, that it designates something that has hitherto escaped our attention:

> If *Sec* caused a more or less anonymous company of readers of whom I was not then thinking, to lose their patience, I would not want to become a cause of impatience to those readers of whom I am thinking today. . . .[28]

And yet, if one begins to think of those readers, will that make them any less "anonymous"? And more "company"? And, above all, will it allow us to avoid: trying their patience?

III

Thus, Sarl did indeed understand. No question here of the essentials being misunderstood. Or rather, if "understanding" is still a notion dominated by the allegedly constative regime of theory or of philosophy, let us not use the word "understood," let us say instead that Sarl was touched.[29]

What does it mean to touch, or want to touch, or not to be able *not* to touch? Freud, whose shadow haunts "the present debate" no less than that of the Sophists, gives us the following account (in *Totem and Taboo*):

> The individual . . . wants to perform this act—the touching—again and again and regards it as his supreme enjoyment, but he also detests it. The opposition between the two currents cannot be readily resolved since—there is no other way of putting it—they are situated . . . so as not to come into contact. . . . The instinctual desire is constantly shifting in order to escape from the impasse and endeavors to find substitutes . . . for what is prohibited. . . . The prohibition itself shifts about as well. Any fresh advance made . . . is answered by a fresh sharpening of the prohibition. The mutual inhibition of the two conflicting forces produces a need for discharge . . . for the performance of obsessive acts. In the case of a neurosis these are clearly compromise actions . . . substitutive acts to compensate the instinct for what has been prohibited. It is a law of neurotic illness that these obsessive acts fall more and more under the sway of the instinct and approach nearer and nearer to the activity which was originally prohibited.[30]

Whether the process and the "law" here described apply *only* to cases of "neurotic illness," or whether it is only more evident in those cases, is a question that now, more than ever, should be held in abeyance. Our previous discussion, if it has demonstrated anything, has pointed to a very general necessity of holding-in-abeyance, to the ambivalent articulation of conflictual processes through instances very similar to the constantly shifting "substitute-" and "compromise-formations" to which Freud here alludes. What is of particular interest, however, in the passage quoted, is the example of *touching* (oneself). If this is the autoerotic gesture par excellence, it is because it recognizes and transgresses the limits separating the self from the other. This explains why

Samuel Weber

touch, for Freud, can engender the symbolic series of acts involving appropriation (of the other by the self), but also why, in order to do so, touch itself must be transformed. Touching alone is not enough: it traces the limit between self and other, but also transgresses that limit. Touching cannot *hold* the other *at a distance*: in order *to hold*, touching must *lay hold of*, must become a grasping or gripping, steadying the other, and with it, oneself.

In this form, with this modification, the *Tasttrieb*, the urge-to-touch, but also to grip, can become the point of departure for more intellectual, sublimated forms of appropriation: for the urge-to-see (*Schautrieb*), which in turn develops into the urge-to-know (or to discover: der *Forscher-* or *Wißtrieb*). Unlike Aristotle and the philosophical tradition to which he gave its name, Freud does not construe the urge-to-know as an elementary instinct of man: "its activity corresponds on the one hand to a sublimated manner of obtaining mastery, while on the other hand it makes use of the energy of scopophilia (*des Schautriebes*)."[31] Through the urge to see, to explore, and to know, man responds not simply to nature as such, but to the peculiar problems of his own nature, problems that are encountered generally as dangers, menaces, or threats:

It is not by theoretical interests but by practical ones that activities of research are set going in children. The threat to the bases of a child's existence offered by the discovery or the suspicion of the arrival of a new baby and the fear that he may, as a result, cease to be cared for . . . make him thoughtful and clear-sighted.[32]

The encounter with *another* child—with the other, perhaps, as such—lets the child react by seeking, in all senses, *to hold on to itself*: seeking, in short, to comprehend. The desire to comprehend is thus inseparable from the need to apprehend—to get a hold on—the other that threatens the self.

The relationship that Freud—and before him Nietzsche—postulates between the *Tasttrieb* and mental activities survives, etymologically, in the formation of the words designating such activities: perception, conception, comprehension, apprehension. All entail the effort of "coming to grips with," "getting a hold of," "getting a handle on." And yet of all of these, it is the last term mentioned—that of *apprehension*—that seems to name the act in its most general, most generic form: the pure and simple gesture of *laying-hold*.

Such, at least, was the function assigned to the term in medieval scholastic philosophy, where the *actus apprehensivus* designated the initial and indispensable *contact* with the object to be known. The term is still used by Kant, in the first edition of *The Critique of Pure Reason*, where the transcendental deduction begins with the description of an original "synthesis of apprehension," by which the manifold impressions of the senses are made into sense, i.e. gathered spontaneously into a unity that itself cannot be the product of the senses or merely empirical.

Apprehension, then, marks that initial, "original" contact with the object that all cognition—and recognition—necessarily presumes. It seems of some interest, therefore, that this word, even today, is anything but univocal. For apprehension, of course, also means: *anxiety*. It signifies the act of understanding, of recognition, of perception: an act by which we catch the meaning of a phrase or ascertain the existence of a thing; and yet it also signifies the concern with or expectation of something adverse, uncertain, and possibly dangerous.

Is apprehension, then, perhaps just what we have been looking for—from the very beginning? Does it mark the place *of* that beginning, precisely in *dividing it*? And if this equivocation makes us *curious*, we will not be disappointed by certain of its other meanings: for instance, to apprehend someone is, of course—in the "physical" sense—to *arrest* that person, in the name of the *law* (in order that he be brought to judgment). Finally, consulting the *OED*, we can find other, equally *physical* meanings, now fallen into disuse: to seize an occasion (we still speak of "embracing" an opportunity); to take possession of; and also, most literally and most physically of all: "to lay hold of, seize, with hands, teeth etc. . . . take down in writing."

Apprehension, then, from the Scholastics to Kant, and in our own language even today, marks the ambivalent spot where a certain repetition defines itself as repetition of the same and recognition of another. But nowhere, perhaps, does this process produce more interesting effects than in the writings of Freud, where it follows a most circuitous route, to be sure. This route is itself, of course, a repetition. Its initial *instance* can be located in *The Interpretation of Dreams*, where Freud, unlike Kant, is not deducing the categories of understanding but rather describing the formation of desire:

A hungry baby screams or kicks helplessly. . . . A change can only come about if in some way or other (in the case of the baby, through outside help) an "experience of satisfaction" can be achieved which puts an end to the internal stimulus. An essential component of this experience of satisfaction is a particular perception (that of nourishment in our example), the memory-image of which remains associated henceforward with the memory-trace of the excitation produced by the need. As a result of the link that has thus been established, next time this need arises a psychical impulse will at once emerge which will seek to recathect the memory image of the perception and to re-evoke the perception itself, that is to say, to re-establish the situation of the original satisfaction. An impulse of this kind is what we call a wish; the reappearance of the perception is the fulfillment of the wish. . . . Thus the aim of this first psychical activity was to produce a "perceptual identity"—a repetition of the perception which was linked with the satisfaction of need.[33]

What is of interest in this description is not so much that it determines the "first psychical activity," the production of the "perceptual identity" (*Wahrnehmungsidentität*), as an effect of repetition and of memory: Kant had already done as much in demonstrating that the synthesis of apprehension was indissolubly bound up with what he called "the synthesis of reproduction in imagination." What is interesting in Freud's description is precisely what is most problematic: the determination of the "perceptual identity" as a repetition of something called an "experience of satisfaction," which itself appears to consist in an alleviation of tension. For a professional philosopher, especially one schooled in the Kantian tradition, this "experience of satisfaction" would doubtless appear to be the hypostasis of a transcendental category as an empirical *event*. Nor would this be simply wrong. But that event has some rather peculiar properties which make it difficult to situate empirically. Most importantly, it can only become effective mentally by being *linked* with "a particular perception" or memory-trace: it is the reproduction of this trace that constitutes both the "perceptual identity" and at the same time, the *wish* that it defines.

In his early psychoanalytical writings, Freud does not raise the question of why or how such a *link* could take place, or what its implications might be. He construes the primitive psyche in terms of a more or less mechanical "apparatus," reacting quasi-automatically to increases and decreases in stimulus and tension. This quasi-automatic operation is described as a function or effect of the Pleasure (or Unpleasure) Principle. The strategic problem inscribed in this "principle," which in fact only described, but did not explain,[34] is that of deriving consciousness without simply taking its place, i.e., postulating another consciousness, or rather another instance possessing the *same structure* as consciousness: namely, the *structure of the same*, a structure that could be identified, grasped, comprehended. If consciousness and whatever was accessible to it, had to be construed as "secondary," the problem was to avoid conceiving its *other* as being "primary." This explains Freud's insistence both on the decisive nature of the "economic" factor, on the intensity of the conflictual forces at work, and at the same time on their unknowable, enigmatic aspect: "We are consequently operating all the time with a large unknown factor, with a capital X, which we are obliged to carry over into each new equation."[35] Freud's much decried emphasis upon this "quantitative" factor indicates not a positivist bent of mind, but the effort to articulate what cannot be comprehended in terms of the traditional, "qualitative" categories of consciousness.

Once the possibility of a psychic order of activity that did not operate in accordance with the concepts and categories of consciousness had been established, however, Freud's effort shifted: instead of describing

psychic functions *apart from* that of consciousness, he sought to rein-
scribe the latter *as a part of* those functions. The focus of this reinscrip-
tion was, of course, the problem of *narcissism* and its implications for the
structure of the *ego*.

In short, after an initial period of describing the non-identity of the
subject in terms of a conflictual order that exceeded and determined its
conscious identity, Freud endeavored to address the problem of just how
a subjective identity could be conceived that did not derive from consciousness, and yet still endowed the subject with a certain *coherence*.
This reemergence of the problem of identity was not without consequences for the theory itself: instead of contemplating conflictuality as
an attribute of the objects or "cases" it studied, it began increasingly to
acknowledge a certain conflict within itself. As the ambivalence of the
narcissistic ego was progressively elaborated, Freud's thinking was increasingly willing to permit its own ambivalences to articulate themselves.

The most celebrated of such articulations is doubtless that which led
Freud beyond the pleasure principle. And yet no less interesting—for our
purposes, at least—is another aspect of this step "beyond," involving not
the spectacular hypothesis of the death-drive, but the revision of Freud's
thinking on anxiety. In his earlier writings, Freud had construed anxiety,
in its "neurotic" manifestations at least (which he distinguished from
"real" anxiety), to be the result of repression. The latter, by setting
libidinal energies "free" at the same time that they were barred from
being discharged, triggered the affect. And yet, if anxiety was the
product of repression, why should anything be repressed in the first
place? The problem of deriving repression was at least one of the factors
that impelled Freud to reconsider the status of anxiety. And of course the
hypothesis of a "primal repression" displaced the problem, but could not
resolve it.

The text in which Freud reversed his previous position is *Inhibition,
Symptoms, and Anxiety*—a text whose remarkable structure is already
suggested by its title (which can be considered as a precursor to the
parataxis of *Sec*). Anxiety was now no longer conceived as an effect of
repression, but rather as its cause. This in turn resituated the entire
conflictual process: if Freud's early writings described it as transpiring
outside of the ego (conceived largely in terms of perception-conscious-
ness), it was now articulated as taking place "within" the ego, albeit one
that was divided and ambivalent.[36] The relation of the ego to that which
exceeded it or was alien to it was no longer that of a (more or less)
simple difference or distinction, but rather one of incorporation: in seeking to incorporate the "symptom," the ego tended to expropriate itself.[37]

What was at stake, then, in the revision of the theory of anxiety was
nothing less than the ambivalent structure of the subject itself. The

earlier distinction of anxiety into two, relatively unrelated forms, "neurotic" and "real" anxiety, was retained, but it was subsumed under a common determination: anxiety was now described as the reaction of the *ego* to *danger*. This *reaction* necessarily entailed the reproduction of an earlier situation. Anxiety was determined as a function of the ego, and as a function of repetition.

If anxiety was thus conceived to be a reaction that reproduced an earlier situation, this could have been taken as evidence for the then popular theory of Rank concerning the birth-trauma. Freud, however, emphatically rejects this hypothesis, while at the same time elaborating his conception of what a *danger* entails. An objective danger to life, such as that of birth, was not per se, Freud argued, psychically effective. Indeed, it was only because the proponents of the birth-trauma projected their adult experience onto the infant that they could endorse this hypothesis. For what they conceived to be evidence for the birth-trauma, Freud continued, were "sensory impressions, in particular of a visual kind"; in privileging such a mode of experience, however, they overlooked the fact that it was highly unlikely "that a child should retain any but tactile and general sensations relating to the process of birth."[38] In their emphasis of visual experience, they were speaking and thinking from the perspective of an already constituted ego, rather than retracing the process by which the ego was constituted, and in which the sense of *touch* was surely more important than that of sight.

It is in this context that Freud, in attempting to describe just what a "danger" for the psyche might consist in, takes up once again his earlier account of the pleasure principle, although this time with a significant modification:

The situation, then, which it [the infant] regards as a "danger" and against which it wants to be safeguarded is that of non-satisfaction, of a growing tension due to need, against which it is helpless. . . . The economic disturbance caused by an accumulation of amounts of stimulation which require to be disposed of . . . is the real essence of the "danger." . . . It is unnecessary to suppose that the child carries anything more with it from the time of its birth than this way of indicating the presence of danger.[39]

As in the earlier account of the formation of the perceptual identity, what is the driving force is an "economic disturbance caused by an accumulation" of tension, an experience of "non-satisfaction." The subject, however, that experiences such non-satisfaction is no longer the quasi-automatic reflex-apparatus, but rather the *ego*. What the "pleasure principle" had been obliged to take for granted—a psychic apparatus that *somehow* was capable of registering, retaining, and reproducing that "experience of satisfaction," and above all, of *binding* it to a memory-trace that became, when repeated, the perceptual identity—is now construed in relation to the ego. To assert that the child must be able, "from the time of its birth," to indicate "the presence of danger," is to pose, from the very start, the rudiments of an ego-function. Or, at least, to abandon the effort to conceive (of) the subject *without* such a function.

It is here, however, that the difference between psychoanalysis and traditional, philosophical modes of thought emerges. For Kant, the impossibility of conceiving the subject—or of *conceiving tout court*—without presupposing something like this *binding*, a state or act of synthesis, was precisely what pointed to the non-empirical, transcendental structure of the categories of understanding:

The synthesis [*Verbindung (conjunctio)*] of a manifold can as such never come to us through the senses. . . . Of all representations [it] alone cannot derive from objects but can only be accomplished by the subject itself. . . .[40]

Kant's conclusion: any form of "analysis" must presuppose a prior synthesis, for the understanding cannot take apart what it has not previously put together.

Freud's psycho*analysis* does not simply deny this: what it argues, is that this prior synthesis never entirely takes place, but only *more or less*. This more-or-less is not, however, a simple question of quantity: it can be described and determined, more or less. It is just this that is at stake in the passage we are discussing, where the earlier account of *Unlust* is repeated and modified as that *reactive apprehension of danger by the ego* which is here called *anxiety*.

Instead, then, of unpleasure being construed as a quantitative increase in excitation or in tension, it is now reinscribed as that aspect of energy that endangers the ego. What is thereby endangered is precisely the function that constitutes the ego: the function of *constitution* itself, of *Bindung*:

The ego is an organization . . . [whose] desexualized energy betrays its origins in its striving for binding and unification, and this compulsion to synthesize increases in proportion to the strength of the ego.[41]

What constitutes a danger for the ego, then, is whatever impairs its ability to bind energy—and thus, itself. Energy, however, can only be "bound" to—or more precisely: *as—representation*.

Thus, we can begin to understand why, in the earlier account, an "experience of satisfaction," the essence of which seemed to consist in a purely *quantitative* change in energy, could and should become "linked" to a *qualitative* "memory-trace," which can then be repeated as the very first mental identity: the perceptual identity. Through the (repetitive) process of re-presentation, the ego constitutes itself.

That process is now given the name: anxiety. It is as anxiety that the ego apprehends "the presence of danger," determining *it* as *its other*:

Samuel Weber

as the loss of its object, as separation, as privation. As anxiety, the *act* of apprehension—necessary a priori of all identity and understanding—is reinscribed as the re-action determining what cannot fully be determined, but what is also never entirely indeterminate.[42] Freud calls this: anxiety *as signal.*

The ego, then, constitutes itself in and as the reactive movement of apprehension, suspended between recollection and anticipation; temporality itself appears as the medium of apprehension, by which the ego, in *defending itself*, gets *it* together, albeit not altogether. And the phases through which the ego passes, in the ambivalent process of its narcissistic constitution, mark its divided and divisive character. At first, such division seems to be situated *between* it and the object: the object that is "lost," from which it is separated. Then, the ambivalence of such "loss" and "separation" is sharpened: castration-anxiety affirms, on the one hand, the "original" presence of what has been lost (the maternal phallus), but on the other it merges possession with dispossession. However, it is only in the "decline" of the oedipus complex, with the emergence of the anxiety of conscience, that the ambivalence of consciousness comes into its own.

IV

"But what about those readers? You've lost sight of them completely!"

"Have I? And I thought that I was talking *about* them all the time, even while I was talking *around* them. For instance: isn't 'reading' just another name for what I have tried to describe as *apprehension*: that ambivalent effort to get it *together* by holding it in *abeyance*, by *arresting* its movement, *re-acting* (to) it—as though it were dangerous, threatening. . . ."

"You're getting carried away again—are you trying to show that you can try the patience of readers even WHILE *you're thinking of them? If that's what you're after, Q.E.D. But now try to be a little more* CONCRETE."

"Okay—if it's examples you want, I can give them to you: two instances to bite into, so to speak. As a start, let's begin with dreams. . . ."

In recalling a dream, we seem to be reproducing something that has already taken place, at a particular time, usually the night before, while we were asleep. This something, however disjointed or absurd it may appear in our memory, will generally be supposed to have possessed a certain formal coherence. That is, it will be considered to have *begun* at a certain point in time, to have *unfolded*, and then to have reached an *end*, or—as is often the case—to have been interrupted; in any case, to have stopped. We thereby tend to cast ourselves, the morning after, in the role of a spectator seeking to conjure up something that was, that we then seem to watch as we would view a film, a sequence of images vis-à-vis, even if we are more or less dimly aware that we cannot simply be the spectator in such a process, but must at least double as the narrator (or, to stay within the film metaphor, as the projectionist). In any case, this vague awareness does not usually alter our sense of being somewhere quite apart and detached from the dream we seem merely to see before our mind's eye, as we remember it.

If, however, we persist in reflecting upon this situation, even if we have not read Freud's *Interpretation of Dreams*, the simple model of a subject facing an object, of a mind repeating something that once was, progressively falls apart. We come to realize that we are not simply the spectator or projectionist of the dream, but the projector, the screen, the camera and film, the actors, extras, stagehands, and stage-props, in short: the entire production crew and the conditions of production (including the various forms of censorship, disseminated, *un peu partout*). What is remarkable in all this, however, is that although the dream is thus "our creation" or "product," we, as creators or as producers, are not situated outside, above, or beyond our *work*. On the contrary: we are, quite literally, part and parcel of a process that "we"—our conscious selves—can never entirely *comprehend*; and yet which at the same time we cannot but *apprehend*. Were we not to apprehend it, in one way or another—and it is perhaps apt here to recall that one of the meanings of the word, now dormant, was to "feel the force of, be sensible of," in short: to be *grabbed* by . . .—it could hardly be *said* to exist, or in any case be discussed *as such*.

And yet, *can* it be said to exist, *as such*? What—*concretely*—can it mean to apprehend a dream that cannot be comprehended? It is to this very question that Freud addresses himself at a decisive juncture in *The Interpretation of Dreams*, in the opening section of the seventh chapter. The passage is decisive precisely because it marks the transition from the more or less descriptive and analytical theory of the workings of the dream itself, to the attempt to elaborate the implications of that theory in what will later be known as a "metapsychology." Before Freud begins to speculate on these implications, he feels compelled to pause for a moment, in order to defend and to secure his preceding work against possible criticism. In other words, Freud engages in a defensive dialogue with the reader.

The first and doubtless the most fundamental objection that he feels obliged to answer goes as follows: The dream itself is never directly accessible to us; all we can know about it is what we can remember, and surely "there is every reason to suspect that our memory of dreams is not

Samuel Weber

only fragmentary but positively inaccurate and falsified." As a result, "there seems to be a danger that the very thing whose value we have undertaken to assess may slip completely through our fingers."[43] Freud's response to this objection is remarkable, not only in its content but in its form: instead of *denying* or rejecting it out of hand, he in a certain sense *accepts* it: he "incorporates" it, so to speak, by repeating it and at the same time transforming it from an objection into a confirmation— one, however, which does not merely leave what it confirms, the incorporating body of the theory, unchanged. In incorporating the other *as other*,[44] the theory itself is altered; in making place for it, it is displaced. This, then, is Freud's response:

It is true that we distort dreams in attempting to reproduce them. . . . But this distortion is itself no more than a part of the revision to which the dream-thoughts are regularly subjected as a result of the dream-censorship. . . . The only mistake (is to suppose) that the modification of the dream in the course of being remembered and put into words is an *arbitrary* one and cannot be further resolved. . . .[45]

Freud does not deny that the process by which we reproduce the dream entails distortion, he *affirms* it: indeed, it is precisely this distortion, he asserts, that allows us any access whatsoever to the dream. For the dream, as a particular form of mental activity, is itself a process of distortion—or, since the German word is more suggestive and less privative, a process of *Entstellung*, which literally and historically, as Freud later took pains to point out, signifies a *change of place* or *dislocation*.[46] The mode of articulation peculiar to the dream, the *dream-work*, entails distortion because the dream is not, as is commonly held to be Freud's view, simply the fulfillment of a wish, but rather the *distorted* fulfillment of a *conflictual* wish. Thus, the distortions of memory, which may seem to bar our access to the dream—and which often in fact *do* just that—are at the same time precisely the condition of possibility of our "knowing" anything about the dream at all, much less our being able to interpret it. If we can interpret a dream, it is only by allowing ourselves to distort it, letting ourselves "go" and not trying to control the direction(s) we go in.

The objection, then, is, in a certain sense, *taken in*. But so is the theory. At least inasmuch as it had set out to demonstrate that the dream is a "meaningful mental structure" (*ein sinnvolles psychisches Gebilde*).[47] As a process of distortion the dream does not so much represent meaningfully (*Sinn darstellen*) as it depresents and disarticulates (*Sinn entstellen*). In so doing, however, it dislocates itself as well: as an ongoing process of distortion and displacement, it *has* no *self*, no clearly defined beginning, middle, and end. The dream only comes-to-be *after the fact*, as it were, in the process of its repetition, recounting, and retelling. The dream, one would be tempted to say, only *is*, *in* and *as* its retelling; but the latter only reproduces the dream inasmuch as it distorts what we might call *its manifestation*, if we were not cognizant of the fact that the dream never manifests itself as such, but only afterwards, in its distorting reproduction. Moreover, this distortion itself can never be fully comprehended, since it will always entail an over-determination, another meaning, an other-of-meaning, which is the conflictual process from which it emerges and in which it merges.

Like anxiety, then, the dream is not easy to get a hold on: the wish that it most directly articulates is inevitably—Freud insists on this— bound up with other wishes, more remote and going back to infancy: "ultimately," to the sequence of desire and prohibition that we have already discussed. Perhaps this is why the question of "anxiety-dreams" returns insistently to haunt Freud's thesis of the dream as wish-fulfill-ment, and the theory of the "pleasure-principle" upon which it is based; a theory which, as I have argued, is re-placed (not invalidated, but displaced and transformed) by the theory of anxiety.

But even if we grant that the dream is only the confluence, the momentary, precarious, labile *arresting* of a conflictual process that ex-ceeds its every manifestation, the fact still remains, and it is decisive, that there *is* a *relative* determination of that process: there is, in short, *the apprehension of it*. And there is, moreover, a *theory* of that apprehen-sion (even if what is being "theorized," of course, is a *certain* impossi-bility of theory—and yet, perhaps also a certain *necessity* of it).

What, then, in Freudian terms, might enable us to conceive this relative determination? The description of ambivalence already pointed to the necessity of "compromise-formations," and Freud introduces a variety of terms in order to render them conceivable: reaction-formation, counter-cathexis, symptom. And yet, perhaps the most elaborate attempt is that which grew out of the *Interpretation of Dreams* itself, as the attempt to *defend* it against the *reaction* of its "first reader," who served Freud as "the representative of the others," Wilhelm Fließ.[48] Fließ had, in a sense, varied the objection we have already discussed, accusing Freud of distorting the dreams he analyzed by projecting his own wit and ingenuity upon them. Out of this charge grew the attempt to settle accounts, once and for all, with the force that had intruded and cast doubt upon Freud's theoretical mastery of the dream: *Jokes [Wit] and their Relation to the Unconscious*.

This brings me, then, to my *second* example or instance. And it really will only be an instance, since I cannot here recapitulate the dramatic story by which the "theory" of jokes arrives at its decisive articulations.[49] Instead, I will have to limit myself to what, for our purposes, are the most pertinent aspects of that theory.

Samuel Weber

Like the dream, the joke is neither an object nor a phenomenon: for its appearance, that is, the actual telling of the joke, is not sufficient to constitute it *as* a joke. Something else is needed. What is required, for a joke to be a joke, or more precisely, since the temporality is not a matter of indifference: for a joke *to have been* a joke, is a particular after-effect: *laughter*. The laughter of the listener decides, *post facto*, whether or not the story that has been told will have been a joke.

Thus, the joke—apparently in opposition to the dream[50]—involves a process that requires what Freud calls "three persons," or in any case a triadic structure: the first person, the joke-teller, the second person, (which need not be a person), the object or butt of the joke, and the third person, the listener, whose laughter decides. What this indicates, in the context of our earlier discussion, is that here, at least, we have an instance of language, the joke, which precisely cannot function in the "radical absence of its intended receiver." And yet, what is decisive is that it cannot function in the full presence of that receiver either. Why?

The answer has to do with the nature of the response of that receiver: the third person is not called upon to make a conscious, deliberate judgment; on the contrary, to the extent to which he reacts with full awareness, his laughter will not count. For, as Freud continually insists, the laughter intended by the joke is one in which the person laughing cannot, at the time, know *what* he is laughing at. Nor is he simply laughing *at* anything, in the sense of an *object*, which is why Freud emphasizes that the particularity of the joke—like the dream—entails not the contents or themes that it treats, but the techniques it employs and the tendencies (*Tendenzen*) it pursues. But the ultimate goal of all techniques and tendencies is the evocation of laughter; and by laughter, Freud means the violent eruption of energy momentarily set free. The successful, "good" joke triggers an explosion of laughter.

Where an explosion takes place, of course, barriers are broken through, resistances overcome, even if only temporarily. In his Jokebook, Freud gives an "economic" account of those resistances and the manner in which they are overcome by laughter. The energy that is normally absorbed in sustaining prohibitions, maintaining the repression of certain thoughts and desires, in short: the "normal" psychic economy and relation of forces is temporarily circumvented by the joke, which accomplishes this by the following general procedure. The attention of the listener, the third person, is aroused, stimulated, and *diverted*. While the listener's attention is thus *absorbed*, the joke, the punch-line, the *pointe* takes place *elsewhere*. This is the element of *surprise*: the listener is literally *over-taken*, since by the time he *comes-to* (his senses), he is *already* laughing; the joke has succeeded, while diverting his conscious attention in representing ideas, thoughts, and wishes that under normal circumstances would be intolerable. The energy otherwise utilized to contain such desires—and Freud emphasizes that censorship, repression, and the like require a constant effort that always must be renewed—is momentarily liberated, unbound, decathected, "released" in an explosion of laughter.

This economic account of laughter, as coherent as it is, leaves certain questions open. Most important of these, and Freud returns to it often, concerns the relation of the "first" to the "third" person: Why, for instance, can a joke not be told to oneself? Why must the third person laugh, while the first person cannot (except *"par ricochet"*)? Freud is sensitive to a certain complicity between joke-teller and listener—both, for instance, must share the same prohibitions, in order to be able to laugh at the same joke—but their relationship remains enigmatic. For instance, Freud never once alludes to the striking fact that, in most cases at least, the joke-situation is clearly defined as such in advance. What is striking here is that the element of "surprise" is not, as one might surmise (if one had never participated in a joke . . .), undermined by the announcement that a joke will be told. On the contrary, such an announcement sets the scene, as it were, for what is to come: it dims the lights of reality, and, if anything, appeals to the curiosity of the listener, promising him the premium of pleasure. But here, as elsewhere, there are no give-aways: if the listener is lured by the promise of pleasure, he must in turn be prepared to assume a certain *risk*. For in accepting the "contract" that binds him to the joke-teller, he obligates himself in a way that no civil contract could permit. He commits himself to an act that he cannot consciously, deliberately control or perform: the "act" of laughter. And yet, should he fail to perform as expected, the onus will not fall upon the "first" person alone. No wonder, then, if—at times, at least—the announcement of a joke can be the cause not just of gaiety, but of a certain apprehension. For if the joke fails to produce laughter, there will have been no joke. And without the joke, the positions of "first" and "third" persons are no longer those of *allies*, but perhaps . . . of *adversaries*.

Or was this perhaps always the case? In the description of what might be regarded as the prototype of the joke—the dirty joke—the "third person" appears at first as an interloper, a rival, or in any case as the one who renders the second person—object of desire—inaccessible. Only later does he become an "ally," who partakes of and sanctions the (aggressive) exposure of the forbidden (and absent, or lost) object. In so doing, the third person enforces what might be called, in the strictest of senses, *the pleasure of re-presentation*.

Who, or what, might be involved in this "third person," whom I have by convention (a convention that is rightly being interrogated today) been designating as "he," although *it* would probably be more accurate? This is a question that Freud's "second" topography, developed many years after his book on jokes, can help to elucidate. At the same time, it is hardly unlikely that such "elucidation," following the strategy of a certain "incorporation," may also dislocate that topography. For if it is unmistakable that the "third person" is not simply a person in the sense of another, conscious subject, another "I"—since he (it?) cannot consciously determine whether or not its role will be performed—our previous discussion makes it less obvious where precisely that person might, in terms of that topography (id/ego/superego), be situated.

On the one hand, as the tribunal of decision, presiding over the fate of the joke, and as the rival turned ally, determining through interdiction, the third person would seem to be identifiable with the superego, internalized (or should it be, "incorporated"?) heir of the paternal prohibition, as well as that which determines the strivings of the ego (as ego-ideal).

And yet, on the other hand, what takes place, not so much *in* the third person as *through* it (*per-sona*), is an explosion of energy that can only come from the id; or perhaps from *it*. Why *it*? Because what is released in laughter, as laughter, does not simply *repeat* a movement of desire that has long since been repressed: laughter itself *is* that repetition, the repeated spasms of another kind of *utterance*, temporarily exceeding all determination as language, in meaningful words and phrases that can be understood. *More or less*, that is. For such laughter is not, as we have seen, utterly independent of what can be understood, and what not.

The third person, then, is neither simply id nor simply superego, if those terms are understood to designate entities that are discrete, clearly distinguished from one another. But of course this is not how Freud worked with them: the superego is always described as forming part of the ego, from which it has split off, just as the ego forms part of the id (its organized portion). And finally, the id comprises part of the superego, as the source of its energy.

What comes together, in this "third person" that seems impossible to situate precisely, even within the tripartite scheme of Freud's second topography, is perhaps the figure of a certain alterity, of a certain ambivalence, dislocating the topography that itself tries to locate the dislocation.

Which is why it is not merely witty to say that Freud's theory of jokes is the Joke of Theory—and why, above all, that is precisely its strength. For it offers us the possibility of conceiving, inasmuch as such is possible, the general scheme of that process of ambivalence. The structure of the joke: *prescribing* that the "first" person must depend upon the "third"—upon *it*—in order to be (to have been) a first person, and that the mode of that "being" is inseparable from a *story*; *describing* how the third person must be curious, attentive, absorbed—must want *to know*, in short, in order to be able to laugh; and finally, *inscribing* both first and third persons in a structure of *sociality*, in which "rules" and "conventions" play their part, precisely *as interdictions limiting the play, but also making its transgression, making* IT, *momentarily possible*—all that can be assembled into a scheme ("very schematically," to be sure) enabling us to talk *about* it, without fully comprehending what we are talking about. At least beyond the fact that what we will never entirely comprehend, we will always try to apprehend.

"Now you've lost me entirely. Just what is YOUR *scheme, anyhow? I begin to wonder if you yourself know—but I suppose you would claim that to be the proof of the pudding; tails you win. . . . And I thought you were going to say something about reading, about readers. . . ."*

"Reading? Readers? I thought I had said it: getting it together, from apprehension to laughter—isn't *that* where *it's at*?"

"?!!"

NOTES

1. *Basic Works of Aristotle*, ed. Richard McKeon (New York: Random House, 1941). I have modified this translation.
2. Jacques Derrida, "Limited Inc," in *Glyph 2: Johns Hopkins Textual Studies* (Baltimore: Johns Hopkins University Press, 1977), p. 177.
3. John Searle, "Reiterating the Differences: A Reply to Derrida," in *Glyph 1: Johns Hopkins Textual Studies* (Baltimore: Johns Hopkins University Press, 1977), p. 208.
4. Ibid.
5. Derrida, "Signature Event Context," in *Glyph 1*, p. 183.
6. Ibid.
7. Derrida, "Limited Inc," p. 194.
8. Ibid., p. 244.
9. Ibid., p. 210.
10. Ibid., p. 200.
11. Ibid., p. 210.
12. Ibid.
13. Searle, "Reiterating the Differences," p. 199.
14. Derrida, "Limited Inc," p. 191.
15. Derrida, "Signature Event Context," p. 195.
16. Ibid., p. 180.
17. Derrida, "Limited Inc," p. 201.
18. Ibid., p. 174.
19. Ibid., p. 200.
20. Ibid., p. 218.
21. Ibid., p. 184: ". . . this power, this *being able*, this *possibility* is al-

ways inscribed, hence *necessarily* inscribed *as possibility* in . . . the functional structure of the mark."

22. Derrida, "Signature Event Context," p. 185.

23. Ibid.

24. Derrida, "Positions," in *Positions* (Paris: Editions de Minuit, 1972), p. 60.

25. Derrida, "Limited Inc," p. 216, and "Fors," in *Le verbier de l'homme aux loups* ed. Nicolas Abraham and Maria Torok (Paris: Aubier/Flammarion, 1976), pp. 17ff.

26. Derrida, "Limited Inc," p. 246.

27. Derrida, "Signature Event Context," p. 189.

28. Derrida, "Limited Inc," p. 179.

29. Ibid., 177.

30. Sigmund Freud, *Totem and Taboo* (New York: W. W. Norton, 1950), p. 30.

31. Sigmund Freud, *Three Essays on the Theory of Sexuality* (New York: Avon, 1962), pp. 91–92.

32. Ibid.

33. Sigmund Freud, *The Interpretation of Dreams* (New York: Avon, 1965), pp. 604–5.

34. See Gilles Deleuze, *Présentation de Sacher-Masoch* (Paris: Editions de Minuit, 1967), pp. 96 ff.

35. Sigmund Freud, *Beyond the Pleasure Principle* (New York: W. W. Norton, 1961), p. 25.

36. The trajectory of this shift can be observed, in condensed form, in the switch in meaning of the word *inhibition (Hemmung)*. In Freud's early psychoanalytical writings, the word is generally used to designate the decisive—and enigmatic—process by which energy is blocked from discharging itself and thus *bound*. (See, for instance, *The Interpretation of Dreams*, pp. 638 ff, where the emergence of the "secondary process" out of the "primary" is described: "All that I insist upon is the idea that the activity of the *first psi*-system is directed towards securing the *free discharge* of the quantities of excitation, while the *second* system, by means of the cathexes emanating from it, succeeds in *inhibiting* this discharge and in transforming the cathexis into a quiescent one." In *Inhibition, Symptom, and Anxiety*, by contrast, "inhibition" is taken into the ego. And yet this "taking-in" also deranges the "in" of the "taker"; for if inhibition is now situated "in" terms of the ego, it is as a "restriction" of its functions (*Inhibition, Symptom, and Anxiety* (New York: W. W. Norton, 1959), pp. 15–16).

37. The effort of the ego to appropriate the symptom is described by Freud precisely as an incorporation, but one which is also very close to a dismemberment: "It [the ego] makes an adaptation to the symptom—to this piece of the internal world which is alien to it—just as it normally does to the real external world. It can always find plenty of opportunities for doing so. The presence of a symptom may entail a certain impairment of capacity, and this can be exploited to appease some demand on the part of the super-ego or to refuse some claim from the external world. In this way the symptom gradually comes to be the representative of important interests; it is found to be useful in asserting the position of the self and becomes more and more closely merged with the ego and more and more indispensable to it. It is only

very rarely that the physical process of 'healing' round a foreign body follows such a course as this. There is a danger . . . in saying that the ego has created the symptom merely in order to enjoy its advantages. It would be equally true to say that a man who had lost his leg in the war had got it shot away so that he might thenceforward live on his pension without having to do any more work" (ibid., p. 25). It should be remarked that Freud describes his analogy *only* as being "equally true"—he does not claim that is equally *false*.

38. Freud, *Inhibition, Symptom, and Anxiety*, p. 61.

39. Ibid., p. 63.

40. Immanuel Kant, *Critique of Pure Reason*, §15, 137b.

41. Freud, *Inhibition, Symptoms, and Anxiety*, p. 24.

42. This is surely the decisive difference distinguishing the thought of Freud from that of Heidegger. Anxiety, for the latter, places the subject (*Dasein*) before something "utterly indeterminate" (*völlig unbestimmt*), thus casting it back upon its *own* Being-in-the-World (*auf sein eigenstes In-der-Welt-sein*). For Freud, anxiety does not entail the *total* in-determination of its object, through which the subject would be confronted with its *own* negativity: it entails the *ambivalence* of a *relative* determination, that of a *certain more-or-less*. And perhaps nothing is more difficult for philosophy to comprehend than this more-or-less. . . . (Cf. M. Heidegger, *Sein und Zeit* [Tübingen: Niemeyer, 1963], §40.

43. Freud, *The Interpretation of Dreams*, p. 551.

44. Ibid., p. 552.

45. Sigmund Freud, "Der Mann Moses und die monotheistische Religion," *Gesammelte Werke*, 18 vols. (London: Imago, 1968), 16: 144.

46. "In the pages that follow I shall bring forward proof that there is a psychological technique which makes it possible to interpret dreams, and that, if that procedure is employed, every dream reveals itself as a psychical structure which has a meaning [ein sinnvolles psychisches Gebilde]. . . ." *The Interpretation of Dreams*, p. 35.

47. Sigmund Freud, *Aus den Anfängen der Psychoanalyse* (Frankfurt: S. Fischer, 1950): "I need you as audience," Freud writes Fließ on January 30, 1899 (p. 236), and on September 21: "Unfortunately, I cannot do without you as representative of the 'other' . . . " (p. 256).

48. This will be discussed in my forthcoming book, *Freud-Legende* (an English translation of which is in preparation).

49. The dream, Freud asserts in his book on jokes, only involves "two persons": the dreamer and the dreamed. And yet, if one reads the descriptions in *The Interpretation of Dreams* carefully, one will discover that there is almost always a third person waiting in the wings: either the analyst, Freud himself, to whom the dreams are being told; or—the reader, to whom Freud is telling his "own" dreams. As we shall see, the divided-divisive structure of the unconscious, the "intra-subjective" alterity of the subject, recurs ineluctably as the "third person," figure of the Other that comes to *take its* place.

TWO

THE DECONSTRUCTOR AS POLITICIAN: MELVILLE'S *CONFIDENCE-MAN*
Henry Sussman

I

GIVEN THE INTENSITY with which signs, pronouncements, and arguments are questioned in *The Confidence-Man*,[1] the titles of its chapters are to be commended for honesty in advertising. The title of the first chapter, for example, describes exactly what takes place within it, "A mute goes aboard a boat." Wearing the cream-colors of neutrality, a man whose fleecy hat suggests the fleecing activity of skulduggery, steps aboard a Mississippi riverboat on an unspecified April Fool's day. This character, whose lack of a voice makes him a writer by necessity, instigates a crisis in interpretation that will preoccupy the entire novel merely by inscribing one line on a blackboard. And at first glance this pronouncement is of "an aspect so singularly innocent" (7) as his own. It possesses the form of an equation, the certainty of a truism, and the stability of an eternal truth:

Charity thinketh no evil.

In the random, almost chance inscription of this pronouncement—and in the ensuing public controversy that compels the mute to list further predications regarding charity—the text provides us with the germ of a scenario that will, like the word "charity," remain constant despite whatever revisions it undergoes. And in this scenario pronouncements—often as unimpeachable as the mute's—are made before a public that must interpret them. *Must* interpret them because these statements, despite the negative form in which the novel's first example is disguised, implicitly harbor an imperative, a call to action. As a legion of later fraud-episodes will attest, the pronouncement, "Charity thinketh no evil," implies, "contribute to the charities that approach you for a donation." It is fitting that the mute's first inscription alone should be able to trigger a minor public disturbance because the wider issue at stake, one continuing throughout the novel, is the status of public or political language. Pronouncements of the same formulaic and moralistic sort will emanate from a wide variety of characters, exhorting their auditors to consummate actions, usually on philanthropic or humanitarian grounds. The auditors who are the targets of the words may be convinced, or, as the complexity of the confrontations increases, they may offer resistance. Even in the novel's first pages, the sides of the conflict ensuing from public pronouncements are delineated. There is the exhortation to action (often disguised in the most neutral predications) and the refusal to act. There is the appeal for belief, the naive reading, the taking of the word at its word, and there is the cynical repudiation of the claims at the basis of the appeal. The continuous sequence of operators in the novel will be accompanied by a less populous but no less adamant string of cynics. However the novel embellishes its dramatic situations and allows its thematic interests to wander, underlying the involutions is always an attempt to persuade and a testing of the interstice between language and action.

In the present and paradigmatic situation of the mute, public resistance induces him to make a series of amendments to the initial pronouncement. Charity "suffereth long and is kind," "endureth all things," "believeth all things," and "never faileth" (7). Paradoxically, as emended or changed, charity is always all-encompassing and enduring. An ideal, charity manifests the universality and eternity of the ideal. Paradoxically again, the invoker of the ideal is the one who relativizes it, who fills in new substitutions on the blackboard of substitution, who is aware of the fluctuations on the stock-exchange of language. Not only the mute, but all of the operators who follow in his path occupy a similarly anomalous position. At the same time that they deploy the duplicitous and fictive potentials of language, they are the most authoritarian enforcers of the ideals orienting the social and intellectual orders of society. The characters in this novel who possess fictive or critical competence disclaim it, and in fact proclaim it in others to constitute a public menace. The most dogmatic promoters of order and authority are those who exercise critical skills, yet who publically renounce them. *The Confidence-Man* is an extended meditation on the relationship between the language of politics, which culminates in action and is therefore fundamentally reductive, and the language of criticism, whose alternation between the perspectives of idealization and penetration is endless.

The Confidence-Man is systematic in the way the encyclopaedic novels most indebted to Hegel's *Phenomenology* are. Not only is it oriented to the ideal—its emptiness as well as its imperatives—but the operators who emerge and vanish in the wake of the mute represent the vital sub-systems making up the social order: commerce, medicine, philanthropy, theology, and higher education. Not only does the novel incorporate a social microcosm, but it dramatizes the functioning of a philosophical system. When the numerous discrete encounters of the first half of the novel give way, in the second half, to the less successful but far more speculative fraud-attempts of a character known as the "cosmopolitan," the universal man, the novel in effect sublates itself to a higher level of generality. Yet this novel, that is so striking in its capacity to encompass, both referentially and conceptually, is punctuated throughout by wild misusages and a language play that points to the insubstantiality of systems, to the groundlessness in reaction to which systems are a cosmetic effort at containment.

The internal organization of the boat that is the setting for the novel's attempts at persuasion is that of a writing-desk: "Fine promenades, domed saloons, long galleries, sunny balconies, confidential passages, bridal chambers, staterooms plenty as pigeon-holes, and out-of-the-way retreats like secret drawers in an escritoire. . . ." A floating writing-machine whose intricately organized spaces encompass activities ranging from the most innocent to the most suspicious moves down a river that grows in the absorption of its tributaries. The activity of the voyage itself is defined by assimilation and exchange.

Though her voyage of twelve hundred miles extends from apple to orange, from clime to clime, yet, like any small ferryboat, to right and left, at every landing, the huge Fidèle still receives additional passengers in exchange for those that disembark; so that, although always full of strangers, she continually, in some degree, adds to, or replaces them with strangers still more strange. . . . (12)

It is appropriate that the movements of an enterprise largely consisting in the effacement of the ideal should be able to unite widely divergent climates and geographical regions. The business of persuasion is no place for fine distinctions. For this reason, within the novel's symbolism, polar opposites merge. East can be superimposed on West, and the difference between black and white is by no means obvious.[2]

Just as the river expands by absorption, the boat receives an endless flow of persons increasing only in their strangeness, their being alien to each other in the sense of the French *étranger*. A catalogue of the different types of strangers fills out the second chapter. But more important than their variety is the fact that the voyage, the river, and the exchange of passengers all proceed by a movement of assimilation. On the most literal level, this is the historical assimilation of the American population. If Melville introduces the confidence game by associating it with a kind of interchangeability in language enabling its chalked-in ideal to be modified by a multiplicity of predicates, he devotes the second chapter to establishing the capacity of the game to be all-encompassing, to assimilate everything. Just as the boat traffics in "a piebald parliament, an Anacharsis Cloots congress of all kinds of that multiform pilgrim species, man" (14), the confidence game will absorb every type of individual, both as operators and targets. It will appeal to dowager windows, college students, and coonskin adventurers. It will employ smooth business-types and wretched juveniles.

The name of the boat is *Fidèle*, and while the craft may wander, it is forever oriented to the *fides* that is both the north-star and center of *confidence*. The array of operators will invoke an equally variegated assortment of ideals in exhorting to action. There will be a rough correspondence between the nature of the pitch and the ideal invoked. The herb-doctor, for example, who peddles homeopathic remedies for all ailments, will extol the virtues of nature, while the "man in a tassled travelling-cap," an agent of the Black Rapids Coal Company, will stress the need for business confidence. But the meta-ideal of the novel, the ideal that directs the targets' response to all other appeals, is confidence itself. The slave trader whose profession is described as "philosophical intelligence" places confidence in its widest context: "Confidence is the indispensable basis of all sorts of business transactions. Without it, commerce between man and man, as between country and country, would, like a watch, run down and stop" (178). If a target *confides* [verb: intransitive] he will do whatever he has been exhorted to do, whether to contribute to a charity, buy a stock or medicine, or make a personal gift. By invoking confidence as the indispensable basis for social order, the operators, who all descend from that writing specialist, the mute, shame their auditors toward a moment of dull, non-resilient collision with their directives. Down the all-encompassing Mississippi floats a boat on which a succession of writers attempt to influence the public with their texts. The stylized interaction between writers and readers becomes a game that in turn encompasses not only all players but all terms deployed in the interchanges. The term common to all rounds of this game, the meta-ideal of confidence or literal acceptance of the word, encompasses all other ideal structures both invoked and emptied by the fiction-makers in the novel. "Here reigned the dashing and all-fusing spirit of the West, whose type is the Mississippi itself, which, uniting the streams of the most distant and opposite zones, pours them along, helter-skelter, in one cosmopolitan and confident tide" (14).

II

The present reading of *The Confidence-Man* assumes in large part the structural scheme clarified by H. Bruce Franklin in his edition of the novel. According to this scheme, the novel is divided into two halves, according to the daytime and night of the unspecified April Fool's day on which it takes place.[3] The text consists of forty-five chapters. Twilight occurs at the beginning of chapter twenty-three.

The Confidence-Man thus joins that significant body of literature in which the text releases the negative potential of its irony against itself. As in *Faust* and *Ulysses*, the nighttime of the work's temporal setting is the night for the determinations crystallized earlier, under conditions of ostensibly greater lucidity. An obscuring and ultimate violation, in the second half, of the patterns at times arbitrarily and mechanistically laid down in the first becomes the culmination of the novel's irony as it sets into play the self-deconstructive potential of language. For the moment, however, we are concerned with delineating the mechanisms crystallized in the first half of the novel, even knowing that they will be exploded. For it is precisely such willful patterns that comprise the rules of the confidence game in general and provide for the variants manufactured by such a matrix.

Judging from the mute's entrance onto the stage of action, it is not difficult to understand why, two chapters later, Black Guinea's appeal for alms should produce both its sympathizers and its skeptics. Numbered among the former are two clergymen and a country merchant, who is soon to become the novel's first major dupe. What is most important about the doubts concerning Black Guinea's authenticity is not merely that they are expressed—but that they initiate a search for references.

"But is there not some one who can speak a good word for you?" asks an Episcopal clergyman (19). Black Guinea can indeed furnish a list of references, one broad enough to encompass virtually all the operators in the novel and then some. And three chapters later, when the Episcopalian succeeds in running down one of the character references in the list, "a gem'man in a gray coat and white tie" (43), this character not only confirms but also bemoans Black Guinea's destitution. This is merely the first of many instances in the novel when the operators assist each other by confirming each other's claims. This can be done either retrospectively,[4] as in the case just mentioned, or prospectively,[5] as when the agent of the Black Rapids Coal Co., approaching a sick old miser, wishes that the herb-doctor were there (101). (The herb-doctor later appears and exhausts the miser into buying his Omni-Balsamic Reinvigorator.) Like the uncannily repetitive *dramatis personae* that populate contemporary American television commercials, the operators collectively contribute to a mutually-confirming fictive utopia.[6] The operators are interreferential. Suspicions aroused by one operator can be displaced along a chain of reference until they can be "corrected" by someone appearing more solid. The interpretative crisis initiated by an operator's claims can itself be displaced elsewhere in the same network until the hermeneutic energy is dissipated in the public consideration of some tangential issue or anecdote. So it is that a target known as the "good merchant" opens for general discussion a sob-story concerning an early operator, the "man with the weed," that he had heard in passing from yet another operator, the "man in a gray coat and white tie." The story relates how that first unfortunate's bizarre and dirt-eating wife, Goneril, unjustly turned the law against him and initiated his wanderings along the Mississippi. The filial ingratitude of *King Lear*, from which Goneril derives her improbable name, is transmuted into a marital infidelity assuming the form of the "mysterious touches" (85) that she gives other men and the legal machinations by means of which she usurps custody of the couple's child. By engaging the good merchant in a critical evaluation of Goneril's story, yet a final operator, the "man in a travelling-cap" is able to divert the good merchant's suspicions regarding *his* intentions. The tangential narrative of Goneril thus connects three operators by bonds of mutual substantiation and also dissipates suspicion along a potentially endless interpretative regress. In their interreferentiality the confidence-men cooperatively fabricate a self-enclosed fictive domain, a utopian *world apart* oriented to the meta-ideal of confidence. The transtemporal quality of the references provides for the endurance of the game. The game has a momentum, a mechanism of its own that is independent of particular participants, themes, or results.

In the first half of the novel the fraud-episodes follow upon each other with the rapidity of slapstick gags. Out of Black Guinea's catalogue of references emerge five operators who fill out the daytime of the novel, occupying the stage for differing lengths of time. Each of these characters bears a unique "trademark," represents an interest, chooses corresponding metaphors and themes for his discourse, and deploys characteristic ploys or gimmicks. The movement that may be extrapolated from the repetitive structure of the fraud-episodes and from the interreferentiality of operators is that of a machine—a language machine dovetailing with a capital machine. A language machine, because the raw material of the fabrication process is words, and more specifically, rhetoric. A capital machine, powered by the constant thrust of the interchanges toward a one-sided exchange of money or its equivalent. As the world-wide vision of the charity business conjured by the "man in a gray coat and white tie" makes clear, the capital machine assembled by the novel proceeds by a logic of endless accumulation. The interreferentiality of the operators in the first half of the novel makes the machine whose input is words, whose product is money, one with interchangeable parts —a creation of the assembly line and the age of mechanical reproduction.[7] It is not accidental, then, that the Missouri bachelor who deflates the herb-doctor's claims for nature before he succumbs to the analogies of the philosophical intelligence officer—and buys slaves—is a technocrat. "Machines for me," he declares (160).

While always reducible to the predatory pursuit of a target by an operator, the fraud-episodes in the first half of the novel vary in their complexity and the degree of their resolution, but above all in the massive battery of ploys available to the community of operators. At their simplest and most mechanical, the fraud-episodes are hit-and-run affairs in which the targets are simply bowled over by the operators. The first time we meet the college student, he is reduced to speechlessness by the deluge of verbiage unleashed in his direction by the "man with the weed." The demand to "drop Tacitus," both the book he is reading and his silence, only renders the collegian more helpless. The operator's exhortation to replace Tacitus with Akenside is a demand to suppress the historical consciousness exemplified by the *Annals* and to cover it over with the circumlocutionary exaltation in humanitarian ideals that fills "The Pleasures of the Imagination." The "man with the weed" thus weaves into his appeal the typical American anti-historicism, the belief in an ongoing state of newness that need not be fettered by precedent.[8] If history cannot be renovated to fit the times, it is best ignored.

Such stripped-down episodes as this one may be complicated by a variety of factors. Debunkers, for example, compound the logical structure of the episodes. While a debunker may throw wrenches into an operator's delivery, establishing the veracity of the debunker becomes as serious an interpretative problem as ascertaining the operator's claim. A model debunker of the first half of the novel is the "soldier of fortune" who comes face to face with the herb-doctor. The autobiographical narrative provided by this cripple is in direct antithesis to the unmitigated optimism displayed by the herb-doctor, who professes "confidence in everybody" and designates himself "the Happy Man—the Happy Bonesetter" (131). The story continues in the line of the demonstration by the Goneril episode that laws are not necessarily tantamount to justice. The demise of the central character, one Thomas Fry, begins when as a cooper he testifies against a gentleman who murdered a pavior in a street fight. Naturally it is Fry, who, as a consequence of his lower class, is "fried" by the judicial system. He ends up in prison while the gentleman goes free. His crime: "While I hadn't got any friends, I tell ye. A worse crime than murder, as ye'll see afore long" (133). Although friendship here has the connotation of crude influence and connections, it will be elevated in the second half of the novel into a fundament of the ideology of confidence.

Thomas Fry's travails go only from bad to worse. His experience is a living example of the hollowness not only of the herb-doctor's discourse but of all of the ideals invoked thus far by the operators. Friendship is not love of one's fellow human beings but influence. Justice is defined by class distinctions. The herb-doctor's response to the tale is characteristic: "I cannot believe it" (135)—a profession of total ignorance of those chinks in the ideal that are the very mortar of language and rhetoric.

But the final turn provided by this story that is in itself a debunking of several varieties of the ideal is yet to come. The cynical penetrator of the optimism claimed to be indispensable to the social order is himself an operator, a minor one, a beggar, but one who reaps a "pretty good harvest" (136). In the encompassing operation of confidence, the debunkers who arise to battle the operators' claims turn out to be fellow-operators, just as the most duplicitous discoursers profess the most extreme sort of prudery. The confidence game not only extends itself temporally in the interreferentiality of the operators: within a given episode its roles are interchangeable.[9] With great fluidity its characters change—or are engineered into changing—their roles. Bystanders can be appropriated by the operators as model dupes. Valiant debunkers can become fellow-operators or dupes. And the operators can be the most implausible pollyannas. Thus, one of the clergymen who supports Black Guinea—and we will never know his "true" allegiance—the Methodist minister, assumes the characteristic pose of the operators. First he shames, then he forces the cynical customs house official into charity (20–21). Such relative, situational roles are in keeping with a confidence operation passing with facility from one theme and social context to the next.

There is no fuller measure of the variety afforded by the operational matrix delineated in the first half of the novel than the array of ploys at the operators' disposal. These range from the bluntest acts of appeal and shaming[10] to highly intricate performances. More conventional ploys include the following: (a) a renunciation of payment for wares;[11] (b) serving as a model of charitable acts by conspicuously giving donations to fellow-operators;[12] and (c) the operators' casting aspersions on their own enterprises and "relenting" as the targets refuse to entertain such doubts.[13] Faced with the failure of their ploys, the operators prove skillful at sloughing over their own errors and resiliant to resistance. The herb-doctor turns an expectation that slips out—that he does not expect the old miser to whom he has just sold medicine to live long—into a warning that the compound will be difficult to find elsewhere (114). Felled by the "sudden side-blow" of the Missouri bachelor, the same operator "recovers" himself with hardly an interruption (122). In so doing he literally demonstrates the capacity of an ideology in which differences are blurred to right or reorient itself in spite of whatever criteria of consistency are applied to it.

The culmination of the operators' nerve in the first half of the novel, the ploy of ploys, occurs when the herb-doctor, encountering resistance from the Missouri bachelor, accuses his debunker of precisely the sort of language play that has characterized the discourse of all operators. "Yes," says the herb-doctor, "I think I understand you now, sir. How silly I was to have taken you seriously, in your droll conceits, too, about having no confidence in nature. In reality you have just as much as I have" (148). In the same gesture in which the herb-doctor professes his naive veneration for nature, he projects his own drollery onto his interlocutor, the Missouri bachelor, whose literality is symbolized by his name: "My name is Pitch; I stick to what I say" (162).

The first half of the novel, in the rapid pace of its episodes, in the division of labor making its operators representatives of specialized interests, and in the compartmentalization of themes by operator, invites comparison and the type of structural analysis generated by such comparisons. After Black Guinea, we meet, in order, the "man with the weed," the "man with a gray coat and white tie," who represents the Seminole Widow and Orphan Asylum, the "man in a tassled travelling-cap," an agent of the Black Rapids Coal Company, the herb-doctor, and the philosophical intelligence officer, who sells slaves. Although the highest interest represented by the "man with the weed" is his own desire for money, his anti-historicism and anti-intellectualism will be the basis for the claims made by all subsequent operators. The "man with a gray coat and white tie" represents "the charity business . . . in all its branches" (54). Advancing his philanthropic ideal with the rhetoric of evangelism, he envisions a world-wide welfare institution that enriches itself from a universal tithe. What philanthropy is to this cosmic fund-raiser, business confidence is to the agent of the Black Rapids Coal Co., who rails against the "destroyers of confidence and gloomy philosophers of the stock market" (68).

Why, the most monstrous of all hypocrites are these bears: hypocrites by inversion; hypocrites in the simulation of things dark instead of bright; souls that thrive, less upon depression, than the fiction of depression; professors of the wicked art of manufacturing depressions; spurious Jeremiahs; sham Heraclituses, who, the lugubrious day done, return, like sham Lazaruses among

the beggars, to make merry over the gains got by their pretended sore heads
—scoundrelly bears! (67–68)

Bullish on America, this character senses that the diametrical opposite of
the ideology of confidence, with its duplicitous profession of well-being, is
financial depression, or, translated into another context, *hypochondriasis*,
the claim of nonexistent damage. Hypochondriacs, such as the "spurious
Jeremiahs" of the above passage or the dusk giant (119, 122), one of the
novel's most outspoken debunkers, intuit harm precisely where an operator sees a panacea. And for the herb-doctor, confidence in nature is the
panacea for all earthly woes. "Trust me, nature is health; for health is
good, and nature cannot work ill. As little can she work error. Get
nature, and you get well" (112). It is the herb-doctor, with his appropriation and disfiguration of Wordsworth ("Nature delights in benefitting
those who most abuse her," 151) who most fully demonstrates the natural affinity of the ideology of confidence for the Romantic code.[14]

Although less specific than the cure-alls peddled by the other
operators, the ideal advanced by the philosophical intelligence officer is
of the widest philosophical scope. For the "doctrine of analogies" sometimes invoked, sometimes retracted in guaranteeing the quality of the
slaves that this character sells is no less than a model of representation
and causality in language. Analogical or representational thought finds
its practical application in the slave market in the trader's need to claim
that a child's present physical attributes necessitate his future superiority
as a slave. Such a claim must be able to proceed, by analogy, "from the
physical to the moral" (167), from physical traits to overall superiority.
Within this type of argumentation, the physical trait must function as a
thoroughly dependable and stable sign. Zeroing in on the penis, the
operator holds firm to the capacity for "anticipation" that it embodies:

The man-child not only possesses these present points, small though they are,
but, likewise—now our horticultural image comes into play—like the bud of a
lily, he contains concealed rudiments of others. . . . (168)

Can it now with fairness be denied that, in his beard, the man-child prospectively possesses an appendix, not less imposing than patriarchal; and for
this goodly beard, should we not by generous anticipation give the man-child,
even in his cradle, credit? (169)

And yet, a complementary posture necessitated by the slave trade demands that the philosophical intelligence officer also adulterate this pure
phallogocentrism. For while it serves the trader's interest to be able to
proceed in an unproblematic fashion from the child to the man and from
the physical to the moral, he must also be able to assert that "blemishes"
in a young slave will not necessarily continue in adulthood. Hence, the
questioning of analogical thought, the repudiation of the Wordsworthian

dictum having the child as "the father of the man" (165), is as necessary to his posture as the transparent model of representational thought. The philosophical intelligence officer's attitude toward language is thus a double-bind. In his own use of language he cannot abide by the notions of causality and referentiality that he must nonetheless presuppose in formulating his sales pitch. Quite typically, this character empties the ideal he represents—that of representational language—in the same gesture by which he invokes it. The philosophical title of the trader, the philosophical nature of the problem he poses, is one of the novel's most direct intimations of the collusion between the critical skills and political repression.

The first half of the novel is an arena in which we observe a metaphysical structure—the ideal—and a linguistic structure—the confidence-game—pass through a sequence of settings and characters, accruing themes and variations all the while. This schematic effort reveals the power of the scheme, in business and in fiction. In the fate of this scheme will reside many of the resources of the novel's economy.

III

In postulating a model of the confidence game, the double gesture by which the operators espouse certain ideals while violating them in their actions has afforded a stable point of departure. Yet the manner in which the operators *represent* the ideal is not nearly as transparent as has thus far been implied. While wondering at the operators' efficacy, the novel nonetheless mocks the pettiness of their crime, the triteness of their machinations. And the ideals propounded by the operators are implicated—by association—as targets for the satire.

By assimilating the structure of the ideal in so many of its manifestations or guises, whether charity, philanthropy, or nature, the novel becomes an encyclopaedic shooting-gallery for the puncturing of the ideal. The only factor mitigating the overall nihilistic thrust of this debunking is the affiliations linking the operators to specific social institutions. The component of the novel offering to be read as an ultimate Nietzschean emptying of the ideal is thus coupled to a concrete social satire or criticism. At the same time that the novel offers a critique of the political uses of the critical skills, the public disclaimer of the linguistic competences at the basis of manipulation, it is also a satire of its characters, the dupes as well as the operators, and, ultimately, of itself.

The continental divide down the center of the text becomes one of the most effective instruments of the novel's irony and self-irony. The adjustments made to the pacing of events, the structure of episodes, and characterization in the second half of the novel are too conspicuous to be overlooked.[15] Both a release of structure and a new wealth of associations are made possible by the eclipsing of daylight in the temporal setting. Episodes become fewer and more attenuated. The stream of targets slows down. The encounters between the cosmopolitan and his interlocutors become digressive. The naked economic motives propelling the exchanges are obscured and to a certain extent effaced by philosophical speculations.

If, as H. Bruce Franklin suggests, the operators of the first half of the novel merely anticipate the cosmopolitan, the novel leads up to a massive anti-climax, for, fitting in with the novel's religious symbolism, the cosmopolitan is more lamb than lion.[16] He is a born loser.[17] The exchanges he enters are reciprocal battles of wits, not economic abductions of passive victims. The two interlocutors who eventually assume the name Charley Noble—suggesting *their* interchangeability—are no less suspicious, cagey, and manipulative than he is. The single weapon in his arsenal is charm; his only strategy, seduction. Hence, the importance of wine and tobacco in his encounters. The cosmopolitan has no gimmicks or trade-marks at his disposal. Consequently, the neat division of labor of the operators in the first half of the novel, the compartmentalization of theme by character, disappears and is replaced by much more fluid convergences of theme. The digressive quality of the cosmopolitan's encounters marks a shift of emphasis in the confidence-operation from rhetoric to story-telling.

Obviously, then, in comparison with previous operators, the cosmopolitan undergoes a reduction in stature. The satire of the second half of the novel thus moves in a double direction, on one hand extending the assault on the ideal, but on the other shifting the thrust of the satire toward the novel itself. The cosmopolitan's failure with both characters named Charley Noble, the fact that his major triumph consists in conniving a twenty-five cent haircut, demonstrate the novel's application of its satire to its anti-hero and hence to itself.

The second half of the novel divides itself into three main scenes. After an inconclusive foray at the Missouri bachelor, the only carry-over from the first half of the novel and a means of affording some continuity, the cosmopolitan falls in with an "acquaintance" who occupies him for some ten chapters. In the course of this interview, the lineaments of the ideology of confidence fill out considerably. The abstract notion of confidence as the indispensable basis of social interaction in any context is now amplified by its *behavioral* dimension, hence the emphasis on conviviality and congeniality.

Strangely enough, the expansionist racism brought to light in the story of the exemplary Indian-hater, Colonel John Moredock, narrated by the cosmopolitan's interlocutor in these chapters (chaps. 25–35) goes hand in hand with a social code of friendship and amiability. The Indian-hater is characterized by the same inconsistency that was manifested by the operators who disclaimed their rhetoric in the same act in which they deployed it. ". . . Moredock was an example of something apparently self-contradicting, certainly curious, but, at the same time, undeniable: namely, that nearly all Indian-haters have at bottom loving hearts; at any rate, hearts, if anything, more generous than the average" (218). The Indian-hater is an example of the capacity to displace violence, to externalize it, to turn it on *another*, precisely for the purpose of protecting an atmosphere of stability, whether described as peace or confidence, closer to home.[18] This is in the direct line of the pattern established by the herb-doctor, who externalizes his drollery, his language-play, by displacing it to *his* other. This is just what happens on a far wider scale in an anecdote introduced into the narrative as a rationalization for Indian-hatred. Chief Mocmohoc suddenly, and for no overt reason, terminates his hostilities against the colony of Wrights and Weavers and offers a truce, one of whose conditions is that "the five cousins should never, on any account, be expected to enter the chief's lodge together. . . . Nevertheless, Mocmohoc did, upon a time, with such fine art and pleasing carriage win their confidence, that he brought them all together to a feast of bear's meat, and there, by stratagem, ended them" (209–10).[19] The Indian chief entertains his neighbors with an ultimate irony. Mocmohoc mocks them with an overt demonstration of the discrepancy in public discourse dramatized repeatedly by the operators in the first half of the novel. Instead of dissimulating this credibility-gap, he gives it its most positive—and negative—statement. The anecdote continues the novel's questioning of the status of legal language. The genocide that the anecdote justifies is a means, on a societal level, of liquidating a segment of the population onto which the duplicity of language in civil life has been projected and externalized. The Indian accoutrements for the taking of wine and tobacco appear four times in the last half of the novel (185, 214, 228, and 240) and suggest, in a way reminiscent of the human lampshades of World War II, the form in which awareness of this operation filters through to the domestic front. The violence translates into absurd Indian baskets and calumets.

Indian-hating, then, is the primary instance of the novel's disclosure of the *other*, that is, the usually concealed but complementary side of the ideology of confidence. In the figure of the Indian-hater, the novel comes closest to the obsessive personality whose most developed example in Melville's fiction is Ahab of *Moby-Dick*. Whether the quest is for the Indian or the "deep-sea denizen" (213), a split personality underlies the monomaniacal, seemingly single-minded project. The hunt is an attempt to restore consistency, to quell an internal discrepancy, whose model is language, by eliminating an external quarry onto which it has been projected. The hunter teeters between obsession and schizophrenia.

It is in the cosmopolitan's encounter with his first main interlocutor that the ideal finds its social applications or manners. Considerable attention is paid to conversation itself as the occasion for the always polite transactions of confidence, as the medium of social interaction. And the conversation between the cosmopolitan, alias Frank Goodman, and Charley Noble passes with facility from one sub-category or theme of confidence to the next. Over a bottle of bad port, which these two characters both abstain from drinking as they urge each other on to greater libations, they entertain such topics as the nobility of the human heart (230) and the needs for humor (232), congeniality (241), and the trite cultivation that prolongs the conversation accompanying the transactions of confidence. This literate veneer is exemplified by the extended discussion of Shakespeare (242–49). Even when the interlocutors seem to argue energetically, their respective positions presuppose the necessity of confidence—as when Charley Noble scores the Missouri bachelor and Polonius for their skepticism and the cosmopolitan defends them in the name of charity.

The effusive friendship between the cosmopolitan and his interlocutor is interrupted only when the former transgresses the single norm in the code of congeniality, when he makes a direct appeal to Charley Noble for money. The cosmopolitan placates the anger of his companion long enough to narrate the tale of yet another character who undergoes abrupt changes of personality, Charlemont, the gentleman-madman. If the figure of the Indian-hater may be described as a paranoid-schizophrenic in the discrepancy between his homicidal isolation and his occasional outbreaks of soppy friendliness, Charlemont is a manic-depressive version of the same incongruity. At the age of twenty-nine, the St. Louis businessman turns morose and begins to fail in his endeavors. He disappears, and his friends speculate that he may have committed suicide. Years later, he returns, "Not only . . . alive, but he was himself again" (262). His restoration is described in terms of a code that is by now well-established in the novel. He can now give himself over to "genial" friendship; his "noble qualities" enable him to prosper "in the encouraging sun of good opinions"; "under the influence of wine" he relates to an acquaintance the secrets of the intervening years. The moral of this *mise en abîme* of the situation in which Frank Goodman and Charley find themselves is, predictably, never to "turn the cold shoulder to a friend—a convivial one" (264), and is for Charley to donate the previously requested contribution. Yet the widest speculative horizon for such instances of discrepancy in character, whether schizophrenic or manic-depressive, is the issue of discrepancy itself—of how both the masquerade and the text in which it is narrated depart from the norms of consistency and representation on which they depend for their effect.

In the second segment of the narrative focusing on the cosmopolitan (chaps. 36–41), he encounters two characters whose personalities are also marked by inconsistency. Espousing the ideals of the American transcendentalists, they nevertheless betray a Yankee pragmatism (265) beneath their admiration for beauty and nature.[20] Just as the philosophical intelligence officer found it necessary both to advance and refute the claim of representation in his discourse, Mark Winsome vacillates between a representational "doctrine of labels" and a "doctrine of triangles" that denies the possibility of "forming a true estimate of any being" from "the data which life furnishes" (271). In his encounters with Mark Winsome and Egbert, his disciple, the cosmopolitan shifts from being the operator to the straight-man. Winsome and Egbert themselves expose the chinks in the ideals they espouse. This is nowhere more evident than when Egbert, now as the new Charley Noble, narrates the story of China Aster in order to deflate the ideal of friendship that the cosmopolitan holds up to him in pressing yet another appeal for money.

The third and concluding installment, both of the cosmopolitan's experiences and the novel, in many senses brings the text full circle. The cosmopolitan's involved haggling with the barber over the price of a haircut returns us to the novel's ur-cynic and to its earliest testing of the status of signs. The hair which is the barber's business is a universal human denominator, and the debate brings the discourse to the level of the anthropological study of man attained in the remarks of the philosophical intelligence officer. The novel's final scene recrystallizes a familiar configuration. The cosmopolitan's representations to a venerable old man who sits reading the Bible under a solar lamp, a recurrence of the sun dawning as the novel begins, are punctuated by a voice of cynicism emanating from an invisible source among the berths. The novel ends as yet a final operator, this time an impoverished boy, peddles "security" devices: "the traveller's patent lock" (341), money-belts, a carry-over from the novel's first scene, and *Counterfeit Detectors*.

The text provides us with no more heavily coded and ironic self-allegorization than the story of China Aster, the simple candle-maker whose demise is sealed when, against his own better instincts, he accepts a loan from his friend, Orchis. China Aster, the star of China whose name itself reflects the illumination business, shines, and is then eclipsed over Marietta, Ohio, "at the mouth of the Muskingum" (291). The name China Aster endows a story of small-town usury with an exotic aura and with the remote setting of parable. The star of the orient is displaced to Ohio, and the Muskingum, combining musk, essence of the male organs, and the lingum of the Indian erotic literature, are two additional instances of the novel's assimilative economy. Although a man, China Aster is endowed with the fragility of fine china. And in the course of the story, he is "screwed," allegorically as well as economically, by his less delicate male associate, Orchis, whose name signifies not only a plant but also a testicle. While China Aster pursues the implicitly speculative *métier* of providing light, Orchis, a shoemaker, attends to the concrete matters under foot.

Having improved his station by winning a "capital prize in a lottery" (292), Orchis sets about convincing his friend of the need for additional capital and to "drop this vile tallow and hold up pure spermaceti to the world" (242). Echoing the "man with the weed's" demand to "drop Tacitus" and the evangelical vision of the "man with a gray coat and white tie," Orchis compels China Aster to accept unnecessary capital on the basis of an artificial consumer demand, the conversion from tallow to spermaceti candles. And repeating previous operators' dissimulation of their motives, notably the herb-doctor's refusing payment for his wares, Orchis secures China Aster's commitment in a most off-handed manner:

"By-the-way, China Aster, it don't mean anything, but suppose you make a little memorandum of this; won't do any harm, you know." So China Aster gave Orchis his note for one thousand dollars on demand. Orchis took it, and looked at it a moment, "Pooh, I told you, friend China Aster, I wasn't ever going to make any *demand*." . . . "You see I'll never trouble you about this . . . give yourself no further thought, friend China Aster, than how best to invest your money." (294–95)

China Aster's compliance with the scheme is, however, not entirely without conflict. Two of the old geezers in town, "Old Plain Talk" and "Old Prudence," serve as China Aster's alter-egos and voice their reservations. Orchis instinctively senses enemies in these skeptics, just as the agent of the Black Rapids Coal Co. was down on "bears." What we have, then, is the "classical" configuration of the confidence-game. Orchis, the operator, exhorts China Aster to accept unnecessary credit, while the two "straight-men," as simple and direct as their allegorical names, offer some resistance. It can hardly be surprising, then, that Orchis addresses to China Aster the following speech, the condensation of an ideology that has elsewhere demonstrated a Protean capacity to change forms:

"Why, China Aster, you are the dolefulest creature. Why don't you, China Aster, take a bright view of life? You will never get on in your business or anything else, if you don't take the bright view of life. It's the ruination of a man to take the dismal one." Then, gayly poking at him with his gold-headed cane, "Why don't you, then? Why don't you be bright and hopeful, like me? Why don't you have confidence, China Aster?" (295)

The machine of capital accumulation is once again greased by the language of effusive optimism. But the story of China Aster introduces a

Henry Sussman

new dimension and level to the functioning of this category. For the first time we have an inkling of the psychological manifestation of confidence, both private and mass-psychological, an anticipation of the Freudian notion of the dream as wish-fulfillment.

But as destiny would have it, that same night China Aster had a dream, in which a being in the guise of a smiling angel, and holding a kind of cornucopia in her hand, hovered over him, pouring down showers of small gold dollars, thick as kernels of corn. "I am Bright Future, friend China Aster," said the angel, "and if you do what friend Orchis would have you do, just see what will come of it." With which Bright Future, with another swing of her cornucopia, poured such another shower of small gold dollars upon him, that it seemed to bank him up all round, and he waded about in it like a maltster in malt. (296)

This capitalist reverie achieves the deepest penetration of the ideology of confidence, invading the inmost sanctuary of the psyche. Attacking China Aster in the defenseless state of slumber, it evades the resistances mounted both by his own good sense and the detachment of Old Plain Talk and Old Prudence, who induce him, like psychoanalysts, to interpret the dream. But to no avail. Having succumbed to the dream, with its images of fertility, abundance, and drunken abandon (the maltster), China Aster is unable to return the check that Orchis has pressed upon him. And when the pointlessness of the loan and the discomforts it causes begin to haunt China Aster, the now-obsessive dream of ever-increasing prosperity returns and reinforces the debtor's compliance to the conditions of the loan (299).

Thus begin two counter-trajectories both deriving their drift from the original friendly loan. For China Aster, the path is of uninterrupted, almost mechanical decline. Unable to keep up with payments on the loan, China Aster must assume greater debts. The battle to keep pace with payments on the principle becomes an equally futile attempt to pay off the interest. Reversals within the broader system of speculation make China Aster's failure inevitable:

. . . he did not try his hand at the spermaceti again, but . . . returned to tallow. But, having bought a good lot of it, by the time he got it into candles, tallow fell so low, and candles with it, that his candles per pound barely sold for what he had paid for the tallow. Meantime, a year's unpaid interest had accrued. . . . (301)

Yet the obvious way out of this trap, simply defaulting on the loan, eludes China Aster, for he is too honest, he has internalized the ideals of politeness and decency promoted by the operators throughout the novel too well: "had China Aster been a different man, the money-lender might have dreaded" (300).

But Orchis is a different man. There is no consistency to his meanderings. Like his fellow-operators and the narrator, Orchis is free to be inconsistent. Of a suspicious temperament, like one of the earlier de-bunkers, he is a hypochondriac. Illness takes him to Europe. Like Charlemont, he returns from his travels a changed man, but in the op-posite direction, "sallow in cheek, and decidedly less gay and cordial in manner" (302). Having converted into a religious "or rather semi-religious" (301) Come-Outer, Orchis demonstrates once again how popular religion, with its evangelical impulse, interlocks with capitalism and its logic of accumulation. In his final manifestation, Orchis, the civilized operator, the operator as good citizen, is both hardened and religious, superstitious and skeptical. He has aspired to and attained the level of big-time capitalism. For it is through "a breach of trust on the part of a factor in New York" (303) that he must subject China Aster to the crushing and final pressure that will result in the latter's fatal sun-stroke. China Aster dies, the candle of his mind extinguished, the sun of optimism within eclipsed by the external sun of harsh economic facts, his children public charges. "The root of all," as is dutifully recorded by Old Plain Talk and Old Prudence on his gravestone, "was a friendly loan" (303).

This story insinuates a sexual dimension into the manipulation that has taken place throughout the novel and suggests the wider psychologi-cal impact of the confidence game. Yet the primary contribution made by the story is not so much elaboration as combining details dissemi-nated loosely throughout the novel into a precise self-allegorization. Beneath the hilarity of the story and the provincial travesty contained in the characters' names, a refined economy is operating. The textual econ-omy of this internalized theater runs parallel to the machine-operation of the confidence-game in the first half of the novel. To the extent that the story parodies the confidence operation outlined in the first half of the novel, it is allegory, self-irony, self-deconstruction. But in the sense that it recalls the ongoing machinations of confidence in all its interlocking domains, it is social criticism and mass-psychology.

IV

If confidence is ultimately a metaphysical category, implying a rela-tion of optimism and unquestioning belief, consistency is its homologue within the sphere of fiction and representation. What confidence is to belief, consistency is to logic and representation—a guarantee of authen-ticity, a moratorium on fluctuations of meaning or value. It is fitting, then, that the category of consistency should come into play not only in the three chapters that the narrator explicitly appropriates for himself, but also in the occasional narrative descriptions that get out of hand, that betray some tampering with narrative "objectivity."[21]

And in his direct entrances onto the stage of the fiction the narrator provides the operators with cover-fire, for if they are walking embodiments of a basic contradiction, a simultaneous profession and emptying of the ideal, the narrator challenges the worth of consistency in a work of fiction, whether the consistency of the characters to themselves or the "severe fidelity" of the work to "real life."[22] Not only do predictable characters and realistic works lack "the play of invention" (94), but there is a certain order of "facts" (95) to which they are not equal and that they finally betray. As positive models for his fiction the narrator invokes the "duck-billed characters" for which no classification is readily available (97) and "the best false teeth . . . those made with at least two or three blemishes, the more to look like life" (197). In promoting the cause of fictive inconsistency, the narrator becomes the voice of the text, its house-organ. The narrator verges on his own brand of idealism in his contention that in serving concrete reality, a work of fiction betrays a profounder one. But the overall thrust of his remarks is toward a declaration of independence from representation and realism made by and for the fictive work (260). Ostensibly "outside" the text, then, and lending it a dimension of credibility lacking in its proper domain, the narrator is assimilated by the masquerade staged by the novel, its array of costumes,[23] its side-show of freaks,[24] its menagerie of animals,[25] and its herbarium of flowers.[26]

Viewed as the theater of the unmasking of the ideal, the text could continue endlessly in a joyous demolition-derby, with each successive incarnation of the ideal shattered in the textual machinery. Yet there is one small catch to this free-play, one small rider on the declaration of fictive independence. And the catch is, precisely, the unholy place where the language games border on power, where the voices of the operators declaim in the interest of identifiable institutions continuing in some form or another to this day. Note that this catch, this bordering, does not reduce or impose closure upon the general debunking. The puncturing of the ideal and the social critique are simultaneous. Melville thus provides us with a compelling variation on a critical program edging closer to established authority. The Nietzschean-Heideggerian-Derridean isolation and triggering of a violence pent up within master-texts or attitudes that were, by implication, too obtuse, inflexible, or blind to account for it— this dis-closure of the duplicity of language moves, in Melville's version, from the morally superior position of the pale or margin to the center of collusion, the seat of power. In Melville's model, the critics *are* the politicians. The wielding of power is inseparable from the critical awareness of the duplicity of language. In *The Confidence-Man*, the neat division of labor whereby the literary or metaphysical fatcats *harbor* the violence while the critics *unleash* it breaks down. Only within the civil neutrality of academic discourse could the utilization of language in suppression and violence come as news to anyone.

Under the master-rubic of *confidence* a veritable menagerie of ideals has ambled through the novel. There have been the great ones and the little ones. Of the wider ideals, we have observed, or at least touched upon: nature, man, charity, philanthropy, and speculation. Of the narrower: friendship, humor, politeness, generosity, nobility, the human heart, patriotism, and, paradoxically, class privilege and racial dominance. Yet we have reserved for last the ideal category perhaps closest to home: "original genius." Melville underscores the importance of this term when he has the narrator, intruding into the action for the last time, underscore these words: "QUITE AN ORIGINAL" (329), the only instance when the narrator offers a direct gloss upon the text. "Quite an original" is the term that in future times will occur to the barber when he describes his fleecing by the cosmopolitan. Yet already that original operator, the mute, was an "original genius" upon stepping aboard the Fidèle (4). Its trajectory encompassing the entire novel, the term "original" genius is vital not only to the text's historical program, but also to its economy of the ideal. To be sure, "original genius" is a function of the novel's concern with various types of origins. There is the demographic origin of the "strangers" mixed by the boat along the Mississippi, a microcosm of the American population. And there is the origin of the language consisting of images, terms, and usages unique to this novel. While *confidence* and its forms is the most prevalent term in the novel, its meaning running from self-assurance, hope, and optimism through trust, discretion, privacy, and secrecy, on into subterfuge and trickery, important word-plays exploit the variations on words less conspicuous and decisive to the overall scheme: *spectacle-speculate-suspect-suspicion*,[27] *extreme*,[28] *strange*,[29] *frank*,[30] and the *press*.[31] In the widest sense, the concern for establishing origins of all kinds belongs to the program of cultural epigenesis in American letters outlined in recent work by John Irwin.[32]

But the originality whose importance is marked throughout the text is coupled to "genius." This word reaches back to the very roots of life, but also up to the transcendental spirit or spark conducted back to this world only by the fit few. Among the definitions of the word offered by the *Oxford English Dictionary* is the following:

5. Native intellectual power of an exalted type, such as is attributed to those who are esteemed greatest in any department of art, speculation, or practice; instinctive and extraordinary capacity for imaginative creation, original thought, invention, or discovery.[33]

Yet this otherworldly gift somehow finding its way to "native" soil also adapts itself to the ideology of confidence. For there is a touch of genius in "geniality," the social skills, the conviviality, in which the always polite transactions of confidence are surrounded. It is in this sense that the operators translate their genius so well into the practical interests and activities of business. The initial Charley Noble is particularly frank regarding the collusion between genius and geniality.

Fill up, up, up, my friend. Let the ruby tide aspire, and all ruby aspirations with it. . . . Be we convivial. And conviviality, what is it? . . . A living together. But bats live together. . . .

. . . bats, though they live together, live not together genially. Bats are not genial souls. But men are; and how delightful to think that the word which among men signifies the highest pitch of geniality, implies, as indispensable auxiliary, the cheery benediction of the bottle. (250)

Geniality has invaded each department and profession. We have genial senators, genial authors, genial lecturers, genial doctors, genial clergymen, genial surgeons, and the next thing we shall have genial hangmen. (251)

And here we are indeed closest to home. For in addition to suggesting the spiritual dimension of genius, Melville implicates here, in a remarkable gesture of authorial frankness, not only his own work's pretensions to genius, but the entire complex of institutions dedicated to the recognition, preservation, and generation of original genius, of which the university is the primary installation. While unstated, in the interest of confidentiality, original genius is the metaphysical orientation of the university. It is in the name of original genius that the university's standards are stipulated. It is around this term that the neutral space is opened in which "any department of art, speculation, or practice" may operate. This neutrality is secured by the protective discursive tariffs making the various disciplines as inaccessible as possible to outsiders. Concurrent with the pursuit and profession by the operators of their respective discursive lines is the encompassing institutional aim, that "each department" be invaded by "genial authors . . . lecturers . . . doctors . . . surgeons," and the like. The university is to the individual disciplines what the cosmopolitan is to the singular operators: the sublation of a system of speculation to a higher level, to the universal. As the sanctuary of original genius, the university provides the social systems of government, finance, defense, health, education, and welfare with the security that their operations are backed by the highest emanations of inspiration.

What does it mean, then, for deconstructive critics to unleash the negativity of language within the text when the audience is the university? What can this mean when the debunking takes place *on campus*, within the insulated zone that is afforded its protection in repayment for self-administered neutrality? Within this space, critics are recognized as the final authorities on language and reading in the land. But what does it mean to teach the critical skills within the temple of original genius when the moves breathlessly announced by the critics of deconstruction are near-timeless principles in the rulebooks of political power *out there*? To be sure, there is a politics of the university proper, but its implications are trivial in comparison with the collusion between the critical skills and mass-manipulation *out there*. Television is the best example of a mass-medium assuming the characteristic pose of the confidence-men. While a complex form of visual and aural language itself, it systematically enforces the obliteration of difference, an erasure of the discrepancies, political, social, and intellectual, that discontent the audience. The *resolution* of all possible sources of tension implemented by television at all levels of programming is the mass-media equivalent to the operators' unsinkable optimism and the processes of assimilation dramatized by the novel. The coordination by which the programs and commericals mutually confirm and arise out of each other is a contemporary version of the interreferential links by means of which the operators support each others' claims. A challenge to the ideology of television is a blow to the metaphysics orienting a culture of now-global proportions. But the deconstructive awareness facilitating such an attack has seldom wandered *out there*. The principles of sound capitalism dictate a reinvestment of such gains back to the "original" enterprise, the pursuit of original genius. This paper joins the Melville literature generated by the university and as such is offered upon the altar of original genius.

There is no more striking example of the assimilative neutrality of the university than its reception of deconstructive criticism. Though it may also demonstrate historical rigor, scholarly comprehensiveness, and technical facility, deconstructive criticism primarily bases its appeal not on these types of guarantee but on a bearing, a contrapuntal rhythm to deterministic operations, on a characteristic mode or voice of irony.[34] It is remarkable, then, given the claims of deconstructive criticism to undermine a 2000-year epoch of Western culture, how, in a few years' time, "critical theory" has become a category to be placed alongside thematic, historical, biographical, formal, and linguistic studies. The untoward voice or posture of deconstructive criticism becomes merely one more commodity among a bewildering array of skills and wares peddled along the arcade of the academic bazaar. This institutionalization suggests that we no longer witness the *rise* of deconstruction but its *wake*. The only direction in which to proceed from the supersaturated academic space may well lie *out there*, beyond the campus, where neutral language gives way to hard language,[35] where the determinisms we observe on an ever-widening *general* scale effect the material, cultural conditions of life. I place *material* and *cultural* in apposition, having no reason to oppose them.

Just as the flaxen mute who emerges out of nowhere on an unspecified April Fool's day anticipates the course of the novel, *The Confidence-Man* has proven prophetic. A product of the age of mechanical reproduction, it harbors the seeds of the manner in which communications and mass-language will function long beyond its time. In its critical scenario, as well, it is beyond its day. Not only does it provide a highly sophisticated and comprehensive mechanism for the deconstruction of the ideal, but it places the critical skills made accessible by deconstruction in the widest social context. It suggests an alternative to the self-serving configuration in which the critic and the assertion of power are always on opposite sides of a pre-given and mystical bar. It demands of those who would trace out the configurations implied by its internal critical scenario a fresh reevaluation of positions—positions within the contemporary critical scene, the position of that scene within the academic super-market, and the overall social setting of the university. Although in a small way, it is for us to determine what "further may follow of this Masquerade" (350).

NOTES

1. All citations refer to H. Bruce Franklin's edition of the novel. Herman Melville, *The Confidence-Man* (Indianapolis: Bobbs-Merrill, 1967). The title will be abbreviated *CM*.

2. See *CM*, p. 11, where "the great ship canal of Ving-King-Ching seems the Mississippi in parts." The ambiguity (and ultimate indifference) of Black Guinea's color is to be found on pp. 20 and 46.

3. Cf. *CM*, pp. xviii, 180.

4. Also see *CM*, pp. 27, 65, 80, 81, 125, 138, 141, 159, 187.

5. Also see *CM*, pp. 20, 32.

6. For a contemporary version of this kind of utopia, see Louis Marin, "Disneyland: A Degenerate Utopia," in *Glyph 1: Johns Hopkins Textual Studies* (Baltimore: Johns Hopkins University Press, 1977), pp. 50–66.

7. See Walter Benjamin, "The Work of Art in the Age of Mechanical Reproduction," in *Illuminations*, ed. Hannah Arendt, trans. Harry Zohn (New York: Schocken, 1969), pp. 217–51.

8. This attitude bears affinities to R. W. B. Lewis's notion of Adamism. See R. W. B. Lewis, *The American Adam* (Chicago: University of Chicago Press, 1971), pp. 9, 41.

9. For role reversals, as well as other forms of reversal in the novel, see John G. Cawelti, "Some Notes on the Structure of *The Confidence-Man*," *American Literature* 29 (1957): 278–88.

10. *CM*, pp. 63, 103.

11. *CM*, pp. 138–39, 151.

12. *CM*, pp. 49, 127.

13. *CM*, pp. 66–69, 78.

14. Also see CM, pp. 73 (a parody of the beginning of Blake's song, "How sweet I roam'd from field to field"), 150 (a reference to Wordsworthian "passion-fits of nature"), 166, and 225.

15. See Walter Dubler, "Theme and Structure in Melville's *The Confidence-Man*," *American Literature* 33 (1961): 307–19. Dubler recognizes the connection between the novel's theme of moral indeterminacy and the various types of dialectical relations it sets into play, but he does not consider the dialectic in which the two halves of the novel are involved.

16. *CM*, p. xx. The figure of the confidence-man can be regarded *both* as a sequence of different characters (as it was in most criticism prior to Franklin's work) *or* as a single composite character who changes guises.

17. The dialectical logic of the novel does not preclude the possibility that the cosmopolitan's "defeats" are pedagogical moves in a strategem that metamorphoses the interlocutors of the second half of the novel into operators as effective as the cosmopolitan himself.

18. Explications of this episode tend toward a moral evaluation of Indians as opposed to Indian-haters and of Melville's intentions, whether he sided with the Indians or their predators. Yet the wider issue at stake is the ideology of confidence and how both groups are encompassed by it. See Elizabeth S. Foster's introduction to her edition of the novel, *The Confidence-Man* (New York: Hendricks House, 1954), pp. lxv–vii, and Roy Harvey Pearce, "Melville's Indian-hater: A Note on a Meaning of *The Confidence-Man*," *PMLA* 67 (1952): 942–48, parts of which are reprinted in Pearce's *Savagism and Civilization* (Baltimore: Johns Hopkins University Press, 1965), pp. 244–50.

19. The connections that Melville observes between language and power are of course close to the tenets and moves described by Machiavelli in *The Prince*. It is no accident that Chief Mocmohoc's strategem is almost identical to one employed by Cesare Borgia in *The Prince*, when he captures the Orsini and Vitellozzo after bringing them together in council. See "Legation to Cesare Borgia" in Niccolò Machiavelli, *The Prince*, ed. Robert M. Adams (New York: W. W. Norton, 1977), pp. 89–91.

20. See Egbert S. Oliver, "Melville's Picture of Emerson and Thoreau in *The Confidence-Man*," *College English* 8 (1946–47): 67–72.

21. *CM*, pp. 50–52, 117–18, 180–83, 184–85, 323.

22. For a good discussion of the implications of the narrator's interjections for the novel's fictionality, see Edgar A. Dryden, *Melville's Thematics of Form* (Baltimore: Johns Hopkins University Press, 1968), pp. 150–95.

23. *CM*, pp. 51, 184–85.

24. *CM*, pp. 107, 149, 181.

25. *CM*, pp. 6, 9, 15, 45, 47, 98–99, 140, 146, 148, 154, 160, 167, 169, 184, 186, 189–90, 198, 200, 250, 257, 266–69, 321, 328, 343, 346.

26. *CM*, pp. 11, 26, 27, 61, 105, 168, 185, 228, 239, 265, 317.

27. *CM*, pp. 19, 44–45, 49, 67, 70, 115, 127, 140, 150, 201, 318, 346, 349.

28. *CM*, pp. 3, 19.

29. *CM*, pp. 3, 6, 16, 36, 41, 62, 84, 100, 105, 135, 195, 224, 230, 265, 272–77, 285, 310, 318.

30. *CM*, pp. 84, 150, 193, 224, 315.

31. *CM*, pp. 201, 235–37, 238–39.

32. See Irwin's forthcoming book on the American hieroglyphic.

33. *Oxford English Dictionary*, s.v. "genius."

34. This is a notion of Richard Klein's that came up in conversation during the summer of 1976.

35. "Hard Language" was the title and subject of a conference organized by Bruce Jackson at SUNY-Buffalo in 1974. The conference examined that facet of language bordering on and influencing many varieties of behavior.

THREE

THE CAESURA OF THE SPECULATIVE
Philippe Lacoue-Labarthe

Alles schwebt.
Anton Webern

THE PURPOSE of my remarks, extracted from a work-in-progress, will be twofold. First, I would like to show—but this is scarcely a thesis, so evident should the thing be, fundamentally—I would like to show that tragedy, or a certain interpretation of tragedy, itself reinterpreted or reelaborated, making itself explicit as philosophical and desiring—above all—to be such, is the origin or matrix of what, in the wake of Kant, is conventionally called speculative thought, that is to say, dialectical thought, or to take up Heideggerian terminology, onto-theo-logic in its final state. It has been known for some time, or at least since Bataille, that the dialectic, the mastering thought of the corruptible and of death, the determination of the negative and its conversion into the force of work and production, the assumption of the contradictory and of the *Aufhebung* [relève] as the very process of the auto-conception of the True or the Subject, of ab-solute Thought—it has been known, therefore, for a long time that the dialectic, the *theory* of death, presupposes (and, no doubt, not entirely without its knowledge) a *theatre*—a structure of representation and a mimesis, an enclosed space, distant and preserved (that is, safeguarded and true if one understands well, as did Hegel,

For Rodolphe Gasché and Samuel Weber

what the German *Wahrheit* means), where death in general, decline and disappearance, is able to contemplate "itself," reflect "itself," and interiorize "itself." This space, this "temple," and this scene were, for Bataille, the space of sacrifice—which, Bataille said, is a "comedy." We all know this celebrated analysis.—On the other hand, that which is a little less known—and which I would like to accent for this reason—is that within the earliest stages of absolute idealism there is a quite explicit foundation for the speculative process itself (of dialectical logic), a foundation based on the model of tragedy. In reconstituting, albeit cursorily, this movement (to the point, certainly, of its denegation—or its disavowal—of theatricality), one can detect, with a certain precision, the philosophical exploitation (raised to the second power) of the Aristotelian concept of *catharsis*. So that, if there is some justice in this suspicion, this is not the only mimesis—or the only "structure of representation"—that finds itself artfully implicated within the dialectic, but the totality of tragedy, including that element which essentially defines it for the whole of the classical tradition, that is, its *effect* proper, the "tragic effect," the so-called "purificatory effect." As might be anticipated, the question in this case would be as follows: what if the dialectic was the echo or the reasoning of a ritual?

But let me immediately say that this is not the essential part of what I have to say.

Indeed, I am much more interested in carrying out the "counter-proof" of this hypothesis. Actually, the work from which I have extracted these remarks does not relate *directly* to speculative Idealism, but rather to Hölderlin, to Hölderlin's theory of tragedy.—I am not unaware that between the latter (Hölderlin) and in truth, the former—Hegel and Schelling—the distance is, for the most part, extremely small or sometimes, indeed, at the extreme limit, non-existent or imperceptible. I am not unaware of this—and yet it is just this which interests me most of all. Because it is, in fact, for the precise reason that Hölderin collaborated in the most intimate manner possible in the building of the edifice of speculative dialectic—on the model of tragedy—that he must be examined.

These assertions would seem to create a paradox. I am therefore bound to explain them a bit: a complete "strategy"—assuming that we keep to this very aggressive and militaristic vocabulary—let us say more simply, an entire procedure is implied here, and it is necessary, if what follows is to be intelligible, that I give some approximate indication of my general direction.

The Hölderlin who seems to me urgently to require examination (and decipherment) today is the theoretician and dramatist (essentially, the one doesn't function without the other), it is the Hölderlin of a certain journey, precise and sure, a journey in the theory and practice of the theatre, in the theory of tragedy and the experience or the testing of a new kind of dramatic writing, included by and in the translation of the Greeks (of Sophocles). But perhaps this is simply a new kind of writing, one which is, as Hölderlin himself and his epoch said, "modern."

It is necessary to recognize that the Hölderlin of whom I am speaking has been largely neglected up to the present day. This is particularly evident in France, which is, in this respect, a perfect echo chamber for the commotion of general attitudes and where, even though care has been taken to translate all of Hölderlin's theoretical texts (beginning even with the famous *Remarks* [*Anmerkungen*] on the translation of Sophocles), no one has risked proposing a version, even a problematic one, of Hölderlin's translation of Sophocles, a version that would be indispensable to understanding what it was he hoped to accomplish. And even in Germany (where commentaries abound), despite the appearance of works of great philological rigor (or probity), it seems that no one has wished to see just what the "stakes" of this dramaturgic labor were, a labor, it must be taken into account, that occupied the greater part of Hölderlin's productive activity in the period of "lucidity" (from 1798, if not earlier, to 1804). Perhaps only a few practitioners of the theatre, in Berlin or elsewhere, have, using Hölderlin as their point of departure, attempted to interrupt and take up again the adventure (an "other" adventure, if you like) of tragedy. But this is quite removed, as you might surmise, from being able to constitute the indication of a general movement. . . .

Having said this much, I would still like to forestall at once any risk of misunderstanding. If it seems to me in fact to be crucial, to be crucial today, to place the accent upon a labor that I, out of sheer convenience, am calling the dramaturgic work of Hölderlin, this is not for the sake of underestimating and subordinating the place held by lyricism in the *oeuvre* of Hölderlin, by overturning the perspective of the classical commentaries (in particular, Heidegger's study, which, in this respect, remains unsurpassable). On the contrary: all the texts written between 1798 and 1800 (while Hölderlin's first dramaturgical effort, *The Death of Empedocles*, was marking time), in which a general poetics (i.e., genre theory) is adumbrated, are quite explicit in their designation of lyric poetry as *the* modern genre par excellence; or rather—since the question posed is precisely whether or not *genre* still is a relevant category—in their designation of *it* as the direction, between poetry and literature, in which the *Dichtung* (writing) required by an epoch that defined itself through its imperceptible but violent difference to Antiquity, had to proceed. If there is such a thing as the *oeuvre* of Hölderlin, and if, as such, it culminates or concludes at some point, then, undeniably, it does so in the lyric. Heidegger, it should be added, is not the only one to insist justly on this, and one can find exactly the same motif in the tradition established by two well-known texts of Benjamin (I am thinking, essentially, of Adorno and Peter Szondi).

To be more precise: how does it happen that in such divergent and, indeed, mutually conflicting commentaries as those by Heidegger, Adorno, and Szondi (I deliberately give Benjamin a place apart) the same privilege finds itself attached to the lyric—and, as a consequence, the same interest is shown in the "last" great poems of Hölderlin—where the critic goes about the task of seeking that which is, indeed, inscribed there, that is to say, a thought? Starting with the same text and using a similar evaluation as the point of departure, how can one extricate (as is the case exemplarily with Szondi) the rigorously dialectical structure of Hölderlin's thought or, indeed, as Heidegger persists in doing, decipher the emergence of an interpretation of truth that is no longer reducible either to the Platonic-Cartesian interpretation of truth (as theoretical and enunciative adequation) or to its speculative and dialectical reelaboration? Might it not be the neglect of Hölderlin's dramaturgic work, its evaluation as a subsidiary, transient phase, including—and in Heidegger this is a deliberate gesture—his "dialogue with Sophocles" and with Greek tragedy—that has prevented us from tracing, at one time, *both* the way in which Hölderlin rigorously dismantles the speculative-tragic matrix he himself helped to elaborate (and this is the manner in which he works through the problematics of tragedy), *and* the fact that in so doing, his long and arduous work of subversion and surbedding could not appeal to any "other" thought as an authority, nor institute difference of any kind?

The question which I am posing therefore has to do with the possibility, in general, of a demarcation of the speculative, of the general logic of differentiation, of the regulated contradiction, of the exchange or the passage into the opposite, as the production of the Identical, of the *Aufhebung* [relève] and of the (ap)propriation, etc.—The question cannot be posed simply as follows: how was Hölderlin able to tear himself away or separate himself from this speculative scheme and from dialectical logic? To pose such a question—and, *a fortiori*, to pretend to give an answer—would inevitably reintroduce the same constraint to which one would prefer not to be subject (that is, the constraint of *opposition*, in general). Moreover, this is the reason why there is a well-known closure of the speculative that is *legally* immune to all assaults. And it is also this inexhaustible power of reappropriation which will have been always menacing the Heideggerian procedure from within and which does not cease to require, today, that we take up once more the question of the relationship between dialectical process and aletheic

structure—indeed, between dialectical process and "event-(ap)propria-
tion" in the sense of the *Ereignis*.

On the other hand, the question that I am asking is really the
following—a "question at the limits," if you like, since it exists at the
limits, indeed, it exists without its own object and ruins in advance any
chance of an answer, at least in the form in which we have come to
expect an answer to be given (in the positive or negative): how is it that
the demarcation of the speculative, in Hölderlin, is *also* its mark (or its
remark)? How is it, in other words, that the speculative (de)constitutes
itself—I mean, dismantles itself, deconstructs itself in the same movement by which it erects itself, installs and constitutes a system? And
what does this imply about the possibility and the structure, about the
logic of truth and property, in general?

The problematic which I have here set up—as well as the procedure
it makes necessary and which cannot be (or can no longer be) "deconstructive" in the rigorous Heideggerian or even Derridian sense of the
term—such a problematic presupposes, therefore, that Hölderlin occupies a rather singular place within a certain history (one which is not
solely empirical, but which is not ideal or pure either, the history of the
culmination of philosophy). This place is so singular, in fact, that it most
probably marks the limit of *critical* potency as such. Yet this is not at all
to say that we should be forbidden to *read* Hölderlin (nothing is more
alien to the procedure just now mentioned than this sort of pious renunciation). If by "culmination of philosophy" is meant the fulfillment of a
program, its realization or implementation, the thought-process entailed
in the bi-millenial questioning of the Same, out of which philosophy in
its entirety has emerged; if the culmination of philosophy is the thinking
of difference in the sense of that "one differing in itself" ('ἐν διαφέρων ἑαυτῷ
—Heraclitus) which Hölderlin made the most constant, most explicit motif of his questioning of the essence of the Beautiful and of Art,
ever since he cited it in *Hyperion*; if, moreover, for reasons that cannot
be developed here but which are presumably familiar enough, the
culmination of philosophy is the stop-gap measure attempting to close
the wound (re-)opened, *in extremis*, by Kant in the thinking of the Same
(i.e., in the Cartesian discourse articulating the self-engenderment of the
subject)—if, in short, it is this patching over of the Kantian *crisis* (the
"jump over Kant," as Heidegger puts it) and of everything in this crisis
tending to sweep away all power of legislating, deciding, and criticizing
—then Hölderlin (this is his singular position, his "case," if you like) will
have represented, in this culmination which he *too* brings about and to
which he "contributes" more than a negligible share, the impossibility of
overlaying this crisis, this wound still open in the tissue of philosophy,
the wound where no healing cicatrix can form, where the hand which

Philippe Lacoue-Labarthe

attempts to close the wound only succeeds in reopening it. It is not that Hölderlin wanted it that way—he wanted, if he wanted anything at all (and for some time he did want something), the resolution of the crisis, in whatever sense you care to understand the term. Nor, still less, is it a matter of his having become the master of this paradoxical gesture (since he will have thought it, for the most part, *as* tragedy itself, or a certain kind of tragedy, at least—but this gesture itself will have carried him beyond any point of control, though I do not say beyond that which one can bear or endure). There is no category, as such, which is pertinent here. We can not speak simply either of lucidity or of *échec*, since this would be to "dis-play" the opposition of power and impotence. And even though these things may have been wholly implied, it is not a "subjective effect," it is probably not even "analysable" in terms of the unconscious, though one could not deny the part played by the repetition compulsion and the ponderous work of the *Todestrieb* within this eagerness for (non)fulfilment.—Only Hölderlin's logic, "his" logic, if it was such in any specific way and if it could be detached, would offer the possibility of an "inter-view." But the "case" is such, in fact, that despite his obstinate insistence on self-*calculation*, he was not able to give rise to any logic that might have belonged to him exclusively and that could have brought about a scission.

It is here, then, that I break off and pass on.

I thus return to the initial purpose of my remarks and simply pose the following question: what does tragedy have to do with the birth of speculative thought and of the onto-logic? Up to what point is one (self)authorized to say that it is tragedy, the re-elaboration of the philosophical or "poetic" (Aristotelian) conception of tragedy, which has furnished the matrix-scheme of dialectical thought?

The entire character of such a question certainly makes it debatable. One could perfectly demonstrate, and have a perfect right in doing so, that it is not primarily within the theory of tragedy that the things of speculation began to be organized. At the very least, it would be necessary for us to recall that the step leading to the speculative was first taken through the question of art, in general (as inherited from Kant's third critique), and, more specifically, through the question of *Dichtung* and the relationship between literature and philosophy. Hegel recognized and underscored this in a well-known homage to Schiller at the beginning of the *Aesthetics*. The supercession of the aesthetic (of taste) in a theory of the Beautiful and of Art, the attempt to bring about a grand philosophical lyricism, the recasting of the poetics of "modes" (as Genette says), and thus the systematization of the poetics of genres, the general problematic of the (absolute) work or the Organon (i.e., the self-engendering, as Subject, of the Work), what could be called, consequently, the "literary operation" (i.e., the invention of literature as its own theory or auto-conception), the will to decision concerning even the old (and still open) debate between Ancients and Moderns: all of these events, which played themselves out in the last decade of the eighteenth century, between Weimar and Berlin (between Schiller's essays on aesthetics and the Athenaeum, the lectures of Schelling and the remarks of Goethe)—all these developments work to constitute the crucible of speculative philosophy and in all probability take precedence over all other, more clearly delineated attempts at operating a transition (such as that of the physics or *Naturphilosophie* of the time). This said, it will not be too difficult to detect, amid this complex and problematic ensemble, the guiding thread of a primary and constant preoccupation, of a single question—none other than that of *mimesis*, at whatever level one chooses to examine it (whether it be that of the *imitation of the Ancients*, of mimesis as the mode of poiesis, *i.e.*, Aristotelian mimesis, or even— and this is not wholly absent from the game—of mimesis in the sense of "mimetism" or *imitatio*). This is precisely why speculative Idealism finds its aperture, jointly and indissociably, as a theory of the Subject, of Art, and of History. But even if this is not always truly clear it is also why tragedy and the theory of tragedy are (from F. Schlegel or Schiller to Hölderlin or from Schelling to Hegel) able to magnetize, fundamentally, this passage, which is itself essentially merged with an attempt to "surpass" ["dépassement"], as they say, *mimetology*. Here I am referring less to the historico-cultural reinterpretation of the origins of tragedy (that is, of the entrance upon the philosophical scene of the Dionysian and all its successors) than to a rereading of the Tragedians themselves—beginning, of course, with Sophocles—for the purpose of isolating philosophical models and documents.

This is the reason why, in following the example offered by Szondi in his *Essay on the Tragic* [*Versuch über das Tragische*],[1] I shall first consider a text by Schelling, dating from the period 1795–1796, which figures in the last of his *Philosophical Letters on Dogmatism and Criticism* [*Philosophische Briefe über Dogmatismus und Kritizismus*]. Szondi, who bases his remarks on this text (but also seems to forget the case of Freud, so difficult to forget), elaborates the argument that if "since Aristotle there has been a poetics of tragedy . . . [Seit Aristoteles gibt es eine Poetik der Tragödie . . . , *VT*, p. 7]"—understood here as a poetics of the tragic effect, based upon the doctrine of catharsis—". . . it is only since Schelling that there has been a philosophy of tragedy [. . . seit Schelling erst eine Philosophie des Tragischen, *VT*, p. 7]." My ambition would simply be to show that, in reality, the so-called philosophy of tragedy remains in reality (though certainly in a subordinate way) a theory of tragedy's effect (thus presupposing the *Poetics* of Aristotle), and that it is only the persistent silence which the theory exhibits in regard to this filiation which allows it to establish itself, over and above the Aristotelian mimetology and catharsis, as the finally unveiled truth of the "tragic phenomenon."

I provide the text of Schelling here.

The question has often been asked: how was the reason of Greece able to bear the contradictions inherent in its tragedy? A mortal—pushed by fate into becoming a criminal, himself fighting *against* fate, and nevertheless punished frightfully for the crime, which was itself the doing of fate! The *reason* for this contradiction, what made it bearable, lay at a level deeper than the one hitherto sought, lay in the conflict of human freedom with the power of the objective world, in which the mortal—assuming that this objective power was a more lofty one (a fate)—necessarily had to be defeated, and yet, because he did not go down to defeat *without a struggle*, had to be *punished* for his being defeated. The recognition of human freedom, the *honor* which fell due to such freedom, followed from the fact that the criminal, defeated only by the superior power of fate, was nonetheless *punished* as well. Greek tragedy honored human freedom by *allowing* its heroes to *fight* against the superior power of fate: in order not to exceed the bounds of art, Greek tragedy had to allow the hero to be *defeated*, but, so as to make good upon this humbling of human freedom—a humbling demanded by art— tragedy also had to let him *expiate* his crime, even the one which was committed because of fate. . . . A great thought was contained in the hero's suffering the penalty even for an *unavoidable* crime, so that he might prove his freedom through the loss of that freedom itself, and so as to be defeated even as he declared the rights of free will.

[Man hat oft gefragt, wie die griechische Vernunft die Widersprüche ihrer Tragödie ertragen konnte. Ein Sterblicher—vom Verhängnis zum Verbrecher bestimmt, selbst *gegen* das Verhängnis kämpfend, und doch fürchterlich bestraft für das Verbrechen, das ein Werk des Schicksals war! Der *Grund* dieses Widerspruchs, das, was ihn erträglich machte, lag tiefer, als man ihn suchte, lag im Streit menschlicher Freiheit mit der Macht der objektiven Welt, in welchem der Sterbliche, wenn jene Macht eine Übermacht—(ein Fatum) —ist, notwendig unterliegen, und doch, weil er nicht *ohne Kampf* unterlag, für sein Unterliegen selbst *bestraft* werden mußte. Daß der Verbrecher, der doch nur der Übermacht des Schicksals unterlag, doch noch *bestraft* wurde, war Anerkennung menschlicher Freiheit, *Ehre*, die der Freiheit gebührte. Die griechische Tragödie ehrte menschliche Freiheit dadurch, daß sie ihren Helden gegen die Übermacht des Schicksals *kämpfen ließ*: um nicht über die Schranken der Kunst zu springen, mußte sie ihn *unterliegen*, aber, um auch diese, durch die Kunst abgedrungne, Demütigung menschlicher Freiheit wieder gut zu machen, mußte sie ihn—auch für das durchs *Schicksal* begangne Verbrechen—*büssen* lassen. . . . Es war ein *großer* Gedanke, willig auch die Strafe für ein *unvermeidliches* Verbrechen zu tragen, um so durch den Verlust seiner Freiheit selbst eben diese Freiheit zu beweisen, und noch mit einer Erklärung des freien Willens unterzugehen. *VT*, p. 13.]

You have no doubt recognized the figure of Oedipus there. Since Aristotle, Oedipus has not ceased to be regularly invoked by philosophy, at least explicitly, as its most representative hero, the early incarnation of self-consciousness and of the desire of knowing. This, as everyone knows, is precisely Freud's attitude as well.

The analysis which Szondi offers of this text demonstrates that the presentation of the conflict or of the tragic contradiction intervenes, at the conclusion of the Schelling *Letters*, in order to offer the possibility (and the model) of a (re)solution, in the dialectical sense of the word, to the philosophical contradiction par excellence, which Schelling calls the opposition of dogmatism and criticism, and which is the opposition in general of the subjective and the objective, of the "absolute I" not yet conditioned by any object and of the "absolute Object" or the "Not-I"—that is to say, so as to remain in the thread of Kantian or Fichtean terminology, of liberty and natural necessity. Indeed, the possibility offered by the fable or scenario of tragedy is that of the maintenance (for the benefit and in the sense of liberty) of the contradiction of the subjective and the objective—since the tragic hero is (as Hegel will also say) "at once guilty and innocent" in struggling against the invincible. The hero, in struggling against the destiny which bears responsibility for his fault, *provokes* an inevitable and necessary defeat and *voluntarily* chooses to expiate a crime of which he knows he is innocent and for which, in every sense, he must pay the price. Culpable innocence and the "gratuitous" provocation of chastisement: these would be the solution to the conflict: the subject *manifests* its liberty "by the very loss of its liberty." The negative, here, converts itself into the positive; the struggle (be it ever so vain or futile) is, in itself, productive. And it is easy to see, if one recomposes the pattern of the scheme thus put in place, that the "conciliation," as Schelling would be apt to say, operates within the very logic of the "identity of identity and difference." The Oedipal scenario therefore implicitly contains the speculative solution. And everything has already been prepared here for this absolutization or this paradoxical infinitization of the Subject, within which philosophy, indeed, will find its culmination.

Such a scheme could be shown to bind, in its entirety, even in Hegel, the "idealist" interpretation (is there any other?) of tragedy— even including that of Hegel himself. Novalis is obeying this same logic when he declares that "the philosophical act par excellence [that is, the speculative act] is suicide," and it is he, quite incontestably, who brings Hölderlin, himself desirous of writing a "true modern tragedy," to the choice of the figure of Empedocles. Yet this is not to say, quite clearly, that Novalis had also caused him, with no more ado, to embark upon the translation of Sophocles and to propose rather tardily *Oedipus the King* as the veritable model for modern tragedy.—But what I find interesting here is that, due to its speculative rehandling (or its transposition, if you prefer, into metaphysical discourse, its ontological translation), this scheme is not basically different from that which Aristotle puts in place when, in the thirteenth chapter of the *Poetics* (1452b), he examines the question concerning what must be sought or avoided in the construction of the fable, if tragedy is to produce "the effect proper to it"—and which is the effect of the catharsis of fear and pity. But for Aristotle as well, you know, *Oedipus the King* itself provides the paradigmatic "beautiful composition"; it is the model of that type of composition called "complex" (as opposed to simple fable) which implies a *peripeteia*, the sudden change or *metabole* of the action into its contrary—and a recognition (the reversal of ignorance and its turning into knowledge, of *agnoia* into *gnosis*). Now if *Oedipus the King* can be granted this privilege, it is because, among all the examples which are said to fulfill this double requirement (these are all cases having to do with the "turning about of fortune"), it is the only one which can evoke the two passions which it is the function of tragedy to "purify." "It is the case," says Aristotle, "of the man who, without being eminently virtuous or just, falls to misfortune, not because of his malevolence or his perversion, but as a result of this or that error (frailty or, indeed, bad luck—*hamartia*) in his actions . . ." (*Poetics*, XIII).—This would seem to be very removed from what Schelling's demonstration actually articulates and, moreover, from what endows it with its thematic originality: namely, the insurrection staged by the tragic subject, against a background of innocent culpability (i.e., the paradox of structural oxymoron identified by Aristotle), and the assumption, in its very injustice, of the rigors of destiny.—But now recall the question with which Schelling began his text: how was the reason of Greece able to *bear* the contradictions of its tragedy? And substitute, for a moment there—while also thinking of the fear and pity Aristotle speaks of, for instance—"passion" for "reason." It is difficult not to see that it is basically a matter, in both places, of the *same* question and that, bearing in mind the ontological translation to which I just alluded, one can detect in Schelling's formulation the following question: how was Greek reason (i.e., basically, how was philosophy . . .) able to "purify" itself of the menace which the contradiction illustrated by the tragic conflict represented? Can we avoid seeing, in other words, that if the appeal to *hamartia* is in no way equivalent to the provocation of an inevitable defeat (in both doctrines the problematic of the *Subject* per se is implied throughout), then the question which bears upon the *tolerance* or the capacity for tolerance, in general, of the insupportable (death, suffering, injustice, contradiction) governs, in both cases, interpretation in its entirety.

Now this has as its consequence that in both cases, it is indeed tragedy itself—the tragic spectacle—which finds itself implicated. Tragedy, that is, the dispositive of representation or of *Darstellung*, the structure of mimesis—which is what Schelling is thinking of when he mentions, though without great precision, the "barriers of art" which Greek tragedy was not allowed to infringe upon. Indeed, only mimesis— that which in Aristotle's view is the earliest determination of the human animal and which opens the very possibility of knowing and of Logos, of reason itself (*Poetics*, IV, 1448b)—it is only mimesis which has the power of "converting the negative into being" and of procuring this paradoxical pleasure, which is essentially "theoretical" and "mathematical" (one which is, moreover, especially reserved for the philosopher), which man is capable of feeling in the *representation*, no matter how inexact, of the insupportable, of the afflicting, and of the horrible, "as, for instance, the vision of the most vile of animals or of cadavers" (*Poetics*, IV, 1448b). It is only mimesis which authorizes the "tragic pleasure." When they become part of the spectacle, in other words, both death and the unbearable (*i.e.*, in 1795, the contradictory) "can be looked at face to face." The spirit [Esprit, Geist] from this point on, far from taking fright, can take its time "sojourning" with death and the insupportable— in this case, indeed, deriving a certain pleasure in any case in purging itself, in recovering its health, in purifying itself, and in preserving itself from its own fear (perhaps too, from the madness which menaces it and probably too from the pity which the Spirit feels if, as Aristotle indicates in passing, there can never be pity except in the form of self-pity). And if, in fact, the nature of the philosophical operation in general—and the speculative one in particular—is fundamentally *economic*, the very principle of this economy will then be the relation of the spectacle and the mimetic semblance; it is precisely the structure of theatricality which makes the theatre available to philosophy—and to the philosophy of Schelling as well, though he does not initiate the thought of the tragic except to create an echo of the poetics of tragedy. Indeed, then Schelling's echo arises from the ancient foundation of ritual and of sacrifice for which, as we have every reason indeed to believe, Aristotle's catharsis is *also* the distant justification and the philosophical transposition. What is more, the one need not exclude the other, as its logical *verification*.

I should now like to go to the counter-proof mentioned in the beginning;—There is nothing simpler, apparently, since, as you know, there is also (by chance, but not by accident) a reading by Hölderlin of *Oedipus the King*. It should therefore be easy to bring the two texts into some sort of head-on confrontation.

But, of course, nothing of the kind is possible.

First of all, a difficulty arises from the circumstance that the *Remarks* on the translation of Sophocles presuppose, as their background, not only (as has often been emphasized) a general introduction, which Hölderlin announced to his editor but never sent him (one which was probably never written and of which, in any case, we have no trace), but also presuppose all of Hölderlin's previous work on tragedy, though this work itself remained in the form of fragments or drafts that, more or less completed and developed, are thus brief, roughly sketched, and obscure, at times, sometimes even totally impenetrable. But the difficulty is also due to the following: that the analysis of *Oedipus*, aside from the fact that it merits a translation which (for the French reading public) should in one way or another be made "accessible," is not supported by anything, in fact, but the very narrow relation between it and that of *Antigone*—just as the converse would, up to a certain point, be equally true.

But only up to a certain point.

This is because the fundamental text with regard to Hölderlin's interpretation of tragedy is, in reality, *Antigone*; it is *Antigone* that represents the most difficult and the most enigmatic of tragedies, of all tragedies, and which in this way constitutes the center, albeit an "eccentric" one (as Hölderlin says)—a kind of pivot, we might say, which is impossible to center, around which gravitates his repeated attempt at theorization—though it is with a great deal of difficulty, constantly being frustrated or thwarted in its course of motion. The reason for all this is that *Antigone* is the most Greek of tragedies (transformed, moreover, as a result, by the translation, in this case a particularly violent translation, as to make it "better suited to our mode of representation," to us as moderns, to make it correspond to this "Hesperian" age which defines our historical locale). One must even go so far as to say: the reason for it is that *Antigone* is the incarnation of the very essence of tragedy, if it be true that tragedy is for ever and ever a specifically Greek genre and, in this way, is "incapable of being reconstituted"—if not totally incapable of being transposed. Moreover, this is why there cannot be a modern tragedy (at least in the rigorous sense) except in and through the translation of ancient tragedy. And this is also why, as a general rule (even if it can be illustrated by only one example), the translation must be all the more violent and transformative since it involves a text more properly Greek.

At any rate, this is what explains the difference in Hölderlin's treatment of the two Sophoclean tragedies he holds on to. It is necessary to note once again, since it is important, that he includes them within an "editorial" dispositive (one, apparently, chosen by Hölderlin) in which—curiously enough—the translation of *Oedipus the King* (in an initial volume) precedes that of *Antigone*. The most modern tragedy thus comes before the presentation of the most ancient. Is there an indication here that a tragedy which is properly Greek, provided it be transformed (if not deformed), is really more modern than a Greek tragedy, like *Oedipus the King*, which "tends" toward the modern? Modern in that its "artistic character," as Hölderlin says, with all "Junonian" rigor and sobriety, is opposed to the natural foundation of the Greeks (to their sacred *pathos*, to their Apollonian impulse towards the "fire of heaven") and better corresponds, in this way, to the unique nature of those Hesperians who, contrary to the Greeks, are "children of the earth" (Beaufret recalls this expression of Kant's)[2] and, as such, are subordinated to the "limit" and immured within an essential finitude?

Such a question, it is true, engages Hölderlin's entire problematic of history, which is, in reality, a problematic of *imitation* within history and which for this reason *is not*, but *remains* irreducible to the dialectical logic to which it seems subordinate. I cannot develop this point any further here, but I cannot help thinking that it is perhaps here that we find the indication that for Hölderlin there was basically no modern tragedy except in the form of a deconstruction, a practical one, of ancient tragedy. And in the same way that there was, without doubt, no possible theory of tragedy and of the tragic except within the deconstruction of classical poetics and its speculative reinterpretation, one not being possible without the other.

I would even like, as long as we have come this far, because the matter seems to me still important for us as "moderns," who, perhaps, must maintain with Hölderlin (this is not to say: with all of his contemporaries) a rapport with the Greeks (this is not to say: with all of the Greeks) analogous to his own.—I would thus like to ask myself in passing if the "modern" would not have to be for Hölderlin the *après-coup*, in the strict sense, of Greek art, that is, the repetition of what went on there without ever taking place and the echo of that unuttered *parole* which nevertheless reverberated throughout Greek poetry.

In any case, this could explain the enterprise of *translation* [*traduction*], precisely, and the perversion of the scheme of imitation (classicist or dialectical) that it presupposes. And this could also explain, no doubt, the secretly and paradoxically greater modernity of *Antigone*, which is, Hölderlin says, more "lyrical" and in which, in fact, Sophocles shows himself closer to Pindar, who was always considered by Hölderlin as the "summit" of Greek art—all of which did not in any way obviate the necessity of *translating* [*traduire*] Pindar as well, or of commenting upon, analyzing, or, indeed, *rewriting* him. Hölderlin felt required to make Greek art say that which it had not said—not in the manner of a kind of hermeneutics attempting to find what is implicit in its discourse, but in quite a different manner, one for which I doubt very much that we as yet have a category—thus it was a matter of saying, quite simply, that which was said (but) *as that which had not been said*: the same thing [chose], then, in its (auto) difference. "Ἐν διαφέρων ἑαυτῷ."

Think, for example, of the historical scheme in the form of a chiasmus to which I just now alluded: it initially presupposed that a certain form of Greek tragedy (which is its regular or canonical form, its truly tragic form, Hölderlin says, at this juncture *Oedipus the King*) was in a position to define the basic determinants of our own human nature. What the Greeks, in effect, conquered against and over the objections of their own nature, and it is their art which defines exactly what the moderns consider to be uniquely their own: the tragedy of a slow bruising, the "wandering about under the unthinkable," and the famous: "that's the tragedy in us, that we depart from the world of the living quietly, packed up in some sort of container" ["Denn das ist das Tragische bei uns, daß wir ganz stille in irgendeinem Behälter eingepackt vom Reiche der Lebendigen hinweggehn. . . ." *HW*, p. 941]. In other words, this is quite the opposite of tragic *sublimation*, of the "eccentric enthusiasm" which defines the initial surge of panic of the Greeks towards the "All-in-One," their brutal and catastrophic transgression, which modern culture rediscovers in its art (the sentimental, in Schiller's sense, or, as Hölderlin would rather say, the elegiac) and its thought (the speculative itself). As Beaufret has emphasized, such a scheme takes up once more, in rigorous fashion, the Aristotelian mimetology, as it is revealed in Book II of the *Physics* (II, 8, 199a) and according to which—one finds here the same structure of differentiation—if art, indeed, imitates nature, it no less has the power of "making good on" or "bringing to term" (*epitelein*) that which nature, by itself, is incapable of "effecting" or "operating."

But now suppose that *Antigone*, once translated and rewritten under the conditions we have observed—suppose, then, that the *Antigone* of Sophocles were *itself* at once the most Greek of tragedies *and* the most modern, and that, in order to communicate this same difference, imperceptible in itself, that repetition implies, one had transformed here or there that which it says so as to better say that which it says, *in truth*.— Now the historical scheme and the mimetology it presupposes begins slowly, vertiginously, to totter, to unravel, and to hollow itself out in an abyssal manner.—And if you still think that the structure of substitution which defines the mimetic relationship in general, the relationship of art and nature, is in Hölderlin's view fundamentally a structure of relief and protection, that it is necessary if man is to be prevented from "taking flame in contact with the element," then you will not only understand what the stakes in Greek art were for him (after all, this art derived finally from a kind of "madness" brought about by excessive imitation of the divine and of speculation), but you also will understand why, in the modern epoch—even though that epoch reverses, in principle, the Greek relationship between art and nature—one must indeed repeat that which is most Greek among the Greeks. Begin the Greeks again.—That is to say, no longer be Greek at all.

I supply these indications, though they strike me as being elliptical with respect to the degree of patience required of us, not only for the purpose of marking the place of *Antigone* as a kind of "hollow." Nor is it for the purpose of suddenly introducing the idea (a false one, at that) that Hölderlin's "theory"—which, as opposed to that of Schelling, explicitly takes into account the problematic of tragedy's effect—might have extricated itself, by some unknown measure of lucidity, from the sacrificial and ritual model of tragedy. Hölderlin did not restrict the function of catharsis, as we have seen, only to the art of antiquity; and the preoccupation with ritual, as is known, was always a constant with him—if it is indeed undeniable, as Girard has pointed out, that his obstinate and oppressive inquiry ("at the gates of madness") concerning tragedy and mimesis cannot be dissociated from Hölderlin's *biography*; indeed, it stems from—in the process of mimetic rivalry which Hölderlin more or less knew he was involved in (*vis-à-vis* Schiller, in particular)— a final attempt to decide or, more precisely, to *regulate* (they are not quite the same thing, and this could well shed light on Hölderlin's *retreat*, too quickly called his "madness")—from a final attempt to regulate the double constraint (*double bind*) which structures the mimetic identification ("Be like me" / "Do not be like me") and sets in motion the "cyclo-thymic" oscillation.—If you like, it seems to me that we could at least acknowledge in Hölderlin that he never denied that we have need of art—though hardly, as Nietzsche said, "so as not to be destroyed by the truth," but rather, in the long run, to gain access to the truth— provided, obviously, that we do not understand truth here in the speculative sense (if this is possible). For it is all too clear that the speculative, which was also, even in its logic, the hope of a possible resolution of the insurmountable contradiction brought on by the "machine" of the double bind (and thus offered the hope of a therapy, indeed, of a possible cure), nevertheless remained, in Hölderlin's eyes, the paradoxical and dangerous "second nature" of the moderns—as paradoxical and as dangerous as their artistic virtuosity had been for the Greeks, through the "fault" of which, the Greeks, having celebrated their natal/native being, saw the "empire of art" which they wanted to institute crumble.

If, in truth, it seems that I have spent too much time on *Antigone*, this is not simply because I thought of Schelling's consternation when confronting Hölderlin's translation of Sophocles, which, he wrote to

Philippe Lacoue-Labarthe

Hegel, "showed his mental derangement." But it is because I was thinking, indeed, of Hegel himself, of the icy silence of Hegel, the person
who, however (that is to say, in these circumstances, "who precisely"),
was about to write, in the year immediately following the publication of
Hölderlin's *Remarks*, those pages of the *Phenomenology of Spirit* de-
voted to *Antigone*, pages which served as the program, up to Nietzsche
and Freud (and even to Heidegger), for the modern interpretation of
tragedy. But it is difficult not to read them as well as the conditioned and
prolix setting aright of Hölderlin's analysis. Even if, as Derrida has
shown in *Glas*,[3] what comes into play in these pages is, at its limit, the
very possibility of the speculative and of the onto-logic—even if it is true
that tragedy (as testimony and as genre) will have always represented,
within this onto-logic, the place where the system fails to circle back on
itself, where the systematic does not quite succeed in its overlay of the
historic, where the circularity (as Szondi says) modifies itself and becomes a spiral, while the closure can scarcely contain the divisive pres-
sures to which it has, perhaps, succumbed without anyone becoming
aware of it. The upshot of all this is nonetheless that (I would like to
say: there is one more reason for thinking that) the speculative will itself
be removed *as well* and be (re)organized upon this gesture of expulsion.
—Heidegger, as you know, was particularly attentive in this regard. But
this, perhaps, is also the reason why he was unable to avoid recourse to a
"sacred" Hölderlin.

Once again, I am not saying this with a view toward extricating
Hölderlin from the speculative and making him, if you will, the "positive
hero" of this adventure. The theory put forward by Hölderlin is speculative through and through.

Let me, then, begin with that aspect of his theory upon which the
analysis set forth in the *Remarks* is based.

Here, indeed, the model is the same structurally (and to be sure,
thematically as well, up to a certain point) as that which we found in
Schelling. Like Schelling, moreover, and in terms which are rigorously
analogous, Hölderlin thought and would have been able to write that
tragic drama exists at a

. . . higher level, where unity itself becomes reconciled with conflict, and both
become one in a more perfect synthetic form. This higher identity is the
drama, which, by comprehending the natures of both antithetical genres
within itself, becomes the loftiest manifestation of the idea and of the essence
of all art.

[. . . höheren Stufe, die Einheit selbst mit dem Widerstreit sich versöhnte, und
beide wieder in einer vollkommneren Bildung eins wurden. Diese höhere
Identität ist das *Drama*, welches, die Naturen beider entgegensetzten Gattun-

gen in sich begreifend, die höchste Erscheinung des An-Sich und des Wesens aller Kunst ist.][4]

At any rate, Hölderlin held that tragedy was ". . . the most serious of the poetic forms [. . . ernster als alle andre bekannte poetische Formen, *HW*, p. 904]"[5] and that what properly constitutes it is that it expresses something "more infinitely divine [ein unendlicheres Göttliche, *HW*, p. 571]" through "more clearly defined differences [drückt sie in stärkeren Unterscheidungen aus, *HW*, p. 571]." Hölderlin basically shared the idea which was common throughout the period of idealism that tragedy is the absolute *organon*, or, to use the expression Nietzsche applied to *Tristan* (a work in which Nietzsche recognized approximately the same thing), the "*opus metaphysicum* par excellence" (*Unzeitgemässe Betrachtungen*, IV). This is the reason why, in all rigor, Hölderlin's theory of tragedy was at once an onto-phenomenology and an onto-organology. As evidence—this fragment of 1799 in which, assuming that we do not dwell too long on the dynamic paradox that it presents (nor on its strange syntax,) we find, here going by the name of a tragic *sign*, the *figure* (in the strict sense, the *Gestalt*—Hölderlin also speaks of the symbol) of the suffering hero who himself becomes a locus for the revelation and the epiphany of that which is:

> The meaning of tragedies is most easily understood as arising out of a paradox. Because all power is justly and equally distributed, all that is original appears not, indeed, with its original strength intact, but actually in its weakness, so that actually the light of life and the appearance belong to the weakness of each whole. In the tragic the sign is, in itself, meaningless, without effect, and yet that which is original is overtly shown. But actually the original can only appear in its weakness, but, insofar as the sign in itself is posited as meaningless=0, the original, the hidden ground of each nature, can also be portrayed. If nature actually is portrayed in terms of its weakest gift, then the sign, when it is portrayed in nature's strongest gift, =0.

> [Die Bedeutung der Tragödien ist am leichtesten aus dem Paradoxon zu begreifen. Denn alles Ursprüngliche, weil alles Vermögen gerecht und gleich geteilt ist, erscheint zwar nicht in ursprünglicher Stärke, sondern eigentlich in seiner Schwäche, so daß recht eigentlich das Lebenslicht und die Erscheinung der Schwäche jedes Ganzen angehört. Im Tragischen nun ist das Zeichen an sich selbst unbedeutend, wirkungslos, aber das Ursprüngliche ist gerade heraus. Eigentlich nämlich kann das Ursprüngliche nur in seiner Schwäche erscheinen, insofern aber das Zeichen an sich selbst als unbedeutend=0 gesetzt wird, kann auch das Ursprüngliche, der verborgene Grund jeder Natur sich darstellen. Stellt die Natur in ihrer schwächsten Gabe sich eigentlich dar, so ist das Zeichen wenn sie sich in ihrer stärksten Gabe darstellt=0. quoted in *VT*, pp. 16–17.]

There would be a great deal to say about such a text—and it would complicate our reading singularly. I do not cite it here, except to point out what it offers on a first reading and to simply touch upon the kind of logic which, on the most obvious level, seems operative here. For it is due to this logic that Hölderlin is able, in yet another fragment contemporary with the one above (1798–1800), to define tragedy as the "metaphor of an intellectual intuition [Es ist die Metaphor Einer intellektuellen Anschauung, *HW*, p. 629]," that is, as the transferring and the passing into that which does not belong to the self ("l'impropre"), with a view toward the appropriation of the "other being" ("l'être") or of "the union (the "absolute alliance") of the subject and the object," since (in a text that is somewhat earlier [*Judgment and Being (Urteil und Sein)*]), such was the concept of intellectual intuition that he took up from Fichte.

In its turn, however, such a definition (presupposing, then, that what is signified by a work, here the absolute, finds its expression by means of a "catastrophe" and reversal in the "appearance" or the antithetical "artistic character") engenders, when it is crossed anew with the distinction between "tonalities" (naive, ideal, heroic) inherited from Schiller, a conception of tragedy which we might call "structural," or, if you like, a general "art of combination" of that which Hölderlin thinks of as the "calculable" in the production of the different poetic genres. Now the logic of this kind of axiology is, in itself, dialectical. It gives rise, for example, to those tables or "graphs" by which Hölderlin attempts to schematize, for each genre, the rule of that which he calls the "change of tones [*Wechsel der Töne*]," where the opposition—in a complex series—of the "fundamental tone [*Grundton*]" and the "artistic character [*Kunstcharakter*]" (of "signification" and "style"), must find its "resolution" in the "spirit" of the genre or, circumstances permitting, in the work itself. It is in this way that tragedy, at least in its canonical structure (the very structure not adhered to by *Antigone*) represents the "naive" resolution—that is, the epic resolution—of the initial antinomy between its "ideal" fundamental tone (the tone of the subjective aspiration directed toward the infinite, the speculative tone, par excellence) and its "heroic" artistic character (here the tone of discord, of *agon*, and of contradiction). Szondi has flawlessly analyzed all of this, and there is nothing to be added here, except perhaps to say, echoing some of Adorno's suggestions in his *Mahler*, that the entire dialectic of tones (and, in a certain way, dialectic in general) is, without doubt, not so alien to the world of great symphonic composition after Mozart. And it is in this way that we can also understand why Adorno was quite justified elsewhere in comparing the "parataxis" characteristic of Hölderlin's late style with the *écriture* of Beethoven's last quartets.

Now, if things are as I have said and if speculative logic does constrain Hölderlin's theory to the point of submitting it to this sort of "organicist" formalism (so close, in principle, to that which one finds in all the attempts, Romantic or Idealist, to "deduce" the genres, works, or the arts in general), how then is it that the analysis of *Oedipus the King*, as presented in the *Remarks*, diverges on this one point so radically from Schelling's proposal, for example? Has Hölderlin been able to extricate himself, by some miracle, from the most powerful of theoretical constraints?

Certainly not.

Must it be repeated again? The theory put forward by Hölderlin—and this would apply to more than just those texts which are usually classified as such—is, in its entirety, speculative. At least—and here you may refer again to *Glas*, p. 188—it can always be interpreted in this way, read in this way, and written in this way. It is probably in just this fashion—above all, when it wished to extricate itself from this constraint—that the theory itself was first read and written. But this is not to say that it was *reread* and *rewritten* in this manner—especially when it did not want to extricate itself from this constraint, in which it also saw its resource, its protection, and, perhaps, its "remedy."

It seems to me, in any case, that in Hölderlin's difficulty of theoretization (that is, in mastering and completing the exposition of his theory), which increases and does not even spare his poetical production or his lyrics—on the contrary, it *disorganizes* them—that in the aggravation of this sort of paralysis, affecting his discourse (trapping it in an ever more rigid logical and syntactical bind)—that precisely in this difficulty Hölderlin, by a movement of "regression," if you like (and I shall return to the fact that this has no pejorative implication here), succeeds in touching something that dislocates, *from within*, the process of speculation. Something that immobilizes the speculative and prohibits it—or rather distends and suspends it. Something that constantly prevents it from reaching the point of culmination and never ceases, in its role of the double, to divert the speculative from itself, to hollow it out in the form of a spiral, to bring about its collapse. Or, perhaps, it is this "something" which interrupts it, here and there, and sets it, if you will, "in spasms."—How can we describe such a movement?

Despite everything, there does seem to be an access open to us, one which necessarily bears both upon the theoretical and the discursive. This is, quite clearly, no more than a course of last resort, inasmuch as we will not be able to avoid, since I seem forced to take this path, detaching the discursive or the theoretical from the remainder—or from its own residue. But I can do no better at this point, where the best thing is to be at once as brief and as lucid as possible.

Indeed, it is necessary at this point to talk of the "regression"—or at least to give some indication of it. So let me at once present the matter schematically, with a minimum of nuance. In those cases where the

Philippe Lacoue-Labarthe

model of speculative tragedy is constructed on the "denegation" of Aristotelian mimetology and catharsis, it is not only that Hölderlin himself insists—eagerly striving to rediscover Aristotle or, in any case, a general theory of mimesis—but this movement of return, this "step backward," leads him, within the confines of Aristotle and the (already) philosophical interpretation of tragedy, at once toward Sophocles (and through him toward the religious and sacrificial function of tragedy) and toward that which *haunts* Plato under the name of mimesis (against which he fights with all of his philosophical determination, until he finds a way of blocking and fixing the concept of mimesis).

All of this, in its way, is quite simple. However, I must hasten to add that the movement of "regression" in Hölderlin does not stop here. First of all, the movement does not take place by itself, nor all at once. For example, it would be necessary to show, with precision, how the successive drafts of *Empedokles* and the theoretical reflection accompanying them slowly and laboriously decompose this "regression." This would take considerable time and would not be easy.—Nonetheless, the transit appears with a degree of clarity, as far as its principle idea and line of direction are concerned. In fact, Hölderlin takes as his point of departure a scenario which is overtly speculative: that of the so-called "Frankfurt plan," which subtends the greater portion of the first version. Empedocles becomes here the very figure of speculative desire and nostalgia for $\hat{\epsilon}\nu$ καὶ πᾶν—suffering because of his temporal limitation and wishing to escape his finitude. The drama is organized, then (I am simplifying), around the interior dialogue of the hero (a dialogue which is totally "elegiac" and still rather close to the style of *Hyperion*). In practical terms, its sole subject is the justification of speculative suicide. This is why "modern tragedy," in its initial phase, is fundamentally nothing but the tragedy of tragedy or even, in a quasi-Romantic way, the tragedy of the theory of tragedy: a work wishing to make itself absolute, in the very power which it delegates to itself to reflect back upon itself and rise to the level of the Subject.—The question is nevertheless often asked: why did Hölderlin choose to abandon this first version and what reason (philosophical or dramaturgical) caused him to modify, at least twice, the first scenario—to the point of abandoning the project entirely (the "échec") and moving on to his translation of Sophocles. Beda Allemann[6] suggests that Hölderlin, aware of a kind of "deficiency with regard to plot," common enough in what are known as *pièces à thèse* (as if there were any other kind), had attempted to "motivate" dramatically the metaphysical resolution of Empedocles. This is not impossible. In any case, what matters is that when Hölderlin reorganizes the scenario in the second draft and, in fact, makes it more complex, what he essentially introduces is the idea that the "aorgic"[7] temptation of Empedocles is a *fault.* As a result, of course, the plot enters into the register of that which is properly tragic. And generally, it has been right to emphasize this. But what has escaped general notice is that the introduction of the fault here is equivalent to the emplacement of a scenario of the "Oedipal" type, that is, of a sacrificial scenario. Empedocles' fault, indeed, is that of publicly declaring himself divine in the presence of the entire population of Agrigentum. In other words, the philosophical transgression has now become a social one—or, which amounts to the same thing (here) —a religious one. Naturally, Empedocles thereby brings upon himself the enmity of the Agrigentans, who impute to his lack of measure the fundamental responsibility for the plague which is ravaging the city and who, in order to rid themselves of the defilement, subject Empedocles (in a quite explicit and detailed manner) to the well-known gesture of the expulsion of the *"pharmakos"*—a gesture doubled, almost immediately, in the ordinary (dialectical) manner, by its rehabilitation to the level of the sacred (hence the final redemption of Empedocles, in the style of the mystical conclusion of *Oedipus at Colonus*).

The transformation that Hölderlin causes his *Empedokles* to undergo goes then, it is obvious, in the direction of a "return to Sophocles" just now alluded to. The remarkable thing, however, is that such a return satisfied Hölderlin no better than the post-Kantian construction from which it initially departed. This is no doubt why, between the second version and his draft of a third, which was probably abandoned rather quickly, Hölderlin attempted to rework his project theoretically in a long, obscure and difficult essay that evidently had to be written separately because of his renunciation of his original design of a "reflexive tragedy." Now it happens that this essay (*Ground for Empedocles* [*Der Grund zum Empedokles*]) presents us in turn a phenomenon analogous to "regression." But it is now a matter of a philosophical "regression" (indigenous to [the history of] philosophy), that is, of the already mentioned "return" to Plato, to the Platonic problematic of the mimetic (or dramatic) mode of saying. There is nothing to give us forewarning that he was about to take this problematic into account. Its abrupt introduction (dis)organizes the dialectical scheme of tragedy.

I am going to quote, for example, this passage: Hölderlin addresses himself here to the structure of tragedy in terms of its difference from that which he defines as the probable essence of the great modern lyric, i.e., the "tragic ode":

> It is the deepest interiority which is expressed in the dramatic poem of tragedy. The tragic ode also portrays the inward in the most positive differences, in actual oppositions, but these oppositions, however, are present more in the simple form and *as the immediate language of sentiment.* The tragic poem conceals the interiority in the portrayal still more, expresses it in more

clearly defined differences, because it expresses a more profound interiority, something more infinitely divine. The sentiment no longer expresses itself directly. . . . Thus in the dramatic poem of tragedy, as well, the divinity expressed is that which the poet senses and experiences in his world; the dramatic poem of tragedy is also an image of the living for him, one that for him is and was present in his life. But as this image of interiority increasingly denies and must everywhere deny its final ground to the same extent, as this image must everywhere become more proximate to the symbol, the more infinite, the more ineffable, the closer the interiority is to the *nefas*, the more rigorously and the more austerely the image must differentiate the human being and the element of his sentiment in order to keep the sentiment within its limits, *the less can the image express the sentiment in any immediate way.* . . . [italics mine—P. L.-L.]

[Es ist die tiefste Innigkeit, die sich im tragischen dramatischen Gedichte ausdrückt. Die tragische Ode stellt das Innige auch in den positivsten Unterscheidungen dar, in wirklichen Gegensätzen, aber diese Gegensätze sind doch mehr bloß in der Form und als unmittelbare Sprache der Empfindung vorhanden. Das tragische Gedicht verhüllt die innigkeit in der Darstellung noch mehr, drückt sie in stärkeren Unterscheidungen aus, weil es eine tiefere Innigkeit, ein unendlicheres Göttliche ausdrückt. Die Empfindung drückt sich nicht mehr unmittelbar aus. . . . Auch im tragisch dramatischen Gedichte spricht sich also das Göttliche aus, das der Dichter in seiner Welt empfindet und erfährt, auch das tragisch dramatische Gedicht ist ihm ein Bild des Lebendigen, das ihm in seinem Leben gegenwärtig ist und war; aber wie dieses Bild der Innigkeit überall seinen letzten Grund in eben dem Grade mehr verleugnet und verleugnen muß, wie es überall mehr dem Symbol sich nähern muß, je unendlicher, je unaussprechlicher, je näher dem *nefas* die Innigkeit ist, je strenger und kälter das Bild den Menschen und sein empfundenes Element unterscheiden muss, um die Empfindung in ihrer Grenze festzuhalten, um so weniger kann das Bild die Empfindung unmittelbar aussprechen. . . . (*HW*, pp. 571–572)]

Here we find a theory of the dramatic figure (of the personage or of "character") in its relationship with the playwright, a kind of "paradox of the dramatist [paradoxe sur le dramaturge]," if you will. It is possible to recognize, in passing, a motif that we have already encountered and that takes the form of that law according to which the style of a work is the effect or the product, the result of the "catastrophe" of its first fundamental tone or of its signification. This is why the more the tragic poet wants to express "the most profound interiority," the more he must travel along the route of mediation of an "alien material." Consequently, it is nothing other than the paradox that founded the speculative interpretation of tragedy and permitted the deduction (or reconstruction) of its organically dialectical structure.—However, even after the first reading, it is easy to see that something prevents the pure and simple renewal of this analytical lease. Even if Hölderlin, using all the means available to him, including the exhaustion of his dialectical resources (the text, indeed, incompletes and loses itself, failing to close with a result of any kind), strives to think of the dramatic character as the means or the mediation used to further the paradoxically adequate expression of the author or the subject, this dialectical primer—perpetually begun, lacks and never ceases to lack a principle of resolution. From this moment, everything takes place as if one had something to do—and there was nothing more to be done—except in a kind of immobilized extenuation of a dialectical process that shifts its feet in an interminable oscillation between the two poles of an opposition, always infinitely distant from each other. The act of suspending is this: quite simply, the incessant repetition of a priming [amorce] of the dialectical process in the—never changing—form of: the closer it is, the farther away it gets; the more dissimilar it is, the more exterior it is. In short, the maximum of appropriation (inasmuch as the perpetual comparison here originates in a movement to the limit, and proceeds necessarily from a logic of excess—of the superlative)—the maximum of appropriation is the maximum of disappropriation, and conversely "The more infinite the interiority, the more rigorously the image must differentiate the human being and the element of his senti- ment."

One can well imagine the analysis which might be undertaken here on the basis of the contradictory structure implicated by the mimetic relationship—on the basis of the "double bind." This obsession with the near and the far (or, what amounts to the same thing, of peril and protection) runs through—in addition to the poems, including even some of the greatest, such as "Patmos"—all of the correspondence (with Schiller, in particular) and constitutes the privileged metaphor (if, at this point, it can still be considered such) of the detailed description that Hölderlin gives of his own cyclo-thymic rhythm. Such an analysis would be perfectly justified—all the more so, in that it would inevitably have to communicate with what is progressively articulated, in that inflection to which Hegel subjects mimetology, with regard to the general prob- lematic of the subject of enunciation.—But nothing would prevent us, by the same token, from recognizing—within this paralysis affecting (with- out end) the very movement of the dialectic and the ontologic, beyond the evidence of the gesture of conjuration—the effect in exchange of mimetology within the speculative, and, consequently, within the general discourse of truth and presence. It is true that Heidegger constantly looked in Hölderlin for the possibility of returning, within the assump- tion of *adaequatio*, to the speculative mode and of leaving at the very interior of the onto-theo-logic. This is why the "logic" of *aletheia* can also be inscribed as the "logic" of *Ent-fernung* [*é-loignement*, or "disdis- tancing"]. But who knows if this "logic" itself (exposed to that which does not cease, in the moments of greatest exigency, to carry it away as

Philippe Lacoue-Labarthe

well)—who knows whether this logic "itself" is not still penetrated by (if not "subordinated to") mimetology? The "logic" in the open-ended exchange of the excess of presence and of the excess of loss, the alternation of appropriation and disappropriation—all that which we might baptize, with the authorization of Hölderlin's terminology (for lack of anything better) the *hyperbologic*, together with everything that keeps it within the circle of the "homoeotic" definition of truth: who knows if this is not the (paradoxical) truth of *aletheia*?

In any case, it is such a "hyperbologic" which evidently subtends the final definition of the tragic proposed by Hölderlin.

Here it is—it is very well known:

The presentation of the tragic rests principally on the notion that the monstrous, the way in which the god and the human being mate, in which the natural force and the most inner part of man become one, boundless, in rage, is understood through the purification, by a limitless scission, of the boundless act of becoming-one.

[Die Darstellung des Tragischen beruht vorzüglich darauf, daß das Ungeheure, wie der Gott und Mensch sich paart, und grenzenlos die Naturmacht und des Menschen Innerstes im Zorn Eins wird, dadurch sich begreift, daß das grenzenlose Einswerden durch grenzenloses Scheiden sich reinigt. *HW*, pp. 735–736.]

What is at stake here is still catharsis. At the same time, however, it is more than that: a "generalization" of catharsis, if you will, but one which can only be such in the abandonment of the terrain upon which Aristotle had constructed his own notion of catharsis, that is, the terrain of the "spectacular" recital. From this point forward, such a catharsis, indeed, proceeds from the taking into account of the "subject" of the tragedy or the dramatic utterance. Moreover, this is why it brings into play along with it, over and above a simple "poetics," an entire conception of the history of the world, of the relationship between man and the divine—or of heaven and earth—a conception of the function of art and the requisite "catastrophe" undergone by the natural in its encounter with the cultural, of the movement of alternation or of exchange, in general, of that which is mine [propre] and that which is yours [impropre]. I cannot go into this any further here. I should emphasize, nevertheless, that only the "hyperbologic," doubtless, is in a position to account for this scheme of "double reversal" upon which Hölderlin founded his later thought and according to which the very excess of the speculative is exchanged into what is itself the excess of submission to finitude—coming to correspond to the "categorical" reversal of the divine is the "volte-face," as Beaufret says, of the human being towards the earth, his pious infidelity, and his extended wandering "beneath the unthinkable," which together define the basis of the Kantian age to which we belong.

No matter what the outcome of such a thought, the lesson of it in regard to tragedy is as clear as can be: the more tragedy identifies itself with the speculative desire of the infinite and the divine, the more tragedy exposes it as the thing rejected within the process of separation, the differentiation, the finitude. Tragedy is, then, the catharsis of the speculative.

But this should also be taken to mean the catharsis of the religious itself and of the sacrificial—a final paradox, then, and one which is not the least surprising of those encountered.

First of all, that which authorizes such a definition of tragedy is nothing other than Hölderlin's reading of *Oedipus the King*. This reading (*Remarks*, II) is based entirely upon a condemnation (there was never a more explicit one) of the indissolubly speculative and religious temptation wherein Hölderlin finds the fundamental mainspring of the Oedipal "fable" and the reason for its "composition,"—comparable, he says, to the unfolding of the "trial of a heretic."

What, indeed, is the fault of Oedipus?

It is, Hölderlin answers, to act "as a priest." Nevertheless, the response is surprising. But here is the beginning of his analysis. It is impeccably clear:

The *intelligibility* of the whole rests primarily upon one's keeping in mind the scene, in which Oedipus *interprets in too unended a way* the word of the oracle and in which he is tempted to an act of *nefas*.

[The transgression, the sacrilege, would then be the excess of interpretation.—P. L.-L.]

The word of the oracle, namely, is:

Phoebus the King has clearly commanded us
To purify the land of the defilement which has been nourished on this ground
And to deny sustenance to what cannot be healed.

This *could* mean [emphasis mine: this is the literal, profane, political translation of the oracle's saying—P. L.-L.]: keep, in general, a strict and pure code of law, keep a decent civil order. But Oedipus, in the next moment, speaks in a priestly fashion:

Through what purification, etc.

[Die *Verständlichkeit* des Ganzen beruhet vorzüglich darauf, daß man die Szene ins Auge faßt, wo Oedipus den Orakelspruch *zu unendlich deutet*, *zum nefas* versucht wird.

Nämlich der Orakelspruch heißt:

Geboten hat uns Phöbus klar, der König,
Man soll des Landes Schmach, auf diesem Grund genährt,
Verfolgen, nicht Unheilbares ernähren.

Das könnte heißen: Richtet, allgemein, ein streng und rein Gericht, haltet gute bürgerliche Ordnung. Oedipus aber spricht gleich darauf priesterlich:

Durch welche Reingiung, etc. *HW*, p. 731]

"And now he gets down to *particulars*," adds Hölderlin, wishing thus to signify that the movement has, from this point on, become irreversible and that Oedipus, indeed, will conduct his own trial on the charge of heresy.—The tragic fault consists, then, in the religious and sacrificial interpretation of the social ill. The tragic hero is destroyed, as Schelling said, by his wishing to carry out the ritual and by desiring a *"pharmakos"* in order to remove the defilement which he imagines to be sacred. He is destroyed not by directly provoking the chastisement, but by setting loose the old ritual of the scapegoated victim. He is destroyed, in short, by his belief in what Girard calls religious "mechanisms," which are, in fact, with regard to a different concept of religion, "sacrilegious" mechanisms, because they presuppose the transgression of human limits, the appropriation of a divine position (Antigone would be an exemplary case) and of the right to institute difference by oneself (this will be the case of Oedipus just as much as that of Creon, while it is also true that such a reading of tragedy definitively prevents one from conceiving of a "positive" tragic hero). This is why he who desires difference and exclusion excludes himself and undergoes relentlessly, to the point of loss, this unlimited differentiation introduced by the "hyperbologic" in its doubling of the dialectical-sacrificial process, so as to prevent its culmination and paralyze it *from within*. Tragedy, because it is the catharsis of the speculative, reveals disappropriation *as* that which secretly animates and constitutes it; tragedy reveals (dis)appropriation. This is the reason why Oedipus incarnates the madness of knowledge (all knowledge is the desire for appropriation) and represents, in his course the "demented quest of a consciousness": perhaps this is nothing other, then, than the insanity of self-consciousness.

From this point forward, the re-elaboration of tragedy, in its turn, cannot fail to reach the dialectical-structural conception of tragic organization. It provokes, in any case, the subordination of the theory of the alternation of tones. Indeed, from the moment when the mimetic structure no longer rightly guarantees the conciliatory and reappropriating "return to the Same"—from the moment when the tragic spectacle presupposes, behind it, the loss without reprieve of every positioning and every assured determination of the utterance and sees itself condemned, as a consequence, to represent the process, which is itself at all times complex and differentiated, of (dis)appropriation, every element will play its part in coercing the dynamic and productive successivity which organized tragedy to give structurally way to a dispositive of pure equilibrium. The structure of tragedy itself becomes immobilized and paralyzed. Yet this does not in any way prevent this "neutralization" of the dialectical dynamic from being constantly *active*. For the tragic structure *also* remains dialectical, and only the deconstruction of the Sophoclean-Schellingian (or Aristotelian) model of tragedy obliges us to (de)structure tragedy in this way.

Yet the movement I have described also reverts to the disorganizing of tragedy, in the strictest sense, to its desystematizing and its disjointing —consequently, to its reconstructing, in the very place where its dialectical organization confirms itself, upon an empty articulation or the default of all articulation—a pure asyndeton which Hölderlin calls the *caesura* and which suspends the "catastrophic" process of alternation:

The *transport* of tragedy is, in itself, empty and the most unconnected. Thereby, in the rhythmic succession of representations in which the *transport* is portrayed, *that which in prosody is called the caesura*, the pure word, the antirhythmic interruption, becomes necessary, in order to embrace the onrushing alternation of representations, at its crescendo, in such a way that it is no longer the alternation of representations, but rather the representation itself which appears.

[Der tragische *Transport* ist nämlich eigentlich leer, und der ungebundenste. Dadurch wird in der rhythmischen Aufeinanderfolge der Vorstellungen, worin der *Transport* sich darstellt, *das, was man im Silbenmaße Zäsur heißt*, das reine Wort, die gegen-rhythmische Unterbrechung notwendig, um nämlich dem reißenden Wechsel der Vorstellungen, auf seinem Summum, so zu begegnen, daß alsdann nicht mehr der Wechsel der Vorstellung, sondern die Vorstellung selber erscheint. *HW*, p. 730]

Such a disarticulation of the work and of the process of succession through alternations which constitutes the work as such—and through which we must travel (by what effect—even here—of "regression"?) from a melodic conception of the work to a rhythmic one—does not suppress the logic of exchange and alternation. It simply brings it to a halt; it reestablishes its equilibrium; it prevents it, as Hölderlin says, from exhibiting its representations in one sense or another. It avoids (as a protective gesture, which does not necessarily mean a "ritualistic" one) the oscillating transport of passion, the *panic*, and the inflection toward this or that pole. The disarticulation represents the active neutrality of that which is in between both poles. This is, no doubt, why it is not mere chance that the caesura is, on every occasion, this empty moment—the absence of "moment," of Tiresias's intervention; in other words, of the intrusion of the prophetic word.

Tragedy, in German, is known as *Trauerspiel*—literally, "game of grief."

A *Trauerspiel*, then, if you will allow me such an association (which, after all, is not as free as it seems) is something different from the "work of grief," the sublimating apprenticeship of suffering and the work of the negative, the two conditions, as Heidegger has shown, of the onto-logic: *Arbeit* (production and work) and *algos*, that is, *logos*.

Why must we be forbidden to think that Hölderlin, when he was (dis)organizing tragedy in this way, will have *"caesura'd the speculative"* (which is not the same thing as surpassing it, maintaining it, or suspending it) and, in so doing, found something of the *Trauerspiel*?

At any rate, we know that Hölderlin wrote the following about Sophocles—its simplicity is disarming.

> Vainly, the high-spirited tried to say gladness in the extreme;
> Here it speaks to me, at last; here is its word, in grief.

> [Viele versuchten umsonst das Freudigste freudig zu sagen,
> Hier spricht endlich es mir, hier in der Trauer sich aus. ["Sophokles,"
> *HW*, p. 36]

Translated by Robert Eisenhauer

NOTES

1. Peter Szondi, *Versuch über das Tragische* (Frankfurt: Insel-Verlag, 1964). Quotations from this work are hereafter identified by the abbreviation *VT*.

2. Jean Beaufret, *Dialogue avec Heidegger* (Paris: Editions de Minuit, 1973–74).

3. Jacques Derrida, *Glas* (Paris: Editions Galilée, 1974), left-hand column, in the vicinity of p. 188.

4. F. W. J. Schelling, "Philosophie der Kunst," in *Sämmtliche Werke*, K. F. A. Schelling, ed. (Stuttgart: J. G. Cotta, 1859), Part I, vol. 5, p. 687.

5. All citations of Hölderlin's work will be from *Werke und Briefe*, ed. Friedrich Beißner (Frankfurt: Insel, 1969), abbreviated *HW*.

6. Beda Allemann, *Hölderlin und Heidegger* (Freiburg: Rombach & Co., 1954).

7. "La nature est conçue dans ce texte [*Ground for Empedocles*] comme la totalité infinie, universelle, inconcevable et surtout non différenciée; elle est *aorgique*, selon le néologisme forgé par Hölderlin pour l'opposer à l'art organique, individualisé, reflexif." Jean Laplanche, *Hölderlin et la question du père* (Paris: Presses Universitaires de France, 1961), p. 114. Note supplied by translator.

FOUR

THE BEHOLDER IN COURBET:
HIS EARLY SELF-PORTRAITS AND THEIR
PLACE IN HIS ART
Michael Fried

IN THE COURSE of the 1840s, when the French painter Gustave Courbet (1819–77) was still in his twenties, he painted and drew a considerable number of portraits of himself. In fact, it is no exaggeration to say that throughout most of that decade, which from a stylistic point of view was one of apprenticeship to the Old Masters, Courbet himself was his favorite subject and the self-portrait his preferred genre. There are of course other well-known instances of painters apparently obsessed with their own images: Rembrandt and Van Gogh come at once to mind. But I know of no parallel to the role of the self-portrait in the development of Courbet's art, and it is one index among many of the still largely rudimentary state of Courbet studies that that role has gone, if not quite unrecognized, at any rate uninvestigated.[1]

The present essay seeks to approach Courbet's art by way of such an investigation. It has two parts. In the first and longer part I analyze a number of self-portraits of the 1840s in an attempt to call attention to certain features they have in common and to account for those features at least up to a point. My handling of the paintings and drawings in question is somewhat arbitrary. For example, I make no effort to discuss them in chronological order, a procedure which would run into perhaps

The writing of this essay was funded by a Fellowship from the American Council of Learned Societies; I am grateful to the Council for its support. I would also like to thank Ruth Leys-Fried and Stephen Orgel for editorial suggestions.

Michael Fried

insuperable difficulties as regards the dating of various objects, but instead move freely from one to another according to the demands of my argument. No doubt similar conclusions could be reached by considering the same works in a different order, or by treating works that I have deliberately omitted for reasons of space. But precisely this is my justification for proceeding as I do. And in the second part of the essay I try as briefly as possible both to show how my account of Courbet's self-portraits contributes to an understanding of his enterprise as a painter and to place that understanding in the larger context of the evolution of painting in France during the period before he came onto the scene.

It should be acknowledged at the outset that the painter and paintings evoked in the pages that follow differ radically from those made familiar by previous studies. Probably the most conspicuous difference concerns the representational modality of Courbet's "Realism," an epithet which the painter and his friends first applied to his monumental canvases of the years 1848–50 but which is often extended to cover the bulk of his production from then on. At the risk of oversimplifying a large body of writing, I think it is fair to say that historians of Courbet's art have construed that modality in one of two ways. Either they have seen in his "Realism" a direct, concrete, empirical, materialist, and, in all those senses of the word, objective portrayal of persons, things, and nature. Or—a minority view—they have stressed the importance of Courbet's alleged narcissism, by which has been meant not simply a habit of self-love but a tendency to identify with his subject matter and in effect to make himself part of the very fabric of his representations. "Dans l'univers matériel, c'est sa propre réalité qu'il reconnaît," Pierre Courthion has written. "Ce qu'il a laissé sur la toile, ce n'est pas la vision d'un monde intérieur, mais l'image physique de sa personne, diluée dans la reproduction du monde matériel."[2] Neither interpretation seems to me satisfactory: the first because it fails to register the prodigious strangeness of Courbet's art and in particular the unique claims which his paintings may be felt to make upon one's entire person as one stands before them; and the second because its emphasis remains merely personal and presents Courbet's activity as in no sense the product of a conjunction of forces. Recently a compromise view has emerged. Jack Lindsay has argued that there exists "a tension inside [Courbet's] Realism, driving him to define people and things as truly as he can, to hold them at arm's length, and yet at the same time to fill them with his own deep energy."[3] But the problem as I see it is not to reconcile the two interpretations— Lindsay's phrases have little explanatory force, and besides the notion of holding reality at arm's length strikes me as positively misleading—but to account equally for what is accurate and for what is unsatisfying in each.

The version of Courbet's enterprise put forward in the second part of this essay will be seen to be capable of doing just that.

Another major point of difference between this essay and previous studies of Courbet concerns the question of his historical position. It has usually appeared to students of his art that very little in the French painting of the first decades of the nineteenth century anticipates or prepares the ground for the great breakthrough pictures of 1848–50— the *After Dinner at Ornans*, *Stonebreakers*, *Burial at Ornans*, and *Peasants of Flagey Returning from the Fair*. At most something is said about the presence of realist tendencies in the art of David and Géricault; about the work of so-called proto-realists in the years preceding the Revolution of 1848; and about the existence during those years of an impasse between Classical and Romantic schools each of which had lost its vitality, an impasse which Courbet is supposed to have shattered almost with a single blow. But I contend that the *After Dinner* and its immediate successors can be made to disclose their essential motivation only when they are viewed as responses to a crisis involving the relationship between painting and beholder whose roots go back beyond David to the middle of the eighteenth century. I do not mean by this to suggest that Courbet's momentous creations ought finally to be incorporated in a formal or stylistic continuum extending, let us say, from Chardin to Manet. Rather I believe that their full momentousness, indeed their absolute resistance to all such attempts at incorporation, become historically intelligible only in the context of the crisis to which I have just alluded. By the same token, it is only thus that we are enabled to grasp the fundamental significance that Courbet's art had for the greatest painter of the next generation, Edouard Manet (1832–83), in whose masterpieces of the first half of the 1860s the crisis in the relationship between painting and beholder came to a head and in a sense was liquidated.

One more point remains by way of introduction. The first part of this essay makes use of concepts and insights initially developed by writers belonging to the philosophical movement sometimes called existential phenomenology. This has come about not because of any general commitment to the latter on my part—I did not set out to conduct an existential-phenomenological reading of Courbet's art, nor do I think that that is what I have done—but because certain ideas formulated in the writings of Merleau-Ponty and his school, chiefly concerning the notion of the "lived body," have seemed to me more nearly adequate than any others to describe crucial aspects of Courbet's self-portraits. In any case, the existential-phenomenological tenor of my analysis of the self-portraits is superseded by another, more embracing emphasis which might be characterized as pictorial and ontological. It is those sorts of

FIGURE 4.1. Courbet, *The Sculptor*, 1844. 55 x 41 cm. Private Collection.

issues that previous students of Courbet have tended to misconstrue or ignore, with serious consequences for our understanding of his achievement and of the evolution of nineteenth-century painting generally.[4]

I

Let me begin by considering a work not given much attention in surveys of Courbet's art—the self-portrait known as *The Sculptor* (1844; fig. 1). In it Courbet has depicted a young man, unmistakably himself, dressed in a costume we are evidently meant to regard as medieval—an ochre jerkin over a white shirt, red tights with thin yellow stripes and jagged bottoms, slipper-like shoes, etc.—and seated on the bank of a small brook. He seems to be sitting on a large object, probably a boulder, over which has been spread a peacock-blue cloak. Two trees spring from the top of the bank to his left (our right), and further back, in a sort of middle distance, there rises and recedes obliquely a wall of rock crowned by other trees. Beyond these, in the upper left-hand corner of the canvas, we are given a glimpse of bright blue sky.

The young man's head is beardless. It lolls back and to the side—its connection with the rest of his body appears somewhat tenuous—while the eyes roll upwards. His expression is one of engrossment in reverie, a condition that in this instance we may suppose to have come about in response to his surroundings or at least to be in harmony with them. In fact, the existence of some special form of interchange or reciprocity between the young man and his environment is strongly implied by perhaps the oddest single feature of this very odd painting. The brook, such as it is, issues from a circular orifice near the young man's left knee, and just above that orifice can be discerned the image of a woman's head and left shoulder (fig. 2). It seems clear that we are meant to see that image, whose orientation implies that the woman is lying on her back with her head nearer to us than any other part of her body, as having been carved by the young man out of the living rock of the bank; and in general there is the suggestion of a double connection, whose precise nature remains unspecified, between the image of the woman and the brook on the one hand and between both of these and the young man, the sculptor, on the other.

Like his expression, the young man's attitude is obviously intended to convey a sense of ease and reverie in the midst of nature. But various aspects of his pose prevent this intention from being realized. In the first place, the young man is shown leaning backward and to his right while turning his upper body to the left, a posture which, especially in conjunction with the lolling of his head, comes across as anything but natural. Indeed, his torso is turned almost sideways, with the physically improb-

FIGURE 4.2. Courbet, *The Sculptor,* detail of woman's head and shoulder.

able and visually unpersuasive result that his left shoulder and the left half of his chest are lost to view. Even more peculiarly, his right arm, depicted in foreshortening, is supported at about the height of his head by a thin branch beneath the wrist. The branch—it is little more than a twig—scarcely seems adequate to the task: our first impression is that the sitter's right hand, drooping this side of the branch and holding a small mallet, is suspended in mid-air; and even after we have understood that this is not the case, it is hard to shake the conviction that his arm lacks support. The young man's left hand, holding a chisel and resting on his left thigh, presents no problems. But the position of his legs is another matter. The left leg is bent sharply at the knee, planting the left foot as far back as it can go, and the right leg is stretched out almost straight, the tip of the shoe just touching the water in the immediate foreground. The effect is rather like a curtsey, which is to say that it is at odds both with the naturalness of the setting and with the ostensible absorption of the young man in his reverie.

Modern writers on Courbet seem obscurely aware that the *Sculptor* is a work of some importance. But by and large they continue to characterize it as immature and Romantic, two terms roughly synonymous in the literature on the painter, and to treat it merely as a foil for his later work. The unhelpfulness of the notion of Romanticism in this context is obvious, while the alleged immaturity of the picture is beside the point. Admittedly the *Sculptor* bears the stamp of Courbet's youth and inex-

FIGURE 4.3. Courbet, *Wounded Man*, ca. 1844–54. 81 x 97 cm. Paris, Louvre. Phot. Musées nationaux.

perience. But those features whose awkwardness and unnaturalness seem most obtrusive turn out under further investigation to be early instances of elements which recur again and again in his art and whose importance for our understanding of his enterprise will emerge as fundamental. Nothing, indeed, is more characteristic of Courbet's oeuvre than the repetition or reuse, throughout all phases of his development and often with only slight variation, of a number of highly specific and, on the face of it, extremely peculiar motifs, poses, themes, formal structures, and the like. In the paintings of his maturity these tend to be integrated with one another and subsumed within an overall "illusion" of reality to a degree that makes them far less conspicuous than in an early work like the *Sculptor*. But they are everywhere to be understood as vehicles of an extraordinary determination—one which, in crucial respects, changed little if at all in the course of his development.

In this connection it is revealing to compare the *Sculptor* with one of the most famous and masterly of the self-portraits, the *Wounded Man* (ca. 1844–54; fig. 3).[5] In obvious respects there is a sharp contr

between the two paintings. For example, the later canvas eschews the fussy detail, bright local color, elaborate costume, and confusions of pose that threaten to divide our attention in the earlier one. Instead we are presented with a single unitary image: the upper half of the body of a wounded man, Courbet himself, reclining on his back in a wooded setting, his head leaning against the base of a tree and his left hand grasping a fold of the dark brown cloak that covers him. In keeping with the internal scale of that image, the later painting is considerably larger than the earlier one; its execution is broad and confident; and altogether it exemplifies the massive simplification of means and effects that took place in Courbet's art in the late 1840s and early 1850s. But these and other differences should not be allowed to obscure certain deep similarities between the two works.

For example, there is the matter of the figure's general situation in the two paintings. Both depict Courbet himself in a natural setting with trees and a patch of sky behind him, and in both he is shown inclined back into the space of the painting along a diagonal that runs from the lower right towards the upper left. The obliqueness of his pose means that the lower portion of his body is thrust significantly nearer to us than his head. In fact it is difficult to escape the feeling of being obliged to look up at his head and face from below, an impression that is particularly vivid in the case of the *Wounded Man.*

There is also an affinity of sorts between the sitter's apparent condition in the two paintings. This is so despite the fact that we do not find in the *Wounded Man* an evocation of intense or even mild reverie. Instead the wounded man's eyes are closed (or almost closed: it is impossible to tell for sure, but one has the impression that he may be barely looking out from beneath his lids), and he appears about to lose consciousness if he has not already done so (*vide* the wound in his breast and the sword behind him to his right). At the same time, we feel that the whole crepuscular scene expresses his state of mind, or to put this slightly differently, that his consciousness although on the verge of extinction nevertheless goes out towards his surroundings. In short, we do not know exactly what to make of his condition; but we seem to be dealing with an abnormal state of mind, one which, like that of intense reverie, implies both a dilation and an extinguishing of ordinary waking awareness.

Then, too, a prominent role is played in both canvases by one of the sitter's hands. In the *Sculptor* it is the young man's right hand, all but suspended in mid-air, that chiefly strikes us, while in the *Wounded Man* we are shown only the protagonist's left hand grasping a fold of his cloak. Especially in the later painting the hand in question is a focus of interest both because of its place in the composition—it is the sole light accent in the lower half of the painting—and because of the vigorous yet

melting plasticity with which it has been rendered. I shall have more to say about the role of hands in Courbet's self-portraits in a few pages.

But the chief point of similarity between the two works that I want to stress at this stage of my argument concerns what I see as the assertion in each of the apparent nearness, the seeming physical proximity, of the painted image to the surface of the painting and, beyond that surface, to the beholder. In the *Sculptor* the extension of the young man's right leg brings the toe of his shoe almost to the bottom of the canvas, which is to say to the portion of the scene lying closest to us. I suggest in fact that the awkwardness and unnaturalness of the position of the young man's legs are chiefly to be understood in this light—that it was above all in order to assert the nearness of the painted image to the picture-surface that Courbet was compelled to represent the young man as if he were seeking to span with his body the distance between the foreground proper, where his trunk and head are located, and the immediate foreground, as defined by the water in the brook that flows towards us in the lower right-hand corner of the canvas. A plainer and far more powerful assertion of the apparent proximity of the image takes place in the *Wounded Man*. To begin with, the entire scene is pitched much nearer the beholder than is the case in the *Sculptor*. What is more, the situation of the wounded man—lying on his back with his head against the base of a tree—together with the truncation of his body at about the waist by the bottom framing-edge, leave no doubt that a significant portion of his body continues to advance towards the beholder beyond the limits of the canvas; it is even possible, given the apparent distances involved, that the lower half of his body is to be imagined as lying closer to the beholder than the surface of the painting. The *Wounded Man* thereby calls into question the absoluteness or impermeability of the picture-surface as an ontological entity, i.e., as an imaginary boundary between the "world" of the painting and that of the beholder. Or perhaps it mainly calls into question the impermeability of the bottom framing-edge—the capacity of that edge to contain the representation, to bring it to a stop, to establish it at a fixed distance from both picture-surface and beholder. There is in this regard a further point of resemblance between the *Wounded Man* and the *Sculptor*. I refer to the way in which in the latter the water in the immediate foreground functions as a natural metaphor of continuity, of the spilling-over of the contents of the painting into the "world" of the beholder, at any rate of the refusal or incapacity of the painting to contain its representation within hard and fast limits. If this seems fanciful, and to many it will, I would point out that large and small bodies of water are deployed to much the same effect elsewhere in Courbet's art—see for example the later *Source* (1868; fig. 16)—and that in general the bottom

FIGURE 4.4. Courbet, *Small Portrait of Courbet*, 1842. 27 x 23 cm. Pontarlier, Hôtel de Ville. Phot. Bulloz.

edges of his paintings have an ontologically problematic status unlike anything to be found in the work of any painter before or since. This is nowhere more evident than in the stupendous *Burial at Ornans* (1849–50; fig. 13), whose bottom framing-edge cuts across the open grave at the center of the extreme foreground, an arrangement which, in conjunction with the apparent extreme proximity of the entire scene, strongly implies the extension of the grave "this" side of the picture-surface. The implication is confirmed by the placing just to the left of the grave of the blade of the gravedigger's shovel, whose handle is to be imagined as projecting towards the beholder's right hand.

Two more early self-portraits throw light on Courbet's preoccupation with nearness. In the precocious and delicate *Small Portrait of Courbet* (1842; fig. 4), the earliest of all the paintings we shall examine,

Courbet has depicted a rather beautiful young man dressed mostly in black and seated upright at a table with a spaniel in his lap. Although the young man's body is angled back into space, his head is seen almost exactly from the front; and, as in very few of the self-portraits, he gazes straight ahead as if to meet the gaze of the beholder with his own. At the same time, his expression of quiet absorption, which we recognize to be one of absorption in his own mirror-image (it will eventually become necessary to qualify this statement), as well as the fact that his eyes although plainly open are in dark shadow, go a long way towards divesting our relation to the young man of any character of confrontation. Another important factor in this is the placement in the immediate foreground, resting lightly on a table which we almost feel we share with the young man, of the latter's right hand and forearm. As in the first two paintings we have discussed, the hand is shown with its back towards us and is modelled finely in light and dark. (It is further set off both by the dazzling cuff of his shirt and by the broader aquamarine cuff of his jacket, a *tour de force* of restrained colorism.) Also as in those paintings, only more conspicuously, it is a focus of the composition in its own right, to the extent of competing for our attention with the exquisitely rendered head and face. And of course one effect of its virtual isolation at the bottom of the painting is precisely to assert the intimate proximity to the picture-surface of the almost silhouette-like image of man and dog as a composite whole.

Another early work, the *Desperate Man* (1843?; fig. 5), presents the young Courbet—eyes wide and staring, nostrils flared, mouth slightly open, one hand gripping his head while the other pulls violently at his hair—looming, almost lunging, directly at the beholder. (Once again, however, the all but palpable interposition of a mirror holds to a minimum any sense that it is *we* who are confronted by him.) The *Desperate Man* has been characterized by Linda Nochlin as "an attempt to capture 'realistically' as it were, an effect of momentary expression in much the same manner as did the young Rembrandt in his series of etched self-portraits of 1630,"[6] and as far as Courbet's use of sources is concerned the comparison with Rembrandt is germane. I contend, however, that we find in the *Desperate Man* an attempt not so much to capture an expressive effect—the longer we study the painting the less readable the sitter's expression becomes—as to dramatize, to portray in action, the impulse towards extreme physical proximity that we have seen at work in the *Sculptor*, *Wounded Man*, and *Small Portrait of Courbet*. Such a notion helps explain the otherwise wholly arbitrary lighting, which calls attention to features—the desperate man's nose and left elbow—that thrust forward towards the picture-surface, as well as the billowing across most of the bottom framing-edge of his loosely-tied blue-gray scarf, which has

FIGURE 4.5. Courbet, *Desperate Man*, 1843? 45 x 45 cm. Private Collection. Phot. Bulloz.

the effect of softening that edge, of making it labile, even of preparing it to be transgressed. It is as though Courbet's object in this remarkable canvas were by an act of almost physical aggression to cancel or undo all distance not merely between image and picture-surface but between sitter and beholder, to close the gulf between them, to make them *one* (or one *again*).[7]

A few pages back, while comparing the *Sculptor* and *Wounded Man*, I remarked that there exists an affinity between the sitter's condition in the two works and went on to note in both a simultaneous dilation and extinguishing of ordinary waking consciousness. At this point I want to try to answer the following questions: What significance may we attribute to the states of mind depicted in those paintings? More generally, how are we to interpret what might be called the expressive tenor of Courbet's self-portraits? And what is the import of that interpretation for our understanding of his enterprise not only in the self-portraits but throughout his oeuvre?—In the first place, it should be clear that the self-portraits we have looked at so far cannot plausibly be construed as explorations either of comparatively stable facets of his character or personality or of more or less transient moods and emotions. Even the *Desperate Man*, which at first glance appears to be a study in the representation of extreme emotion, is better understood in other terms; while *The Sculptor*, *Wounded Man*, and *Small Portrait of Courbet* are all manifestly uncommunicative on the level of character or personality.[8] (The contrast in this regard with the autobiographical Rembrandt and Van Gogh is acute.) Now it is often held that Courbet was at bottom a painter of inanimate matter—in René Huyghe's words, of "*things*, in all their powerful materiality."[9] And the impassivity of the self-portraits, their virtual blankness as regards the sorts of interest most closely associated with the genre, indeed the air of somnolence that pervades *The Wounded Man* and is at least hinted at in the *Sculptor*, may seem to suggest that Courbet saw in himself as subject simply another material entity, albeit an intimately familiar one whose features he candidly admired and which he could scrutinize at his leisure and depict as often as he wished. Nothing, however, could be further from the truth.

I am convinced, and I shall do my best to persuade the reader, that the expressive tenor of Courbet's self-portraits is most accurately understood as the product of an attempt to evoke within the painting his intense absorption in his own live bodily being—his bodily liveness, as it has been called. Seen in this light, Courbet's undertaking in the self-portraits is roughly analogous with subsequent attempts by researchers in various fields to overthrow the legacy of Cartesian dualism by articulating, through radical reflection on the contents of consciousness aided by the findings of experimental psychology and medical pathology, the fundamental importance of the fact that human beings are incarnate, that they inhabit bodies which are from the first orientated to and implicated in the physical world. That feat of articulation, one of the cardinal achievements of existential phenomenology, leads to a recognition of the essential unity or interwovenness of body and world as the latter is given to us in perception, a recognition whose relevance to Courbet's treatment of subjects other than himself is implicit in much of what follows. But what I want to emphasize here is the deep accord that may be shown to exist between crucial and hitherto unremarked aspects of Courbet's self-portraits, including their seeming impassivity, and the conception of the "lived body" developed in the writings of Scheler, Straus, Merleau-Ponty, et al.[10] This is not to say that Courbet actually held such a conception in the abstract. On the contrary, it will become evident that from his beginnings as a painter, as in the *Small Portrait of Courbet*, he found himself compelled to seek to express in and through the medium of the self-portrait a consciousness of being one with his body which it is extremely unlikely he could have expounded in words. (A major instance of the verbal expression of that consciousness in Courbet's time is *Leaves of Grass*.)[11]

Some of the most telling evidence in support of this reading of the self-portraits concerns the depiction by Courbet of the sitter's *hands*. The use of the motif of hands for quite specific ends is one of the recurrent features of Courbet's art to which I earlier alluded, and it says a great deal about the importance of the self-portraits for any broader comprehension of his work that the key to the meaning of the motif lies precisely there. Simply put, the treatment of hands in the self-portraits tends to be of two kinds: either a single hand is presented in a state of apparent passivity or relaxation and at some distance from the rest of the sitter's body, as if in that way the existence of the hand as a source of internal sensation or bodily feeling could be brought into focus (made an object of absorption); or one or both hands are shown in a state of relative tension or activity—e.g., grasping, pulling, clasping, pressing, etc.—in an attempt not merely to delineate the performance of specific tasks and operations but, more significantly, to evoke as it were from within the sensation of effort itself. Early instances of the former are found in the *Small Portrait of Courbet*, in which the distancing of the hand from the rest of the body is accentuated by the horizontal table-edge that makes a separate zone of the bottom portion of the canvas, and the *Sculptor*, in which the apparent suspension in mid-air of the sitter's right hand has a similar effect. The latter approach is adumbrated in the *Desperate Man* and developed in another self-portrait of a few years later, the *Cellist* (1847; not illustrated), but it is above all in the enigmatic *Man with the Leather Belt* (fig. 10), a painting I shall discuss in detail further on, that hands that are tense and active but divorced from any practical activity are highlighted as a motif. In the *Wounded Man*, a picture that has in it something of both approaches, the sitter's hand not only serves as an epitome of his lived body; there is even a sense in which it takes the place of his body, which, except for the head and upper torso, is mostly hidden from view. More precisely, it is the sitter's body *as object* whose contours the painter has obscured under a rather formless dark brown cloak; and it is his body *as actually lived*, as possessed from within, that has been given expression in the powerful yet delicate hand that emerges from beneath the cloak to grasp firmly but not tightly a fold of the heavy, somewhat indeterminate stuff of which it is made. The ambiguity or doubleness of that gesture, which may be read as directed simultaneously outward towards the world and "inward" towards its own lived physicality, is characteristic of Courbet's art. So for

FIGURE 4.6. Courbet, *Sieste champêtre*, early 1840s. 26 x 31 cm. Besançon, Musée des Beaux-Arts. Phot. Musées nationaux.

that matter is the double nature of the cloak itself, which would seem to belong unequivocally to the world of objects but whose darkness, lack of definite contours, and role in obscuring the body as object suggest that it belongs as well to the realm of the body as lived—e.g., that it functions as a natural metaphor for the impossibility of the wounded man's perceiving his body simply as another object.[12]

Or consider the small but very fine and wonderfully nuanced charcoal drawing known as the *Sieste champêtre* (early 1840s; fig. 6), in which are depicted Courbet and a young woman who has been called Justine asleep against a tree. The angle at which Courbet's head leans back against the base of the trunk, the general orientation of his body, and the implied extension of his legs towards the surface of the sheet, all correspond closely to similar features of the *Wounded Man*, and in fact recent X-rays have revealed that the latter was originally conceived as a painted version of the *Sieste champêtre* and that several years after it was begun, perhaps in the late 1840s, perhaps around 1851, Courbet decided to do away with the figure of Justine.[13] It will be remarked at once that Courbet has again depicted one of his hands—the right hand, resting palm up on his thigh—in a manner that attracts our attention. On first view its openness and slight awkwardness are felt to evince the sitter's perfect unconsciousness. But something in those qualities—an intimation of poise, even of attentiveness—soon makes us almost uncomfortably aware of the hand as a potential locus of sensation and hence as a sign of the male sitter's possession from within of his own live body.

Another feature of the *Sieste champêtre* that deserves emphasis in this connection is its depiction of *sleep* (another motif that recurs throughout Courbet's art, as Huyghe was the first to note).[14] Except for a few early drawings, one of which we shall analyze shortly, I know of no other work in which Courbet portrayed himself as unambiguously asleep. But we have seen that he was strongly inclined to represent himself as engrossed in reverie or as semi-conscious, conditions that have much in common with sleep; and I now suggest that we may regard that inclination as aiming to present the body's liveness in its simplest and most elemental form—as a "primordial presence" which itself has the character of somnolence and which far from being extinguished in sleep is in effect given free rein. There is also a sense in which in the state of sleep a "primordial" relation to the world is allowed to reassert itself by virtue, first, of one's lying down—i.e., abandoning the upright posture that establishes human beings in perceptual opposition to the world of objects—and second, of one's surrendering all control of bodily functions as if to a power or rhythm outside oneself.[15] The role of the woman in the *Sieste champêtre* is significant in this regard. On the one hand, she is part of the world outside the principal sitter; on the other, she presumably has been possessed by him—the contented repose that the two figures share seems frankly post-coital—and in any case she appears almost physically to meld into his body to an extent that foreshadows her eventual elimination from the *Wounded Man*.

Still another aspect of the *Sieste champêtre* that leads me to see in it an image of the body as actually lived is the male sitter's pose and general orientation: lying back with his head propped against the tree and his legs extended towards the surface of the sheet. It may seem that Courbet thus presents his body in perspective and in a sense this is true. But I suggest that it is truer to Courbet's purposes in both the *Sieste champêtre* and *Wounded Man* to say that we are thus invited to become aware that the sitter's view of his own body, should he awaken and open his eyes, would itself be perspectival. That is, Courbet appears to have wished to direct attention to the fact that the sitter's body as an object of outward perception is always presented to the sitter himself from the same oblique angle—that he occupies towards his body a fixed and unchanging point of view, whereas his relation to all other objects is a function of his ability to approach or withdraw from them, to survey them from different sides, and in general to adopt towards them a multiplicity of points of view according to interest and desire and limited only by contingent circumstances. (This is what was meant a page or so back by the reference to the impossibility of the wounded man's perceiving his body simply as another object.) In short I am suggesting that the pose and orientation of the male sitter in the *Sieste champêtre* and *Wounded Man* were partly motivated, not by a resolve to depict his body in a perspective aimed at the viewer, though to a certain extent such a perspective proved unavoidable, but by a desire or compulsion to manifest what might be summarized as the resistance to all variation of perspective of the sitter's body seen from his point of view. The experience of that resistance belongs to the body as actually lived, and in fact provides a sort of immediate foreground relative to which the perception of objects in perspective is to be understood as taking place.[16]

We are now in a position to appreciate the significance of another important and previously ignored feature of Courbet's self-portraits, namely, that the painter appears to have taken steps in them to minimize any sense of confrontation between sitter and beholder. The sitter is characteristically portrayed either reclining with his head leaning against a tree, as in the *Sieste champêtre* and *Wounded Man*, or seated with his body at an angle to the beholder and his head tilted back or to the side or both, as in the *Sculptor, Man with the Leather Belt, Cellist*, and a painting that until now has not been mentioned, *Courbet with Black Dog* (1844; not illustrated). Sometimes, notably in the *Sieste champêtre, Wounded Man*, and, most of all, *Courbet with Black Dog*, the beholder feels himself to be looking up at the image from below. And even the few paintings in which the sitter seems at first to engage the beholder directly, e.g., the *Small Portrait of Courbet* and *Desperate Man*, contrive in one way or another to call this initial impression into question. In all these cases the beholder senses more or less acutely that the customary relationship—roughly, of mutual facing—between himself and the sitter has been placed in abeyance. It is as though Courbet's self-portraits attempt by various means to establish or insinuate another, fundamentally different relationship between sitter and beholder, in which the two are not even approximately faced off but on the contrary are *made congruent* with one another as never before or since in Western painting. And since the *first* beholder, not just chronologically but ontologically, was Courbet himself, I am led to see in that relationship of congruence a further manifestation of what I have been claiming was his desire or

FIGURE 4.7. Courbet, *Lovers in the Country*, 1844. 77 x 60 cm. Lyon, Musée des Beaux-Arts. Phot. Bulloz.

compulsion to evoke in and through the medium of the self-portrait his entire absorption in his body as lived, as possessed from within. A look at a few works we have not yet considered will help make my meaning clear.

In the *Lovers in the Country* (1844; fig. 7) Courbet has portrayed himself and his mistress Virginie Binet in a forest landscape at dusk. Both figures are in profile, their bodies cut off well above the waist by the bottom framing-edge. He is nearer to us than she and seems about to eclipse her completely, a possibility made all the more imminent in feeling by the degree to which his body turns towards hers and thereby obscures it from view. The poses of the figures and the composition as a whole are highly unconventional and have been seen by commentators as verging on the absurd. By now, however, it should be clear that the most salient features of the *Lovers in the Country* are variants of those we have been tracing in the self-portraits generally. For example, Courbet seems to have been at pains to assert the apparent proximity of the lovers to the picture-surface and, implicitly, to the beholder; the male sitter's left hand clasping the woman's right one is a further instance of the use of hands to convey a sense of bodily liveness; while the lovers' expressions connote rapture and/or absorption (he seems enraptured, she seems pensive), states which involve the sort of modification of ordinary consciousness that we have seen before. In addition, the fact that the male sitter has been depicted in profile with his head tilted towards the surface of the canvas exemplifies the tendency to avert a face-to-face confrontation with the beholder which I have claimed is at work throughout Courbet's self-portraits. Indeed the last observation does not go far enough. It is only the head of the male sitter that has been depicted in profile. The rest of his upper body has been portrayed largely from behind, an extraordinary compositional stroke which because our attention goes first to the lovers' faces is easily overlooked. Yet nothing in the *Lovers in the Country*, certainly not the lovers' expressions, is finally as arresting as the seeming obliviousness with which the figure of Courbet turns a considerable expanse of back towards the beholder. And I see in that act of turning evidence that the painter—the painter-*beholder*—Courbet found himself compelled to seek to make his representation of himself congruent with the orientation of his body as he stood or sat before the canvas by installing that representation in the painting as nearly as possible *from the rear*.

This interpretation finds support in another work of roughly the same moment, an oil sketch also known as the *Lovers in the Country* (ca. 1844; fig. 8), in which Courbet and a female companion have been portrayed literally from the rear.[17] But the most fascinating document in this regard is not a painting nor even a finished drawing but a page from a small sketchbook that Courbet appears to have used in the early 1840s (fig. 9).[18] The page has on it four separate and distinct images, each with a different internal scale. Starting at the lower middle of the page and moving counter-clockwise these are:

1. A scene of five figures, evidently village bourgeois, all but one of whom are standing before an open plot of ground with a tree behind them in the middle distance and more trees, buildings (including the belfry of Ornans), and hills in the far distance. The long shadows cast by the standing figures suggest that the hour is near dusk, and it is conceivable that the party is watching a sunset. The lone seated figure, a young

104

Michael Fried

FIGURE 4.8. Courbet, *Lovers in the Country*, ca. 1844. 54 x 40 cm. Whereabouts unknown. Phot. from *Autoportraits de Courbet*.

man, is somewhat apart from the others and rests his head on his hand as if lost in thought.

2. A depiction of Courbet sleeping, his head pillowed on a knapsack. We are shown only his head and shoulders, turned partly to the side; his hat rests lightly on the other side of his head, pushed there when he lay down; and he has a pipe in his mouth. The bulk of his body is to be understood as advancing at an angle towards the surface of the sheet. It is not clear whether the setting is intended to be indoors or outdoors: what seem to be folds in a curtain behind and to the left of the sleeping sitter appear to become the trunks of trees towards the right, but neither reading is certain. This image is the most heavily shaded and in general the most elaborated of the four. A comparison with the *Sieste champêtre* strongly suggests that it was a source, perhaps *the* source, for Courbet's representation of himself in that drawing.

3. A woman's head, gazing upwards seemingly in reverie, drawn rather faintly in almost pure outline with shading just outside her profile. In feeling though not in pose, as well as in its relation to the depiction of Courbet, this image anticipates that of the woman carved into the bank of the brook in the *Sculptor*. More immediately, though, it seems to

FIGURE 4.9. Courbet, *Sketchbook Page*, early 1840s. 14 x 21 cm. Paris, Louvre. Phot. Musées nationaux.

be an early version of the figure of Justine asleep with her head on Courbet's shoulder in the *Sieste champêtre*.

4. A relatively close-up study of Courbet's left hand, held palm upwards, forefinger extended, the other fingers loosely bent. This image too is a likely source for the *Sieste champêtre*—specifically, for the crucial motif of the male sitter's right hand resting palm up on his thigh.

We are thus given separate images of the sleeping Courbet and of his hand, as though the distancing of the hand that we have observed in several self-portraits is here manifest as an actual disjunction. But what makes the last image truly remarkable is that the hand has been depicted from Courbet's point of view, or, better, from the point of view *of his body*: I am thinking not only of its scale (largest among the four images) and position on the page (at the bottom left, i.e., in the appropriate sector of the immediate foreground of the page considered as an image of his perceptual field) but also of the orientation of the hand relative to the painter-beholder (pointing away from him, into the "world" of the drawing). In all these respects Courbet's depiction of his hand records as directly and naively as could be imagined his consciousness of being one with his body. And more nearly explicitly than any other single work in his oeuvre, the sketchbook page reveals the extent to which for Courbet the project of self-portrayal normally, almost rou-

tinely, entailed an attempt to reconcile the immediate notation of that
consciousness with the conventions of the self-portrait as the latter had
evolved over the centuries. It suggests that Courbet's determination to
evoke in the self-portraits his absorption in his own live bodily being
tended naturally to find expression in images which from an artistic point
of view may be characterized as disjointed, multi-scalar, radically proximate, and bizarrely orientated; and that his task in the self-portraits
therefore involved transforming the raw material of those images into
ostensibly integrated, illusionistically more or less coherent, and, if often
highly unconventional, at least not distressingly eccentric representations. The working up into the *Sieste champêtre* of at least three of the
four images on the sheet we have just examined[19] gives a fair idea of the
kinds of operations by which that task was carried out.

Further light on those operations may be thrown by a consideration
of Courbet's most ambitious painting of the period, the *Man with the
Leather Belt* (1845–46?; fig. 10). Alluding broadly to traditional proto-
types, the artist has portrayed himself approximately life-size seated
alongside a table whose near edge runs parallel to the picture-surface.
The sitter's upper body is turned away from the table, and, as so often is
the case in the self-portraits, is at an angle to the beholder as well. His
head, too, is turned in the direction of his body, though his gaze appears
to be directed back (and down) towards the beholder. Once again,
however, we do not feel that we meet that gaze; rather, it seems to slide
past us to our left, as if the sitter were exclusively concerned with his
own thoughts and feelings. His right elbow rests naturally enough on a
leather-bound portfolio but his right hand, its back and top plus the back
of his wrist modelled powerfully under bright illumination and turned
towards the beholder in a gesture of uncanny force, appears to touch but
not quite to support his right cheek and jaw. The effect of both gesture
and illumination, as well as of the slightly too large size of the hand and
its placement just above the center of the canvas, is to make the hand
itself and the seemingly unmotivated turn of the wrist extremely conspicuous. In the lower right-hand corner of the canvas the sitter's left
hand, also brightly lit, grips his broad leather belt, the accessory that
gives the painting its name. In this it resembles the left hand in the
Wounded Man, only with the impression of physical effort infinitely
more intense. On the table to the sitter's right (our left) stands a small
cast of a sculpture, the original of which has been identified as an
écorché then thought to be by Michelangelo. A piece of white chalk in a
holder lies on the portfolio. And a length of cloth covers one corner of the
portfolio before falling past the edge of the table at the lower left.

Even before reading this description the reader will have recognized
that there exists an intimate connection between the *Man with the*

FIGURE 4.10. Courbet, *Man with the Leather Belt*, 1845–46? 100 x 82 cm. Paris, Louvre. Phot. Musées nationaux.

Leather Belt and the works discussed in the previous pages. For example, the sitter has been placed very close to the surface of the painting, so close in fact that we tend to assume without thinking about it that the greater portion of his lower body thrusts forward beyond the plane of that surface. Our sense of his proximity is reinforced by the deliberateness with which the corner of the leather-bound portfolio, in this as in other respects a metonymy for the sitter, juts beyond the edge of the table; while the length of cloth that falls past the table-edge is another of those elements that serve to call into question the impermeability of the bottom limits of the picture. The sitter's expression, which I have characterized as one of self-absorption, is analogous to others that we have seen; this is also true of the tilt of his head, the cloudedness of his gaze, and the obliqueness of his pose relative to the beholder. As in most of the paintings we have examined, however, it is chiefly the sitter's hands which attract our attention, and again I suggest that they evince Courbet's determination to make manifest within the painting his intense conviction of his own bodily liveness. The left hand gripping the belt with a disproportionate expense of physical effort may be seen as struggling to maximize its identity not as an object but as an agent: it seems to be striving to produce what Sartre refers to as "that famous 'sensation of effort' of Maine de Biran," by which would be revealed to the sitter not merely "the resistance of objects, their hardness or softness, but . . . [the hand] *itself*."[20] As for the sitter's right hand, its largeness recalls that of the image of the left hand on the page from the early sketchbook; its state of tension, divorced from any practical rationale, evokes its possession from within still more persuasively than does the action of the hand gripping the belt; and its orientation within the painting, conspicuously, almost painfully turned away from the beholder, exactly matches what we know must have been the orientation of Courbet's right hand, and implicitly his entire body, as he stood or sat before the canvas.[21]

Finally, the *écorché* may be held to summarize the painting's principal concerns. Its pose, which resembles that of the man with the leather belt, suggests the notion of an effort in and through which the body is brought forcibly up against its structural limitations and is thereby made aware of the latter at the level of feeling. The fact that it depicts a figure who has been flayed is consistent with the primacy of internal sensation over external perception posited by my reading of the painting as a whole. And the placing of the *écorché* so that it faces away from the beholder may be interpreted as an acknowledgment that the sitter has been portrayed, though not literally from the rear, in a pose that in decisive respects is congruent with the original orientation of the painter-beholder.

I said at the outset that I did not intend to examine all of Courbet's self-portraits of the 1840s. But no account of his work in that genre would be adequate without some discussion of the famous and splendid *Man with the Pipe* (1849?; fig. 11). On first viewing it one is struck by the simplicity of that painting as compared with, say, the *Man with the Leather Belt*. Nevertheless, most of the features that have emerged as significant in the self-portraits as a group are also present in the *Man with the Pipe*. The sitter's expression has always been perceived as one of intense reverie and self-absorption ("He is dreaming of himself as he

FIGURE 4.11. Courbet, *Man with the Pipe*, 1849? 45 x 37 cm. Montpellier, Musée Fabre. Phot. Musées nationaux.

smokes his pipe," wrote Courbet's contemporary, Théophile Silvestre).[22] Although his eyes are partly open, the whites are lost in dark shadow, a characteristic touch which, as in other pictures we have considered, devalorizes the gaze. The overall impression conveyed is of a state of somnolence that has nothing to do with fatigue and everything to do with the evocation of a primordial or *somatic* order of activity—the automatic processes by which the body sustains itself, by which it lives. Another crucial and familiar feature of the painting is its vigorous assertion of the apparent proximity of the sitter to both picture-surface and beholder. In this the *Man with the Pipe* is fully as extreme as the *Desperate Man* and immeasurably more persuasive in its extremeness than the earlier work. But what I want chiefly to emphasize is Courbet's handling of the sitter's pose and orientation. Our first impression is that the sitter faces us more or less directly, though as usual his head is slightly tilted back and to the side. Gradually, however, we become aware that his upper body is turned at a fairly sharp angle to the plane of the painting, that his left shoulder is appreciably higher than his right one and pushes forward to the immediate vicinity of the picture-surface, and that his left arm, of which we see very little, seems drawn across his body in a kind of contrapposto. These asymmetries are given further point by the leftward thrust of his pipe and the direct illumination of only the left tip of his collar. And they are driven home by the fact that whereas we glimpse over the sitter's right shoulder a distant horizon at dusk, we can just about make out behind the sitter's left shoulder what appears to be the trunk of a tree, against which he is perhaps to be imagined as leaning. (The darkening over time of already dark pigment has made this hard to see even when standing in front of the painting; it is barely discernible in a good black-and-white photograph and may not be discernible at all in the accompanying illustration.) Furthermore, Courbet seems to have done all he could to make visible a portion of the sitter's back by showing us a bit of jacket that lies above and behind the seam of the left shoulder. All this suggests that once again the painter-beholder sought to build into the painting something of the orientation of his body as the latter was stationed before the canvas by depicting the man with the pipe to however slight an extent from the rear.

One last feature of the picture deserves special mention: the pipe. We have seen that Courbet drew himself with a pipe in his mouth on the page from the early sketchbook; a pipe also appears, held in the sitter's hand, in the self-portrait called *Courbet with Black Dog*; others are smoked in works we have not been able to consider;[23] and on one notable occasion in the late 1860s he actually used the image of a pipe as a symbolic self-portrait.[24] This is not the place for a digression on the iconography of the pipe in his art. My point is simply that whatever else may usefully be said about its significance, it functions in the *Man with the Pipe* as a metonymy for the sitter's lived body, the heat and light of the slowly burning tobacco being perceived as natural indices of the somatic order of activity mentioned above. In two other paintings of the late 1840s, the *Portrait of Baudelaire* (ca. 1847?; not illustrated) and

After Dinner at Ornans (1848–49; fig. 12), a pipe plays a roughly comparable role. But a discussion of those paintings would take us far beyond the limits of this essay.

II

In the previous pages I have presented Courbet's self-portraits of the 1840s as the work of an instinctive phenomenologist: a painter who, far from desiring simply to reproduce his outward appearance, analyze his character or personality, or record the external signs of certain transient internal states (passions, emotions, moods, etc.), found himself driven to seek to reconstitute within the painting his absorption in his bodily liveness as he stood or sat before the canvas. That effort of reconstitution was guided less by the data of vision than by what I have loosely called internal sensations, as well as by a primordial "consciousness of a whole and of more or less vague structurization"[25]—the orientated "body-image" analyzed at length by Merleau-Ponty.[26] The devalorizing of the sitter's gaze, in fact the frequency with which Courbet depicted himself with his eyes closed or all but closed, are expressions of that emphasis on the body as experienced from within rather than as observed from without. One might almost say that Courbet has been presented in this essay as having painted the self-portraits with his eyes closed, or at least as having used the sense of sight merely to guide his brush across the surface of the canvas and not at all, or only very little, to determine the object of his representations. This in itself qualifies the earlier statment that the sitter in the *Small Portrait of Courbet* appears absorbed in his own image in a mirror. Altogether the paintings we have just considered, with their determination to match rather than reflect the orientation of the painter-beholder, have less of the character of mirror-images of their creator than any self-portraits ever made. I have also called attention repeatedly to the assertion throughout the self-portraits of the apparent nearness of the sitter to the surface of the painting and implicitly to the beholder, and that too I understand in terms of Courbet's drive to reconstitute in paint his immersion in his own live bodily being. At any rate, it seems clear that the elimination of distance between image and beholder promotes the fundamentally corporeal mode of apprehension that the self-portraits as I have described them are intent to elicit.

At this juncture further questions arise concerning the significance of Courbet's undertaking in his self-portraits of the 1840s. Should that undertaking be seen as having had for its ultimate aim the satisfaction of purely personal needs and drives? Or is it possible to locate Courbet's intense preoccupation with his own embodiedness in the wider context of the state of French painting in his time?—I believe that the answer to the first question is no, despite the fact that Courbet's self-portraits express some of the fiercest propensities of his nature, and that the answer to the second is yes, with the qualification that this is not to say that Courbet imagined those paintings to be responding to the historical situation that I shall argue prevailed at the outset of his career. We have seen how Courbet's early self-portraits issued from a personal compulsion that in almost every sense may be called blind. But that blindness itself soon proved to be the vehicle of a more than personal vision, and it is the essence of that vision, the significance of his self-portraits for the enterprise of painting, that I mean to sketch in the remainder of this essay.

As I see it and have tried in part to demonstrate in previous studies,[27] the evolution of painting in France in the nineteenth century up to and including Courbet is largely to be understood in terms of the dialectical unfolding of a problematic of painting and beholder which emerged as an issue for French artists and critics as early as the mid-1750s and which received its classic formulation in Diderot's writings on drama and painting of the 1750s and 1760s. The fundamental question addressed by Diderot concerned the conditions that had to be fulfilled in order for the art of painting successfully to persuade its audience of the truthfulness of its representations. He concluded that nothing was more abortive of that act of persuasion than when a painter's dramatis personae seemed by virtue of the character of their actions and expressions to evince even a partial consciousness of being beheld; and that the immediate task of the painter was therefore to extinguish or forestall that consciousness by entirely engrossing or *absorbing* his dramatis personae in their actions, activities, and states of mind. A figure so absorbed appeared unconscious or oblivious of everything but the object of its absorption, as if to all intents and purposes there were nothing and no one else in the world. In this sense the task of the painter could be described, and in a remarkable passage in the *Essais sur la peinture* (1766) actually was described, as one of establishing the aloneness of his figures relative to the beholder. A figure, group of figures, or painting which satisfied those demands deserved to be called *naïf* (or *naive*), an epithet which for Diderot was almost synonymous with *sublime*. Whereas if the painter failed in that endeavor, the figures in question appeared mannered, false, and hypocritical; their actions and expressions were seen, not as natural signs of intention or emotion, but merely as *grimaces*—feignings or impostures aimed at the beholder; and the painting as a whole, far from projecting a convincing image of the world, became what Diderot deprecatingly called *un théâtre*, an artificial construction whose too obvious designs on its audience made it repugnant to men of taste. And in general Diderot held that it was necessary for the painting as a whole to obliviate the beholder, to neutralize his presence, to establish positively insofar as that could be done that he had not been taken into account. Hence the importance in Diderot's writings of an ideal of compositional unity according to which the various elements in the painting were to be combined to form a perspicuously closed and self-sufficient structure which would so to speak seal off the "world" of the painting from that of the beholder. And hence also the importance of an ideal of unity of effect, chiefly involving the handling of *clair-obscur* or light and dark, directed to the same end. I have elsewhere summed this up by saying that Diderot's conception of painting rested ultimately upon the supreme fiction that the beholder did not exist, that he was not really there, standing before the canvas. Or perhaps we should say that it rested on the paradox that only by establishing that fiction in the painting itself was the painter able to bring the beholder to a halt in front of it and to hold him there in the virtual trance of involvement which Diderot and his contemporaries regarded as a sine qua non of major accomplishment.

French painters found themselves engaged with these and related issues from the mid-1750s on. It was not until the 1780s, however, that the leading French painter of his generation, Jacques-Louis David, in a series of history paintings the most important of which was the *Oath of the Horatii* (1784–85), temporarily resolved that problematic in ways that his contemporaries and immediate successors found paradigmatic for ambitious painting. To a far greater degree than has ever been recognized or is at first apparent, the history of French painting between the late eighteenth century and 1839, when the young Courbet arrived in Paris to pursue his vocation, is the story of the vicissitudes, modifications, and transformations of the orginal Davidian paradigm. As even a glance at David's masterpieces of the 1780s will confirm, that paradigm, like the Diderotian conception, was emphatically dramatic in nature; and it is perhaps not surprising that a tradition based on such a paradigm should have found it increasingly difficult, and in the end no longer possible, to overcome the theatrical and grimacing in Diderot's and David's sense of those notions. Even David seems to have found the task of representing figures entirely absorbed in action and passion and therefore apparently unaware of the presence of the beholder ever more difficult to accomplish: his former student Delécluze tells us that by the early 1800s David had come to regard as *théâtral* aspects of the *Horatii* itself and to inveigh against the modern taste for strong expression, which he more than anyone had validated, as leading invariably to *grimace*; while the transition from the intensely dramatic "Roman" style of the *Horatii* and related works to the far less overtly dramatic "Greek" style of the *Sabines* (finished 1799) and *Leonidas* (begun ca. 1800 but not finished until 1814) follows exactly the same development. The later paintings were not on that account safe from the charge of theatricality. On the contrary, as Stendhal's criticism shows, the *Sabines* struck many of David's younger contemporaries as theatrical precisely because it marks a withdrawal from action in favor of the pose.[28] Stendhal's repeated calls for the redramatization of painting were anticipated by the art of the most prodigious French painter of the Restoration and one of the master figures of Romanticism, Théodore Géricault, much of whose oeuvre can be seen as an attempt to overcome the theatricalization not just of action and expression but also of the painting-beholder relationship itself through sheer intensity of visual drama. But the ontologically extreme character of the *Raft of the Medusa* (1818–19), with its suggestion that the suffering colossi on the raft are seeking rescue *from being beheld by us*, is powerful testimony to just how extreme the situation had already become.

It is worth spelling out the critical nature of the situation. On the one hand, the dramatic conception of painting put forward in Diderot's writings of the 1750s and '60s and decisively realized in David's canvases of the 1780s remained fundamental to painting of major ambition. On the other hand, the fiction of the beholder's nonexistence that had been the soul of that conception had become all but unattainable. (The conventions by which David had sought to establish that fiction now merely revealed its untenableness.) By 1824, when Géricault died, most French painters of subjects involving the human figure in action, Davidian Classicists and young Romantics alike, appear to have accepted the theatricalization of action and expression as a condition of their art, perhaps without even recognizing it as such; while throughout the 1830s, in the work of Delaroche and other *metteurs-en-scène* of historical subjects, the theatrical was not merely tolerated but embraced with open arms. It is also true that there existed during this latter period a current of dissatisfaction with these developments. But the pictorial expression of that dissatisfaction, as in the art of Corot and Rousseau, was almost wholly confined to landscape, a genre which enabled painters to elude rather than to confront the issue of theatricality.

This above all is the state of affairs with which, from the outset of his career, Courbet's paintings seem to me to engage. Specifically, I see in the work of his maturity, which along with others I regard as having begun with his monumental "Realist" canvases of 1848–50, a sustained attempt to establish a new and revolutionary paradigm for ambitious painting based on the *non- or anti-dramatic* representation of figures absorbed not in action or passion but in what may be thought of as *quintessentially absorptive* states and activities, and by so doing to trans-form fundamentally, to *de-theatricalize*, the relationship between paint-ing and beholder as he found it.[29] And I see in the self-portraits ana-lyzed in the previous section of this essay an incipient or preliminary stage of that enterprise—one whose focus, in obvious respects, was ex-tremely narrow, but whose concentration upon the central problem of the painting-beholder relationship was partly for that reason especially intense.

Let me be as clear as possible about the nature of the last of these claims. I do not say that the young Courbet understood himself to be exploiting the self-portrait for these ends. It seems far more likely, as was suggested by the analyses of individual works conducted in the previous section of this essay, that Courbet's early reliance upon the self-portrait as well as the extraordinary uses to which he put it were dictated by desires and compulsions which themselves flowed inexorably from his native mode of being-in-the-world—from his existential-phenomenologi-cal identity, so to speak. But that identity was not something apart from his identity as painter-beholder; on the contrary, the two appear to have been or to have soon become indissoluble (I see the *Man with the Leather Belt* as putting a seal on that development); and this suggests *both* that the desires and compulsions charted in the previous section were involved virtually from the first in the problematic of painting and beholder whose origins I have just attempted to trace *and* that those desires and compulsions were exacerbated, made all the more imperious, by the state of that problematic by the time Courbet entered the scene. Nor do I mean to say that Courbet found in the conventions of the self-portrait a ready-made solution to the task of de-theatricalization which I see the works in question as initiating. My claim is rather that, far more than the conventions of any other genre, those of the self-portrait made perspicuous certain crucial issues associated with his spectatordom and, by virtue of that fact, enabled him to come almost physically to grips with those issues and within broad limits to shape them to his needs. In particular, by calling for the depiction within the painting of a figure that would at once double and (at least approximately) face the painter-beholder, the conventions of the self-portrait appear to have provoked in Courbet a heightened awareness both of his radical sepa-rateness from and of his opposite orientation to the painting before him. And it was by subtly but profoundly subverting those conventions while ostensibly coming to terms with them that Courbet succeeded, not in definitively resolving those issues—what would it mean to say that they were so resolved?—but in making them subject to the operations of painting as never before.

More generally, Courbet's efforts throughout the self-portraits to reconstitute within them his absorption in his body as actually lived are ultimately to be understood in terms of an attempt *to transpose himself bodily into the painting*—to do away with what I have argued had become the largely theatricalized relationship between painting and beholder in favor of one in which the latter *disappeared into* the former. Indeed, to the extent that Courbet may be held to have succeeded in *that* undertaking—and once again we cannot quite imagine what perfect success would mean—there existed no painting-beholder relationship or at least there existed none outside the self-portraits themselves, in which, as I have tried to show, the subversion of basic conventions of the genre derives from and in that sense recalls the original presence before the painting of a painter-beholder. I realize, of course, that the proposition that Courbet in his early self-portraits attempted to transpose himself bodily into the painting as much as says that he sought to suspend or dissolve one fundamental aspect of his bodily facticity, i.e., that he was situated "here" (in front of the painting) rather than "there" ("inside" the painting or spatially coincident with it). But it does not deny, in fact it positively assumes, that Courbet did everything in his power to make his bodily facticity the overriding theme of the self-portraits. It further assumes that only the pictorial crisis summarized above could had driven him to take so extreme a step.

In sum the self-portrait was at the outset a privileged genre for Courbet because his struggle against his own identity as beholder found there a natural—a counter-conventional—home; and it remained privileged until, starting in the late fall of 1848 and almost certainly receiving vital impetus from social and political developments,[30] he discovered that he was able to conduct that struggle across a wide range of (primarily absorptive) subjects and in paintings whose dimensions compared with those of the self-portraits are sometimes immense. In this connection it is surely significant that the first of the breakthrough pictures of 1848–50, the *After Dinner at Ornans* (fig. 12), is to all intents and purposes an expanded or transcended self-portrait;[31] that two of the other three of those pictures, the *Burial at Ornans* (fig. 13) and the *Peasants of Flagey Returning from the Fair* (1850, 1855; not reproduced),[32] portray intimate friends and/or members of his immediate family, with both of whom Courbet may be said to have identified to an unusual degree; and that he continued to produce self-portraits, some of them works of considerable size and importance, throughout the remainder of his career. At the same time, Courbet's breakthrough pictures broaden or generalize—make less narrowly personal—the determination to abrogate the painting-beholder relationship that I have just claimed lies at the heart of the early self-portraits. One might say that *they aspire to abolish the impersonal or objective conditions constitutive of the very*

FIGURE 4.12. Courbet, *After Dinner at Ornans*, 1848–49. 195 x 257 cm. Lille, Musée des Beaux-Arts. Phot. Musées nationaux.

possibility of spectatordom, and that their wider subject matter, vastly enlarged dimensions, more intense evocation of materiality, and ostensibly objective representational modality—in sum all those characteristics that have seemed to most commentators the essence of their "Realism"— express that aspiration more deeply than any other. Certainly the *Burial* seems intent on abolishing the chief such condition, namely, that there be some place to stand, a position or point of view, in front of—more generally, outside—the painting. That is, the apparent extreme nearness of the entire image together with the centrality of the open grave and its truncation by the bottom framing-edge, features at which we glanced much earlier, express what I interpet as a resolve to cut the ground out from under the feet of the beholder and by so doing to leave him no place to stand or for that matter to recline *outside the painting itself*.[33] For such a beholder, if it still makes sense to use the word, the bottom framing-edge becomes, not a juncture between two "worlds," which is what I have been calling it until now, but the nether limit of the only "world" left existing, that of the painting.

FIGURE 4.13. Courbet, *Burial at Ornans*, 1849–50. 315 x 668 cm. Paris, Louvre. Phot. Musées nationaux.

FIGURE 4.14. Courbet, *L'Atelier du peintre*, 1855, detail of central group. Paris, Louvre. Phot. Musées nationaux.

Having gone this far, let me go just a bit further and propose that painting after painting by Courbet may be interpreted as seeking to achieve an analogous result: to annihilate or make untenable the "world" of the beholder, understanding by the concept of a "world" not so much a collection of objects as a multiplicity of possible standpoints; or at the very least to revoke all distance between painting and beholder as a step towards absorbing the beholder into the painting in a new, almost corporeal way.[34] And since as we earlier remarked the first beholder was Courbet himself, it is not in the least surprising that certain authors have been moved to emphasize the importance of what they call his narcissism, meaning by that a tendency to apprehend reality through a series of implicit analogies with his own person and in general to make himself part of the fabric of his representations. Nor is it surprising that Courbet seems to have regarded both the products of his activity as a painter and that activity itself as without precedent or parallel. Thus the *Atelier du peintre* (1855; fig.14), another expanded self-portrait and his most ambitious attempt to explain that activity (to himself as much as to anyone else), has at its center the relationship between a painter who appears to have begun physically to merge with the painting on which he is work-

FIGURE 4.15. Courbet, *The Stormy Sea*, or *The Wave*, 1869. 117 x 160 cm. Paris, Louvre. Phot. Musées nationaux.

ing and a painting that seems in the process of flowing into its creator. The use of bodies of water in motion to promote this sort of union, hinted at in the *Sculptor* and thematized by the unfinished picture on the easel in the *Atelier du peintre*, helps account for one's conviction that more than the objective representation of nature is at issue in Courbet's paintings of river landscapes, breaking waves (fig. 15), and the Sources of the Loue and the Lison. Those canvases, like a multitude of others in Courbet's oeuvre but more concentratedly than most, *want something of us* as we stand before them. I have tried to say what it is they want—and I am compelled yet again to add that we cannot quite conceive what it would mean for them to attain their object.[35]

Finally, it is not surprising that contemporaries found Courbet's paintings conspicuously lacking in unity, which is to say in *closure*.[36] The ontologically problematic status of the bottom framing-edge throughout his oeuvre is one manifestation of the denial of closure on which the success of his enterprise partly depended. Others are the largely additive mode of picture-construction employed in, for example, *The Quarry* (1857; not illustrated), yet another expanded self-portrait,[37] and his characteristic use of *clair-obscur*—more precisely, of black—for purposes other than securing a unified dramatic effect.[38] Even the astoundingly cohesive factures of Courbet's paintings, by which is conjured up the ontological density of the entire visible/tactile realm—of Courbet's body and world in their interwovenness—are felt to wall the beholder not out but in. But perhaps the most striking manifestation of the denial of closure is the presence in several of the early self-portraits as well as in subsequent canvases of major importance—the *After Dinner* is an obvious case in point[39]—of figures depicted to a greater or lesser extent from the rear. In each of the latter, as in the self-portraits, the essential impulse seems to have been to eliminate all sense of mutual confrontation between subject and beholder; indeed, we are made to feel that the painting in its entirety presents itself to us as if from the rear: or to put this another way, that the space of the painting, like that of the lived body, is an orientated space, in which the relations among objects are chiefly to be comprehended in terms of an implicit relation to a beholder—originally a painter-beholder—whose separateness, distancedness, and altogether whose capacity for spectatordom it is the ultimate aim of the painting to annul. The inadequacy of the notion of narcissism as applied to Courbet's art consists in part in its oversimplification of that aim.

The ravishing *Source* (1868; fig. 16), whose close affinities with a number of the self-portraits discussed in the first part of this essay should be apparent, is a particularly lucid example of such a work. By no means coincidentally, the *Source* also epitomizes the place of nature in Courbet's later art—but a full treatment of that topic must await another occasion.

In Edouard Manet's seminal masterpieces of the first half of the 1860s, Courbet's enterprise is reversed in almost all respects. Most important, Manet seems intuitively to have recognized that Courbet's attempt to abolish the very possibility of spectatordom was doomed in every instance to (ontological not artistic) failure, or at any rate that success in that attempt was literally inconceivable, and that it was therefore necessary to establish the beholder's presence abstractly—to build into the painting the separateness, distancedness, and mutual facing that I have associated with the painting-beholder relationship in its traditional or unreconstructed form—in order that the worst consequences of the theatricalization of that relationship be averted. The *Old Musician* (1861–62), *Déjeuner sur l'herbe* (1862–63), and *Olympia* (1863), with their eschewal of both action and absorption in favor of self-presentation, their problematizing of illusion, voiding of psychology, and denial of traditional modes of signification, and their characteristic facture in

Michael Fried

FIGURE 4.16. Courbet, *The Source*, 1868. 128 x 97 cm.
Paris, Louvre. Phot. Musées nationaux.

which each stroke of the painter's brush competes for presentness with
every other, acknowledge perhaps more deliberately than any paintings
before them that they were made to be beheld. And yet the extreme
provocation that those works continue to offer to all with eyes to see
consists more than anything else in their ontological completeness,
which in a manner of speaking makes the literal presence of the beholder supererogatory.[40]

NOTES

1. Three recent exhibition catalogues contain information pertaining to
the self-portraits: *Gustave Courbet (1819–1877)*, Rome, Villa Medici, October
1969–January 1970, introductory essay by Palma Bucarelli, biographical and
other notes by Hélène Toussaint; *Autoportraits de Courbet*, Les Dossiers du

département des peintures 6, Paris, Louvre, 1973, text by Marie-Thérèse de Forges with a report of X-ray analyses of the *Wounded Man* and *Man with the Leather Belt* by Suzy Delbourgo and Lola Faillant; and *Gustave Courbet (1819–77)*, Paris, Grand Palais, September 1977–January 1978, and London, Royal Academy, January–March 1978, introductory essay by Alan Bowness, biography by Marie-Thérèse de Forges, and catalogue notes by Hélène Toussaint. (Hereafter I refer to the second of these as Forges, *Autoportraits*, and to the third as Toussaint, *Courbet*.) See also the article by Forges, "A Propos l'exposition 'Autoportraits de Courbet,' " *La Revue du Louvre et des musées de France* 22 (1972): 451–62. In addition, various early self-portraits are discussed in three recent studies of the painter: Linda Nochlin, *Gustave Courbet: A Study of Style and Society*, Diss. New York University 1963 (New York: Garland Publishing, Inc., 1976); T. J. Clark, *Image of the People: Gustave Courbet and the Second French Republic, 1848–51* (Greenwich, Conn.: New York Graphic Society, 1973); and Jack Lindsay, *Gustave Courbet, His Life and Art* (New York: Harper & Row, 1973). Unless otherwise noted, I accept the dating of individual works proposed by Toussaint in the catalogue cited above. I might add that I have deliberately kept scholarly footnotes to a minimum, and that I have given the titles of paintings in English except in a few instances where the French originals seemed to me more natural. Finally, illustrations of works by Courbet mentioned but not illustrated in this essay may be found in Toussaint, *Courbet*.

2. "Comme un pommier produit des pommes," in *Courbet raconté par lui-même et par ses amis*, ed. Pierre Courthion (Geneva: Pierre Cailler, 1950), II: 18–19.

3. Lindsay, *Gustave Courbet*, p. 126. See also Lindsay's account of Courbet's alleged achievement in 1849–50 of a "new sense of the object" (p. 87).

4. To expand slightly on this point, I have not tried to show that the phenomenological "lived body" is what Jacques Derrida would call "an effect of *différence*, an effect inscribed within a system of *différence* (*Positions* [Paris: Les Editions de Minuit], 1972, p. 40, my translation). I do not doubt that this could be done; what I question is the utility of the operation for a reading of Courbet's art. Similarly, I have not been drawn to the notion that paintings such as Courbet's or Manet's are most usefully to be interpreted as instances of a special sort of *écriture*, but instead have continued to see them as objects whose ultimate claims on us justify the invoking of what might be called a metaphysics not of presence but of *presentness*. On the other hand, the argument of the second part of this essay may be summarized by saying that the "lived body" as manifested in Courbet's art is itself a function of the problematic involving the relationship between painting and beholder to which I have already alluded. Or to put this another way, the "primordiality" of the "lived body" is subordinated to the primordial convention (no quotation marks this time) that paintings are made to be beheld. In general, this essay seeks to call into question the notion, hitherto taken for granted, that Courbet's enterprise was essentially one of representation. But the alternative to a theoretics of representation argued for in these pages is one not of textuality but of presentness. For the distinction between presence and presentness in the context of abstract art of the 1960s see Michael Fried, "Art and Objecthood," in *Minimal Art: A Critical Anthology*, ed. Gregory Battcock (New York: E. P. Dutton & Co., 1968), pp. 116–47. On presentness generally see Stanley Cavell, "The Avoidance of Love: A Reading of *King*

Lear," in *Must We Mean What We Say? A Book of Essays* (New York: Charles Scribner's Sons, 1969), pp. 267–353; and Cavell, *The World Viewed: Reflections on the Ontology of Film* (New York: Viking Press, 1971).

5. Recent studies suggest that Courbet began work on the canvas that eventually became the *Wounded Man* around 1844; that the definitive composition was arrived at only in the late 1840s or early 1850s; and that the painting may have been touched up as late as 1854 (see all three catalogues cited in n. 1). However, the basic conception seems to me characteristic of the 1840s rather than the 1850s, and I have not hesitated to include the *Wounded Man* among the paintings considered in this essay.

6. Nochlin, *Gustave Courbet*, pp. 14–15.

7. Another self-portrait of roughly this moment, the *Fou de peur* (Forges, *Autoportraits*, Cat. No. 35), thematizes what I suggest was Courbet's sense of a vertiginous gulf between sitter and beholder—and ultimately, I shall argue, between painting and beholder. In that work, which may be seen as glossing the *Wounded Man*, Courbet has depicted himself in the act of leaping from the edge of a cliff; he seems to be springing directly towards the beholder; and the image as a whole suggests that he has been driven to his mad act by contemplating the abyss before him.

8. It doesn't trouble me that this view is in implicit conflict with the well-known passage from Courbet's letter of May 1854 to his patron Alfred Bruyas, in which several of the early self-portraits are characterized in highly charged moral and psychological terms. For one thing, Courbet tended to say to Bruyas the sorts of things he believed the latter wanted to hear. For another, even if Courbet's statement could be taken at face value, we would not be justified in allowing it to govern our reading of the self-portraits either individually or as a group. And yet the passage from the letter to Bruyas has been used by historians in just that way. For the text of the letter see Pierre Borel, ed., *Le Roman de Gustave Courbet* (Paris: Editions E. Sansot, 1922), pp. 37–38.

9. René Huyghe, "Courbet," in the exhibition catalogue, *Gustave Courbet (1819–1877)*, Philadelphia, Museum of Art, and Boston, Museum of Fine Arts, 1959–60, n. p.

10. From a large literature I shall cite only a few texts. Arguably the most important general work is Maurice Merleau-Ponty, *Phenomenology of Perception*, trans. Colin Smith (London: Routledge & Kegan Paul, 1962). Three shorter pieces by Merleau-Ponty that bear specifically on painting are "Indirect Language and the Voices of Silence," in *Signs*, trans. Richard C. McCleary (Evanston, Ill.: Northwestern University Press, 1964), pp. 39–83; "Cézanne's Doubt," in *Sense and Non-Sense*, trans. Hubert L. Dreyfus and Patricia Allen Dreyfus (Evanston, Ill.: Northwestern University Press, 1964), pp. 9–25; and "Eye and Mind," trans. Carleton Dallery, in *The Primacy of Perception and Other Essays*, ed. James M. Edie (Evanston, Ill.: Northwestern University Press, 1964), pp. 159–90. See also Merleau-Ponty's late attempt at self-revision, left unfinished at his death, *The Visible and the Invisible*, trans. Alphonso Lingis, ed. Claude Lefort (Evanston, Ill.: Northwestern University Press, 1968). Three useful collections of essays by various writers are *Essays in Phenomenology*, ed. Maurice Natanson (The Hague: Martinus Nijhoff, 1966); *Readings in Existential Phenomenology*, ed. Nathaniel Lawrence and Daniel O'Connor (Englewood Cliffs, N.J.: Prentice-Hall, 1967); and *The Philosophy of the Body: Rejections of Cartesian Dualism*, ed. Stuart F. Spicker (New York: Quadrangle/The New York Times Book Co., 1970).

11. Another essay would be needed to prove the point, but I know of no closer or more significant analogy between major bodies of work in different arts than that between Courbet's paintings and Whitman's poems.

12. For a discussion of the impossibility of perceiving one's body simply as another object see Merleau-Ponty, *Phenomenology of Perception*, pp. 90–92.

13. In her recent catalogue, Hélène Toussaint questions the traditional notion that the *Sieste champêtre* immediately precedes or is contemporary with the "première composition" of the painting that ultimately became the *Wounded Man*, and suggests that it ought instead to be seen as a record of that "composition" executed at the moment when the painting was decisively altered to its present form (*Gustave Courbet*, Cat. No. 136, p. 224).

14. In his introductory essay to the exhibition catalogue cited above (n. 9), Huyghe equates Courbet's preoccupation with sleep with his alleged materialism: "It seems as though Courbet, adoring the visible and the concrete, wished to place all nature on an equal footing, and to quench the spark of the spirit whenever it showed itself in a human being, so that nothing should disturb the worship of matter" (n.p.). Obviously I do not concur with this equation. But Huyghe's discovery in the same essay that "Courbet's essential, obsessive theme is sleep" (ibid.), although overstating the case, marks a real advance in understanding. Cf. in this connection the discussion of sleeping figures in French painting of the 1750s and '60s in Fried, "Absorption: A Master Theme in Eighteenth-Century French Painting and Criticism," *Eighteenth-Century Studies* 9 (1975–76): 139–77.

15. The phrase "primordial presence," used in a somewhat different context, occurs in the *Phenomenology of Perception*, p. 92. Merleau-Ponty also refers there to "that quasi-stupor to which we are reduced when we really try to live at the level of sensation" (p. 215), and distinguishes bodily from external space in the following terms: "Bodily space can be distinguished from external space and envelop its parts instead of spreading them out, because it is the darkness needed in the theatre to show up the performance, *the background of somnolence* [my italics] against which the gesture and its aim stand out, the zone of not being *in front of which* precise beings, figures, and points can come to light" (pp. 100–01). On the significance of the upright posture versus lying down see Erwin Straus, "The Upright Posture," in *Essays in Phenomenology*, pp. 164–92, and Straus, "Born to See, Born to Behold," in Spicker, ed., *The Philosophy of the Body*, pp. 334–59. On sleep as a surrendering of control and certain analogies in sense experience see Merleau-Ponty, pp. 211–12.

16. See Merleau-Ponty, *Phenomenology of Perception*, p. 92.

17. Cf. also the early painting known as *The Great Oak* (Toussaint, *Courbet*, Cat. No. 6), in which a reclining Courbet is portrayed from the rear.

18. Paris, Louvre, Cabinet des dessins, RF 29234, fol. 23. Cited and briefly discussed by Forges, *Autoportraits*, Cat. No. 9, pp. 12–13.

19. And perhaps all four images if, as seems possible, the *Sieste champêtre* was intended by Courbet to evoke the hour of dusk.

20. Jean-Paul Sartre, *Being and Nothingness*, trans. Hazel E. Barnes (New York: Philosophical Library, 1956), p. 304. Sartre argues that the "sensation of effort" does not exist, i.e., that one can see one's hand touching objects but not know it in its act of touching them, or, as he goes on to assert, "The body is lived and not *known*" (p. 324). Neither the distinction itself nor the arguments by which he tries to establish its validity need concern us here.

21. Especially in view of the last point, the sense of strain or tension conveyed by the sitter's right hand and wrist may also be associated with the *activity of painting*, understood not as a general function by which all pictures are made, but rather as a vehicle of Courbet's absorption in his bodily liveness for as long as was required to bring the *Man with the Leather Belt* into being. (I do not mean by this to subordinate his absorption in the activity of painting to his absorption in his bodily liveness; it would be at least as accurate to say that in Courbet's self-portraits, indeed throughout his oeuvre, the latter has been made a medium of painting.) Similar allusions to (Courbet's absorption in) the activity of painting may be present in other works, notably *Courbet with Black Dog*, in which the sitter's right hand holds a pipe exactly as Courbet's right hand would have held a brush, and the *Burial at Ornans*, in which the shovel cut through by the bottom framing-edge and whose shaft is to be imagined as extending towards the beholder's right hand seems a natural analogue to the painter's brush or knife.

22. Théophile Silvestre, "Courbet d'après nature," in *Courbet raconté par lui-même et par ses amis*, ed. Paul Courthion (Geneva: Pierre Cailler, 1948), I: 44 (my translation).

23. For example, a drawing in the Fogg Art Museum (Forges, *Autoportraits*, Cat. No. 32); an early painting, the *Draught Players* (ibid., Cat. No. 37); and the superb drawing in the Wadsworth Atheneum (ibid., Cat. No. 45).

24. Shortly before leaving Munich in 1869, Courbet is said to have been asked by some artists for a token of his having been there, and to have painted a portrait of his pipe with the signature: "COURBET, sans idéal et sans religion." The story is first told by Champfleury [Jules-François-Felix Husson], *Souvenirs et portraits de jeunesse* (Paris: E. Dentu, 1872), p. 179.

25. Max Scheler, "Lived Body, Environment, and Ego" (a translation by Manfred S. Frings of Chapter 6 of *Der Formalismus in Ethik und die materiale Wertethik*), in Spicker, ed., *The Philosophy of the Body*, p. 165.

26. Merleau-Ponty, *Phenomenology of Perception*, pp. 98ff.

27. The account of developments in theory and painting put forward in the following pages summarizes arguments developed at length in Fried, "Thomas Couture and the Theatricalization of Action in Nineteenth-Century French Painting," *Artforum* 8, no. 10 (1970): 36–46; Fried, "Toward a Supreme Fiction: Genre and Beholder in the Art Criticism of Diderot and His Contemporaries," *New Literary History* 6 (1975): 543–85; and Fried, "Absorption," cited in n. 14.

28. For a brief analysis of Stendhal's art criticism in this context see Fried, review of *The Artist and the Writer in France: Essays in Honour of Jean Seznec*, ed. Francis Haskell, Anthony Levi, and Robert Shackleton, in the *Art Bulletin* 59 (1977): 289–91.

29. In a book-length study of Courbet's art now in preparation, I attempt to demonstrate both the radically non- or anti-dramatic nature of Courbet's enterprise and the primacy in his work throughout his career of quintessentially absorptive subject matter. Significantly, Courbet was not alone in his time in exploiting absorption: two slightly older contemporaries, Millet and Meissonier, also responded to the theatricalization of action and expression by resorting to absorptive themes and effects. But whereas they continued to present those themes and effects within pictorial frameworks that remained essentially dramatic (i.e., to *stage* them), Courbet seems intuitively to have grasped that the evocation of absorption was powerless in itself to bring about

the de-theatricalization of the painting-beholder relationship he sought and that it was necessary as well to eliminate every vestige of drama at the level of pictorial structure, the dramatic as such having become hopelessly theatricalized. Hence what seems to have been his determination to establish the apparent extreme nearness of the image to the picture-surface not just in the self-portraits but throughout his oeuvre, a determination manifest in the breakthrough pictures of 1848–50 and reaching a further stage of explicitness in the *Demoiselles des bords de la Seine* (1856–57). In that painting, as elsewhere in Courbet's art, the pursuit of nearness calls into question the very illusion of solid forms in space; but the efflorescence—the seemingly endless proliferation—in the close vicinity of the picture-plane of colored or semitransparent tactile surfaces prevents us from experiencing the etiolation of illusion as a lack. On the contrary, our conviction is of a sensuous fullness verging on surfeit. In the nonpareil flower-pieces of the 1860s this development is carried to a still further extreme.

It should be noted that something distinctly analogous to the preoccupation with absorption evident in the work of Courbet, Millet, and Meissonier is also present in the art of mid-*eighteenth*-century French painters such as Chardin, Carle Van Loo, Vien, and Greuze, which is to say that there took place in the 1840s and '50s a return to a master theme that first emerged as an object of conscious concern roughly a century earlier, before what I have elsewhere described as the progressive assimilation of absorption to expression got under way ("Absorption," esp. 169–74). The return is made explicit in Meissonier's costume-pieces set in the age of Louis XV, but both Millet and Courbet had eighteenth-century leanings which we are a long way from appreciating at their true worth.

30. By far the most intensive and original recent treatment of Courbet's relation to social and political developments in the late 1840s and early 1850s is T. J. Clark's *Image of the People* (cited in n. 1). In obvious respects Clark and I pursue sharply different approaches to the task of interpreting Courbet. But in fact our approaches have at least this in common, that each of us begins from a sense of what I earlier called the prodigious strangeness of Courbet's art as well as from a conviction of the inability of traditional readings of his enterprise to begin to account for that strangeness. For the political significance of Courbet's "Realism" see also the pioneering essay by Meyer Schapiro, "Courbet and Popular Imagery," *Journal of the Warburg and Courtauld Institutes* 4 (1941): 164–91.

31. Recently it has been argued that the second figure from the left, traditionally seen as Courbet, in fact represents his friend Urbain Cuénot (Forges, *Autoportraits*, p. 35; Toussaint, *Courbet*, Cat. No. 18, pp. 94–95). I find the visual evidence less than persuasive, as does Alain De Leiris in his review of Forges' catalogue in the *Art Quarterly*, n.s. 1, no. 1 (1977): 138.

32. It was first proposed in the catalogue to the Rome exhibition of 1970 that the Besançon *Peasants of Flagey Returning from the Fair* is a version painted in 1855 of a no longer extant original of 1850 (Cat. No. 11, pp. 24–27). See also the discussion in Toussaint, *Courbet* (Cat. No. 42, pp. 130–33).

33. I mention reclining because it often seems to me that Courbet's paintings seek to have us renounce the upright posture in favor of another, fundamentally different position such as lying back. In the case of the *Burial* there is a sense in which the open grave invites such a renunciation, though I do not suggest that the beholder is to be understood as occupying the grave

or anything of the sort. In general it is as though the upright posture as such were in conflict with Courbet's aims, presumably because, as Straus has argued in the essays cited in n. 15, there exists a functional connection between that posture and beholding. In his words: "Sight the animal has in common with man, but in the upright posture seeing is transformed into beholding" ("Born to See, Born to Behold," p. 339). A somewhat related point is that Courbet is known to have painted the *Burial* in an improvised studio that constrained his movements. "I am working blindly [à l'aveuglette]," he wrote to Champfleury in 1850, "I have no room to stand back [je n'ai aucune reculée]" (Clark, *Image of a People*, p. 166, my translation). This is not to say that the features of the *Burial* to which I have drawn attention are to be interpreted merely as reflecting the physical circumstances of its making. On the contrary, I suggest that Courbet accepted those circumstances largely because he saw in them—in the obstacle they presented to his beholding the work in progress—an anticipation of his ultimate goal and perhaps also a means of achieving that goal.

34. On one occasion during his last years in Switzerland, Courbet was led by his young assistant Pata to what the latter considered a fine point of view. Courbet is reported to have laughed and said: "You remind me of poor Baudelaire, who, one evening in Normandy as the sun was setting, led me to a cliff overlooking the sea. He conducted me before a gaping opening framed by jagged rocks. 'There is what I wanted to show you,' Baudelaire said, 'there is the point of view.'—Wasn't that bourgeois of him! What are points of view? Do points of view really exist?" (Charles Léger, *Courbet* [Paris: Editions G. Crès, 1929], p. 191, my translation). The repudiation of the very notion of a point of view is consistent with Courbet's enterprise as I have described it; the characterization of the notion as bourgeois is suggestive but should not be pushed too far.

35. The account of Diderot's thought presented earlier in this essay contains a major simplification which I now want to amend. Briefly, Diderot by 1767 may be said to have held simultaneously two seemingly quite different but in fact internally consistent conceptions of painting. According to the first or *dramatic* conception (the one summarized earlier), the task of the painter was to absorb his figures in action and expression and by so doing to establish the fiction that the beholder did not exist, that there was no one in the world except the personages in the painting. The second conception, which I call *pastoral*, applied to certain "lesser" genres such as landscape and scenes of ruins and held that the task of the painter was in effect to induce the beholder to enter the painting, to wander or sit down or recline within it, to engage its inhabitants in conversation or meditate in solitude, in short to participate in whatever manner was appropriate in the depicted scene. What the two conceptions have in common is that to the extent each is realized *there remains no beholder* in front of the painting: in the first case because he has been negated or obliviated, in the second because he has been drawn into the picture. Now there is an obvious though incomplete similarity between the fiction of entrance and incorporation basic to the pastoral conception and what I have claimed is the relation to the beholder that Courbet's paintings seek to accomplish, and in the longer study of Courbet's art now in preparation I explore both the similarity and the differences between the two in some detail. For a fuller exposition of the pastoral conception see Fried, "Absorption and Theatricality: Painting and Beholder in the Age of Diderot," *Studies on Voltaire and the Eighteenth Century* 152 (1976): 753–77; and Fried, a

book bearing the same title forthcoming from the University of California Press.

36. This was often expressed by the charge that his paintings amounted merely to *morceaux* as opposed to *tableaux*. See Fried, "Manet's Sources: Aspects of His Art, 1859–1865," *Artforum* 7, no. 7 (1969): 72–73, n. 99.

37. For an illuminating analysis of the additive procedures by which Courbet arrived at the final composition of *The Quarry* see Bruce K. MacDonald, "The Quarry by Gustave Courbet," *Boston Museum Bulletin* 67, no. 348 (1969): 52–71.

38. Courbet's use of black in the *Burial* is discussed by Clark, "A Bourgeois Dance of Death: Max Buchon on Courbet," in *Courbet in Perspective*, ed. Petra ten-Doesschate Chu (Englewood Cliffs, N.J.: Prentice-Hall, 1977), pp. 102–3.

39. Other paintings in which a principal figure is depicted largely or entirely from the rear include the *Stonebreakers* (1849), *Bathers* (1853), *Meeting* (1854), *Le Bord de la mer à Polavas* (1854), *Cribleuses de blé* (1855), *Trellis* (1863), *Girl with Gulls* (1865), and *Sleep* (1866).

40. See Fried, "Manet's Sources," passim; and Fried, "Thomas Couture and the Theatricalization of Action in Nineteenth-Century French Painting," p. 45.

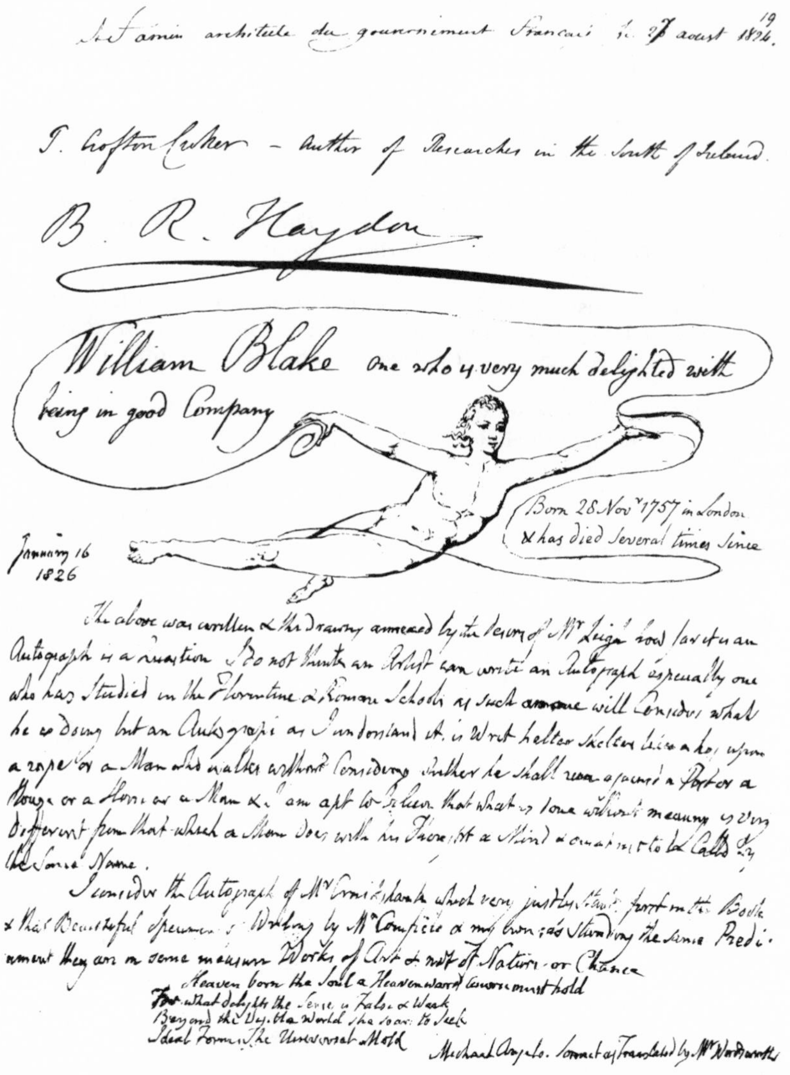

FIGURE 5.1. Blake's autograph in William Upcott's album. Henry and Albert A. Berg Collection. Copyright 1969 The New York Public Library, Astor, Lenox, and Tilden Foundations. Reprinted, with permission, from Lola L. Szladits and Harvey Simmonds, *Pen and Brush: The Author as Artist* (The New York Public Library, 1969).

The annotation to the autograph (fig. 1), transcribed by Erdman in *The Poetry and Prose of William Blake* (p. 675), reads:

The above was written & the drawing annexed by the desire of Mr Leigh how far it is an Autograph is a Question I do not think an Artist can write an Autograph especially one who has Studied in the Florentine & Roman Schools as such an one will Consider what he is doing but an Autograph as I understand it, is Writ helter skelter like a hog upon a rope or a Man who walks without Considering whether he shall run against a Post or a House or a Horse or a Man & I am apt to believe that what is done without meaning is

FIVE

THE "PREDICAMENT" OF THE AUTOGRAPH:
"WILLIAM BLAKE"
Peggy Meyer Sherry

As for textuality in general, the signature represents perhaps *the* case, the place of crossing (topical as well as tropic) of the intrinsic and the extrinsic.

Derrida, Glas

How do we distinguish one face or countenance from another, but by the bounding line and its infinite inflexions and movements. . . . Leave out this [l]ine and you leave out life itself; all is chaos again, and the line of the almighty must be drawn out upon it before man or beast can exist.

Blake, Descriptive Catalogue, XV: Ruth

Individuality is an arabesque we have discarded.

Hofmannsthal, Das Theater des Neuen

FROM THE EARLIEST Blake criticism to the latest studies of his work, readers repeatedly call our attention to the imprint of immediacy in his

---

very different from that which a Man Does with his Thought & Mind & ought not to be Calld by the Same Name.

    I consider the Autograph of Mr Cruikshank which very justly stands first in the Book & that Beautiful Specimen of Writing by Mr Comfield & my own; as standing [in] the same Predicament they are in some measure Works of Art & not of Nature or Chance

    Heaven born the Soul a Heavenward Course must hold
    For what delights the Sense is False & Weak
    Beyond the Visible World she soars to Seek
    Ideal Form, The Universal Mold

Michael Angelo. Sonnet as Translated by Mr Wordsworth

engravings. In a relatively forgotten but still charming commentary, *William Blake, 1757–1827: A Man without a Mask*, the late Jacob Bronowski asks us to take note of what he calls the "handwriting" in the pictures that illuminate the prophetic books:

I begin at the pictures only because, however we take them, we cannot miss the strong grain of the everyday, the craftsman's manner, the handwriting in them. It is the more striking, the more visionary Blake's pictures claim to be.[1]

Informed by the rigor of a more technical analysis and by his unparalleled overview of the range of Blake "originals" still in existence, David Erdman, in his monumental commentary *The Illuminated Blake*, presents the sum of his discoveries about the general structure and the fine detail of picture after picture in an introduction that remarks:

The very web and texture and color of his thinking derive and spin out and exfoliate from the daily acts of his labors on copper, from the minute particulars of the intimate, delicate, thread-thin and steel-strong interconnection of life and art.[2]

Erdman effectively illustrates Bronowski's generalization about the persistence of the everyday in the visionary, when he proceeds to point out the veritable workshop of drawing and coloring going on in the margins of *Jerusalem*, Plate 36, indicating that this page "exemplifies" Catherine and William Blake's daily employment, if also "the Last Vintage and annihilation of mortal melancholy."[3] Clearly, we are dealing in Blake's work with what critics never cease to find an irresistible extreme of the question of the intrinsic versus the extrinsic, the universal versus the individual, the product in relation to the process of production, and the work of art to the living hand responsible for its creation.

The problem with the majority of readings given to Blake's work from Bronowski to Erdman during the revival of interest in him since the late 1940s is that Blake is more ironic than most of his commentators, more tuned to the ontological ambiguities of art than they. Submitting to the imprint of a strong personality they see in his "style," his critics become apologists for what they see as the triumph of continuity between the polarities outlined above in an unfolding unity of vision.[4] It should be precisely that sense of "handwriting," however, and the aura of "his daily labors on copper" that signal rather the problem of distance in his technique and renders the question of the "line" as problematic and interesting a way of studying the form of the illuminated text as it has become recently for some readers of narrative structure.[5]

The first paradox of that seemingly indelible mark of personality, of that distinct authorial presence or "signature" in every design, is a function of those very craftsman's methods by which Blake chose to realize his artistic ideas—the drafting, engraving, etching, printing, and coloring necessary to each new edition of an illuminated book. Granted that we are dealing here with manual rather than more advanced technical reproduction (modern technology has found Blake's books notoriously difficult to reproduce in reasonably priced facsimiles or to convert into paperback editions available to the common reader), it is nevertheless a fact that "to an ever greater degree the work of art reproduced" by whatever means "becomes the work of art designed for reproducibility."[6] The notion of an "original" Blake is limited from the outset, therefore, to the difference between a reproduction made by the artist himself and one in imitation of it by another's hand or by machine. To the extent that the idea of authenticity is based upon the presence of an original, in fact, there is no one "authentic" imprint of the prophetic books, for, like the photographic negative which exemplifies this same point in Walter Benjamin's essay, "The Work of Art in the Age of Mechanical Reproduction," the copper plates of the engraver are "negatives" from which many copies can be made.[7] Critics like Erdman, who has studied the variations in inking, coloration, and linear detail from copy to copy of each book, are often stumped in the effort to distinguish between accident and intention,[8] partly because the purely mechanical means of reproduction are themselves a kind of editing process not entirely under the artist's control. Repeatability impersonalizes and even negates authorial possession or that initial labor of the living hand.

Blake can, of course, be contrasted with the more commercial or established engravers of his time in that he was unwilling to submit his technical standards, and the special set of values they often imply, to what one of his recent critics dubs the "artistic machine" of his profession.[9] Blake critics are all familiar with the case of Schiavonetti, who, in engraving Blake's designs for Cromek's special edition of Blair's poem "The Grave," toned down the outlines and "corrected" the depth perspective in accordance with the prevailing techniques of the day, only to earn from Blake the nickname of "Assassinetti."[10] That Blake chose to reproduce his visions through the mechanical processes of book-making, however, should in itself be a warning against ascribing cult value to them or endowing them with the mysteries of aura. It is precisely the evidence of process, of reproducibility, that in calling attention to itself makes the *Gebrauchswert*, or "use value," of his books political rather than cultic. Hence what Erdman calls the "workshop symbolism" pervading text and picture deserves a critical emphasis that requires no apology for being reductive to questions of art for its own sake,[11] because this imagery of writing, engraving, painting, and finally reading constitutes a rejection of art as theology.

That Blake's workshop methods can be said by this reasoning to be more political than cultic should call attention to the fact that they are

Peggy Meyer Sherry

informed by the same critique of hierarchies which critics have found to inform the "arguments" of his poems. While those arguments attack the priesthood of "natural religion" and political tyranny and reexamine the relations of body to soul, man to gods, imaginative energy to law, and man to nature, the presentation of them in text and picture dramatizes the relation between figure, voice, inscription, concept, and the very structure of the book that results from, and requires an awareness of, these relationships. The process of signification thereby revealed is, of course, no more mimetic of what is said in the text than the text is a poeticized treatise on history, religion, and politics; it is a function of the drama of drawing, writing, and reading as a mental drama as well, in which the differential play of the signifier can both articulate the aleatory desires of unconscious discourse and submit to the more structured movement of a reflexive and symbolic statement. While the emphasis, of course, changes in Blake's career from historical and political themes to more explicit exploration of the psychological problems underlying both these realms of experience, so the styles of illumination from book to book also change, making it difficult to generalize about form-making, textuality, or readership. The basic methods, nevertheless, remain the same from beginning to end, allowing us to return again and again to the problem of the "line," for instance, and the questions it implies, no matter which plate of the illuminated texts we are looking at.

Although it would be a mistake to expect Blake's familiar insistence upon the bounding line to be borne out by the style of every plate in every engraved text (the figures in the pictures to *Urizen*, for instance, are much less clearly and delicately delineated than in the earlier *America* or the much later *Job*), the aberrations in praxis from such an insistence only call our attention more strongly to the ambivalence which makes the line possible, an ambivalence familiar in terms of Blake's own myth as the struggle between Los and Urizen, or the potential of the line for both a metamorphic realization and a deadening measurement of energy. Blake provides us with perhaps his most unmediated gloss on the problem of the line in a text which may appear to be very marginal to his production as an artist, but is, in fact, inscribed with the ontological ambiguities of even his most central works, namely, his own signature or autograph in William Upcott's album (fig. 1).

The road of excess leads to the palace of wisdom.
Blake, *The Marriage of Heaven and Hell*

In the year before his death in 1827, William Blake, at age sixty-nine, inscribed a friend's album with this autograph: "William Blake one who is very much delighted with being in good company Born 28 Novr 1757 in London & has died several times since."

This auto-graph, or self-inscription, has more than the usual appeal of a celebrity's signature with its implications of authenticity, immediacy, and singularity. It was no doubt considered a unique addition to Mr. Upcott's collection, a conversation piece among friends as puzzling and delightful in its way as the visionary heads Blake sketched into John Varley's notebook, "twixt earnest and joke," while sitting at his table one evening.[12] It both enters into the spirit of "good company" with a complimentary flourish and pulsates in its own prophetic space on the page, delighting the sense and bemusing the mind, for what it offers is far in excess of the basic requirements of an autograph.

By several extra and seemingly easy movements of the pen, the proper name "William Blake" extends into a pleasing design, constructed out of a flowing pattern of verbal tags, linear flourishes, and the flying-dancing form of a naked youth with streaming hair. One has the sense that Blake has "signed" his "name" not once, but many times in succession, and through this fanciful reduplication, or multiple inscription, of self has opened up a textual-pictorial space which engages the name in a pattern of repetition and figuration. The reader is invited to discover its movements both within the design of the autograph and within the larger space of the illuminated pages of the poems in which that design is, in its turn, further engaged. It is as if the gesture of the animated autograph were inviting one to read and turn the page, like the tiny interlinear figures who so often appear to be doing this in the prophetic books.[13] Only here the "inflexions and movements" of the line seem to be interweaving the illuminated poetry with Blake's own name in a manner both playful and necessary:

One sees that the name, in a singular manner the so-called proper name, is always caught in a chain or a system of differences. It becomes an appellation only in the degree to which it may inscribe itself within a figuration. Whether it be linked by its origin to the representation of things in space or whether it remain bound within a system of phonic differences or social classifications apparently detached from ordinary space, the properness of the name [le propre du nom] does not escape spacing. Metaphor both shapes and undermines the proper name.[14]

Given the argument of this quotation, every proper name, not just the name of an artist, not only generates figuration but is caught within it. Dramatizing how the movement of the line is implicated in this figuration of the name, the inscription of an autograph like Blake's only intensifies the evidence for the inextricability of identity from displacement, or difference, asserted above. The act of inscription can be said to do this, as we shall observe, by its very excess of movement beyond the name itself, creating a space resonant with the significatory dynamics of the line in the illuminated books. In distinguishing between the aleatory scribble of the ordinary autograph ("Writ helter skelter like a hog upon a rope") and the more structured spacing or "considered" design of the artist, Blake is, of course, suggesting that the system of differences in which his own identity inscribes itself is incapable of immediacy, is not "of Nature or Chance." Even in the autograph, then, which, as a flourish of the pen, would seem to bring the drama of the line much closer to authorial presence than engraving and printing do, individuality of origin is displaced by the potential for figuration in the actions of writing, drawing, and reading inscribed there.

Even without prior knowledge of the illuminated poems, the reader of Blake's autograph will be stopped by the way it structures itself. First of all, it seems to be a series of opening and closing spaces that succeed one another and are linked by the flow of one line. This same line both defines the letters and images that constitute its design and contains them, but rather than resulting in a static whole with a fixed center it remains rhythmically open. As if plotting the movement of the reading eye in the inscribing movement of the hand, the course of the line allows a repeated progression and doubling back upon itself, suggesting that it can be read over and over again in different ways.

There are too many interesting digressions and remarks about technique and style throughout Blake's blurbs, annotations, and letters for us to gather all of them into one discussion here, but it is worth noting some of them now that seem to shed light on the relation of the reader to the possibilities for figuration that delineate themselves in the autograph. One of the few places in his notoriously polemical annotations of Reynolds' *Discourses* in which he, in fact, agrees with Reynolds has to do with the matter of outline. In response to Reynolds' declaration in the third "Discourse" that "a firm and determined outline is one of the characteristics of the great style in painting," Blake's gloss reads, "A Noble Sentence   Here is a Sentence Which overthrows his Book."[15] We know from the blurb on "Ruth" in the *Descriptive Catalogue* (cited in one of the epigraphs to this article) that for Blake the "great and golden rule of art" is "the more distinct, sharp and wiry the bounding line, the more perfect the work of art."[16] Blake, of course, radicalizes this notion in a way that Reynolds does not by identifying the movement of the line in the same blurb with intellect, ethics, cultural progress, and "life itself." Hence when he remarks there that "neither character nor expression can exist without firm and determinate outline," he is referring both to the depiction of human form in painting—the immediate context of the quote—and to the daily acts of perception itself. Blake is suggesting that his own eye, at least, draws in order to perceive the world, just as his hand wields a pen or burin to make a picture.

How then does the line, for Blake, submit to reading and interpretation? The line is "determinate" in that it always gives rise to some sort of figuration, but Blake makes it clear in his annotations to Reynolds's *Discourses* that there are dangers in how we approach that process:

To Generalize is to be an Idiot   To Particularize is the Alone Distinction of Merit—General Knowledges are those Knowledges that Idiots possess.[17]

In the same annotations he remarks that "the Greatest Artists" are the "most Minutely Discriminating & Determinate" and that "Minute Discrimination is not accidental."[18] All of these comments could be understood in terms of the line to imply that it is a mistake to generalize one reading too quickly, that attention to particulars means attention to the ways in which linear determination can be "minutely discriminated," or the ways in which a drawing allows readership to take place. As Blake says in these same notes, "Every Eye Sees differently As the Eye—Such the Object."[19] Hence there is always more than one reading possible, depending on what presuppositions the reader brings to organize the outlines of the picture before him, on the perceptions he "draws" of the world around him, or the actions he "inscribes" in the "page" of experience. The line itself, however, retains a stubborn otherness to all readings. As Blake says in a letter written in the last year of his life to George Cumberland, "A Line is a Line in its Minutest Subdivision[s] Strait or Crooked It is Itself & Not Intermeasurable with or by any Thing Else."[20]

Let us now turn to the autograph and ask how the drama of its line can be organized into different figurations, by retracing specific moments from the signifying processes at work in a range of plates from the illuminated books. For Blake, as we have just seen, the importance of outline is its determining power, its ability to define. If we pursue the earlier observation that the autograph seems to structure itself in a series of opening and closing spaces, we discover that the defining movement of outline both encloses and is ruptured by that which it defines. Rather than completing a circle around the proper name and appositive clause that seem both to flow from it and generate it, the framing line of the design breaks open into the delineation of a naked youth whose outstretched arms both complete the circle and hold it open to further flourishes and continued spacing. There is a kind of balance or symmetry in the total effect. The youth's body hovers between the double line of text in the upper left corner and another double line of text in the lower right, to which he provides a visual and bodily rather than a verbal syntactical link. Thus although he is a reflexive component in the movement of the line like the verbal signifiers in the texts of the inscription, he also seems to burst forth from between the texts as the visual embodiment of what they signify. And although he could be said to be a visual supplement to the name, grammatically in apposition to it like the clause beginning "one who . . . ," the energy generated by his pose could also be said to give him grammatical priority, making the name and other textual fragments supplementary to him. Clearly the autograph exemplifies a tension between text and body, verbal and visual signifiers, in which each both supplements and displaces the other in a powerful pulsation of enclosure or contraction and opening or expansion, reflected in the curling progress of the framing outline itself. The line defines, however, only insofar as it sets up this tension. Its determining power remains to be completed by the reader, for its design remains open both visually and verbally; it neither completes the circle it begins around the name nor the sentence that could have rounded out the text that is there.

Because of these dynamics, the reader finds it difficult to retrace any one signifying moment from the illuminated books without also seeing the opposite moment inscribed. The rapidity with which one reading thus erases the other quickly threatens to leave us at the "margin of nonentity" where the ontology of the signature hovers and upon which the irony of the line always verges.[21] But because autograph and illuminated text "read" one another, the risk of insubstantiality is also the wealth of an excess of signification that leads to a more minutely discriminating sense of how the illuminated poetry shares in the "predicament" of the autograph.

Perhaps the first reading that would occur to a Blake lover, and one that necessarily erases itself in the light of the foregoing discussion of individual identity, would go as follows. The youth who bursts through the inscription could also be said to draw together its framing line like the ends of a scroll or banner on which the text is to be displayed. He rises in flight through the space of the page, lifted by the literal balloon of thought over his head, and accompanied by the loose flourishes of the excess line and verbal tags that flutter around him like the string and ribbons of a kite tail. Although far too simple to satisfy the reader of the illuminated poetry, the appeal of figuring the autograph as an animated cartoon is its resonance for the reader of the letters with one to Thomas Butts:

I labour incessantly. I accomplish not one half of what I intend, because my abstract folly hurries me often away while I am at work, carrying me over mountains and valleys, which are not real, into a land of abstraction where spectres of the dead wander. This I endeavor to prevent; I, with my whole might, chain my feet to the world of duty and reality. But, in vain! the faster I bind, the better is the ballast; for I, so far from being bound down, take the world with me in my flights, and often it seems lighter than a ball of wool rolled by the wind.[22]

The fanciful flight of this gloss is only a distraction from the labor of reading, a nostalgia for autobiography and for the simulated spontaneity the eye would like to see in an autograph but is forbidden to do so by the artist's own annotation. Although the tension between binding and flight, weight and levitation, so important to the dynamics of the line could be used to deconstruct this confessional moment from life in the terms of art, to rest here threatens a return to the familiar platitude about the everyday in the visionary, allowed by the way in which the letter weaves its rhetoric of balloon-ballast, balls of wool, and "a land of abstraction where spectres of the dead wander" into a fabric at once personal and sublime.

To break more directly into the problematics of the line as a source of difference and figuration, let us return instead to the point already made that the youth in the autograph is both a reflexive link and a disruption of its text, both a completion and a breaking of its framing outline that holds open the possibility of a larger design. This phenomenon is a function of the signifying relation of text to body, the acts of drawing and writing (and engraving, as the larger design leads us into the illuminated poetry), and the epistemology of reading, suggesting—as Blake's remarks on the line imply—that they are inseparable. While the entire *Book of Urizen* (1794), as Blake's "creation myth"[23] or the "Genesis . . . of Blake's 'Bible of Hell',"[24] presents a powerful commentary on these questions, certain plates from it provide particularly useful glosses to the predicament of the autograph—Plate 1 or the title page (fig. 2), because as so many of his title pages, it is inscribed with an authorial mark or "signature," and Plates 10 (fig. 3) and 13 (fig. 4), because the human form that figures in each is iconographically comparable to the one in the autograph. In addition, each of these plates has direct implications for writing, engraving, and reading.

As Robert Simmons has elaborated in his article on *Urizen*[25] and Anne Mellor in *Blake's Human Form Divine*,[26] this early work is a veritable study in the formal and conceptual problems of symmetry and closed tectonic form. Morris Eaves's provocative commentary on the title page alone[27] gives some idea of the complex measurement of symmetrical mirrorings by which Urizen is introduced to the reader; and we can see for ourselves, from the image of the old man ensconced on the open book in the foreground while writing in a second with one hand and engraving in a third with the other, that reading, writing, and engraving are very much implicated in these measurings. While the design of the page seems to be unusually measured and enclosed within itself—the body framed by stone decalogues and receding arches, both cave-like and branch-like, but growing in turn from the book in which it seems to be rooted by the flow of its beard into the illegible squiggles on the

FIGURE 5.2. Title page of *The Book of Urizen* (copy B). Courtesy of the Pierpont Morgan Library.

page—it nevertheless remains for the reader to articulate its satiric or symbolic import. He must watch how his own relation to text and picture may be prophetically inscribed in the old man's relation to the books that surround him. The caption Blake attached to this picture when including it in a separate collection of pictures, "which is the Way / The Right or the Left,"[28] calls our attention to the reversals and mirrorings of meaning attributable to the movements of the line, not just by the difference between stage and audience perspective but by the processes of engraving and printing and the movements of the reading eye.

That the processes of book-making are themselves a theme of this poem is evident not just from the title page, but from all the pages which include text as well as pictures. These pages display their text in a double column, usually divided by tendrils (roots or even beard?) to suggest the binding fold between the facing pages of an open book. The analogy is most literally illuminated on Plate 5, where a Jehovah figure displays a half-open book, heavily inscribed with hieroglyphs, directly above the text. In a displacement of this self-referential image for the awesome authority and weight of written language (the leaves of the book look more like stone tablets than paper), Plate 10 (fig. 3) presents as a visual trope for the drama of engraving, and reading, an inscription in stone.

Like the line that inscribes both the letters and the tendrils, dividing the signifying chains of letters in half to delineate book form, the body depicted at the top of this plate is also an inscribing and dividing agent. However, although its environment of stone recalls the underground caves of the "Printing House in Hell," described on Plate 15 of *The Marriage of Heaven and Hell*, its earthly bondage suggests none of the enjoyments of its devil-poet cousin, who basks in the flames of creative energy on Plate 3 of that earlier poem. It is struggling to support and break apart heavy masses of rock, like an Atlas figure locked inside its own burden.[29] It suggests both the bodily vitality of the act of engraving on the hard surface of the metal plate in the workshop, and the energy of the act of reading necessary to liberate bodily tropes from the stony order of written signs in books. As an image of struggle, however, it labors on a threshold of signification rather than completing a figuration in either of the above senses. Like the tropes that figure the birth of Orc on Plates 1, 2, and 6 of *America*, it could be said to sprout bodily from the tendril that splits the text reflected by the rocks, but far from being a spontaneous eruption, it seems to belong rather to the painfully reflexive pressure of the text it illuminates. Like its doubles, the devil in *The Marriage*, Plate 3, and the youth in the autograph, it inscribes an expanding gesture, but this gesture has none of the fiery immanence that could be attributed to the former nor the airy transcendence we could ascribe to the latter. And unlike its near-twin in *The Gates of Paradise*, who figures the element Earth, its head has not been articulated but disappears into the rock around it.

The text it illuminates records the labor of Los, "forging chains new & new / Numb'ring with links, hours, days and years" (10:17–18). That these chains refer not just to the linear measurement of post-lapsarian time but also to the order of language and the structure of the body is the kind of trope we would expect, given the "intermeasurability" of these references in the design of the title page. As Mollyanne Marks's article on the structure of *The Book of Urizen* suggests, the analogy between history and narrative is a function of the poem's self-parody, in the conflict it dramatizes between the forces of the mind, falling from the synchronic vision of eternity into the fragmented vision of chronological or narrative time.[30] We can carry this argument farther into the reflexive

FIGURE 5.3. Plate 10[12] of *The [First] Book of Urizen*, "Ages on Ages roll'd over him." Courtesy of The Library of Congress, Rosenwald Collection.

drama of the "creative process" by asking how the shaping of language and the body inform the drama of the "fall," both by completing it and by preventing absolute chaos, since, as Harold Bloom has pointed out,[31] Los must forge defining support for the falling mind of Urizen. Although there is not space for adequate discussion of this question here, we can begin to ask how the self-parody of the poem begins with the problem of language itself, both in relation to a synchronic vantage point outside of time or in "eternity" and to a chaos which has to be structured. Blake's sense of the signifying process of the letter and of the line ironizes both of these relationships.

In the Preludium to the poem he displaces the authority of a transcendent synchronic viewpoint onto the "Eternals" who dictate his inscriptions: "Eternals I hear your call gladly, / Dictate swift winged words, & fear not / To unfold your dark visions of torment" (2:5–7). Such a gesture of displacement is typical of Blake's openings, but let us take for comparison its occurrence in the "Introduction" poem of Songs of Innocence, since there the pose of the figure to whom such authority of vision is ascribed is iconographically parallel to the youth in the autograph, as one can see from the frontispiece where he is represented in a dialogue with the piper.

Although, like the youth who is a visual supplement to the name "William Blake," the child on the cloud who commissions the piper to become a poet is a projected double of the piper himself, the child is also needed as a transcendent embodiment of the fiction of origin upon which both writer and reader of the songs depend, the innocent aura or presence intended to pervade diction and theme in their texts. This fiction is a displacement of identity through poetic figuration by which the voice, or bodily word, can be kept separate from the fallen act of writing; the ingenuousness of the child counters the knowledge of the piper who must "stain the water clear" to write his songs down. But since the childlike body fills the balloon of thought over the piper's head instead of a text, we could infer that the act of inscription is really trying to transcend itself by the figuration of word as body, a movement that has already suggested itself in the autograph. The predicament of the autograph repeats itself here, if we look at the title page to Songs of Innocence, since the signature implied on the frontispiece is less hidden. A piper in a wide-brimmed hat of the style Blake is said to have worn[32] lounges inside the "I" of Innocence and appears to produce from the mouth of his pipe the first flourish of the letters in the word for which the child on the cloud is the visual trope. The piper figure is, however, himself only a visual trope, as a supplementary flourish of the letter "I," which also happens to be the first person personal pronoun, pointing to an authorial self. Thus the signifying relation of text and body is here, as in the autograph, reversible and mutually supplementary.

In *The Book of Urizen*, as in the *Songs*, the problem of identity is also already caught from the beginning in the displacements of language, or the signifying chains it forges and engraves, identifying the "infinite inflexions and movements" of the line with the "fallen" world of "life itself." On Plate 10 (fig. 3) we find: "In chains of the mind locked up, / Like fetters of ice shrinking together / Disorganiz'd, rent from Eternity, / Los beat on his fetters of iron" (10:25–28). Already imprisoned within the fetters he is shaping with his hammer, Los appears in the repetitions of the text not as a separate identity but within a play of difference with Urizen, in which he seems now outside his opponent forging him a body and now within his rocky skull trying to free his own body. The body which is developing also emerges in a play of difference among bodily signifiers, in what reads as a dismembering thrust into a vortex of signification that can be ordered only with difficulty into the overall symmetries of human or book form:

> The pangs of hope began,
> In heavy pain striving, struggling.
> Two Ears in close volutions.
> From beneath his orbs of vision
> Shot spiring out and petrified
> As they grew . . . .
> In ghastly torment sick;
> Hanging upon the wind;
> Two Nostrils bent down to the deep. (11:19–24, 26–7; 13:1)

The signifying process itself seems to struggle in hope and torment at a threshold of symbolically structured statement and narrative order, for the very hammer of repetitions by which the narrative progresses closer and closer to its goal also seems to be the intensification of difference by which it refuses to progress.

We can read a deep ambivalence in this moment of hope and torment. It is informed on the one hand by the famous lines from *Jerusalem* on the redeeming power of language: "Los built the stubborn structure of the Language, acting against / Albions melancholy, who must else have been a Dumb despair" (40:59–60). But in *Urizen* itself these labors also threaten simply to secure the circularity and rigidity of solipsism, to fix every impulse into the symmetries of a sterile narcissistic ego. In yet another repetition of the struggle on Plate 10 (fig. 3), the text even seems to provide a description of the figure on the title page of the poem:

> Restless turnd the immortal inchain'd
> Heaving dolorous! anguish'd! unbearable

> Till a roof shaggy wild inclos'd
> In an orb, his fountain of thought
> In a horrible dreamful slumber. (10:31–35)

The uncertainty held open by the threshold figure on Plate 10 seems to have all but vanished here in the deadening weight and symmetry of the design already discussed. Morris Eaves suggests that Urizen/Los is in the "horrible dreamful slumber" referred to by Plate 10, and, in fact, is no longer actually writing or engraving because the way he reads has stymied him, put him to sleep, even killed him.[33] The word as full presence in breath and body, the redeeming Logos or Christ, language's "positive" potential, has been written to death according to this reading and the scene on the title page is its graveyard. In fact, Eaves sees Urizen's two hands as crucified by the very tools they employ, nailed against the stony tablets they inscribe.[34] Body and breath may seem to escape this systematization subliminally in the "semiotic chora"[35] of linear patterning which inscribes and reinscribes the initials "W" and "B" throughout the design—in the loops that define the inner bend of the tree trunk, the curves of the decalogue behind Urizen's back, his shoulders and knees, and finally the lines of text on the book open beneath him. Yet even the unorganized sounds these letters articulate fall into the trap of narcissistic symmetry, since they are not only the author's initials but even mirror one another in shape, suggesting a self-parody so extreme that the self can do nothing but sign its name all over the page it designs, rendering every shape in the design, including its own image, nothing, of course, but a supplementary flourish to the marginal non-entity of a letter.

Far from beginning in the synchronic order of eternity, the drama of the line in *Urizen* arises within a temporally and spatially disorganized moment of language, on a threshold of signification from which several resolutions suggest themselves as more or less ironic gestures towards transcendence. The vertical expanding pressure inscribed in the design on Plate 10 can be read as an attempt at the resurrection of the Logos and a liberation from the signifying chains that imprison the processes of both engraving and reading. The "spacing" or system of differences which, as we have suggested, both distinguishes and identifies Los and Urizen and seems to constitute the body through dismembering creation, moves towards an ironic reflection of this possibility, however, as Los and Urizen become one later in the poem. There is a gesture toward transcendence through temporal organization as ironic as this one in what Anne Mellor has noticed as the poem's repeated attempt to return to more and more originary levels of its creation myth.[36] Thus it could be trying to escape time through the retrogressive revisions of the very signifying chains that bind it. In an opposite movement, the same mystifi-

cation can be read in the transcendent gestures of prophecy which attempt to control the future, as Los and Enitharmon begin to propagate
and bind down the bodily links of succeeding generations of their own
kind in the later chapters of the poem.

The problem of signification is reopened by the design on Plate 13
(fig. 4) even more explicitly in terms of "spacing" and measurement in
the fallen world of language, again by allusion to workshop processes,
but here to etching rather than engraving. Just as the figure on Plate 10
struggles on the threshold as a dividing agent, so the figure on Plate 13
(fig. 4) could also be said to engage in a crucial dividing and structuring
process. The text on Plate 13, unlike any of the other plates in *Urizen*
with text on them, is divided not only vertically by a defining line of
tendrils, but horizontally across the middle by a human figure in the act
of separating forms. As Simmons has ingeniously noted, this figure is not
only at the center of its own page, but of the entire volume by verse and
plate as well.[37] If, as some editions show, this figure is pushing the sun
and moon into their places at the margins of the sky and thereby setting
the cosmic clock of the fallen world, then it is just another measuring
agent of an imprisoning order; it moves towards the moon while looking
at the sun, establishing fixed oppositions such as nighttime and daytime,
past and future, beginning and end, the reflecting object and the source
of light, signifier and signified. At the center of a book dependent upon
enclosing symmetries and mirrorings, it is the hinge of them all, and, if'
Simmons's observation that the watery effect of the outlines alludes both
to the moment of reflection and self-love in the Narcissus myth and to
perception in the "sea of time and space" (the Blakean trope for the
fallen world), then the solipsistic circle of Urizen's domination over and
by his own creation is complete.

There is an alternative reading inscribed in the design, however,
which is clearer in editions where the figure simply seems to be parting
brightly edged clouds in a night sky.[38] Then the emphasis is on "spacing" or the articulation of differences in a signifying process which is not
tightly measurable by fixed references and set oppositions. The central
role of the human figure suggests rather the subjectivity of time and a
relative perceptual order that need not have a causal linear continuity.
Because it is opening space by parting dark clouds which seem to be
brighter on the other side, this figure may even embody the desire for
full presence or the resurrection of the Logos. The frontispiece to Ed-
ward Young's *Night Thoughts* is a more explicit reference to just this
idea, as there Blake depicts Christ as a radiant youth leaping from his
bier and parting the clouds as he rises. Unlike its iconographic double
there, of course, the figure in Plate 13, of uncertain sex, has its back to

The "Predicament" of the Autograph: "William Blake"

FIGURE 5.4. Plate 13 of *The Book of Urizen* (copy B). Courtesy of the Pierpont Morgan Library.

Peggy Meyer Sherry

the reader as if to invite the act of reading itself. It defines the structural dynamics of the line and the text only insofar as the hinge is also the break, the articulation of parts by separation and difference which leaves room for unfixing references and for figuration that plays into a vortex of signification through which every reader passes differently.[39]

Whereas this second notion of Plate 13 (fig. 4) as the "hinge" of the book and the text makes it possible to undercut the deadening authority of the written law, depicted in the visual trope of an oppressive Jehovah on Plate 5, the engraving process to which Plate 13 can be said to allude undercuts in turn the opposite authority of the word as living breath and body or Christ. Unlike the text, which is black on a light background, the design on this plate is defined in white outlines on a dark background. If the figure in the picture is in effect a "negative" of the text, as the reversal of black and white would suggest, it can be taken as prior to it, the copper plate as a "negative" which looks watery, perhaps, because it is still submerged in the acid bath of the etching process. As a negative, however, it is not the original of the text, but an allusion to process and repeatability, as discussed earlier in this article. Its outlines emerge under the corrosive power of the acid only as it is submerged, suggesting once again that definition is a function of the fall and that the line taking shape is not a revelation, but only an imprint of the infinite (cf. Plate 15 of *The Marriage of Heaven and Hell*), a bodily signifier of absence, arbitrarily separate from any origin in eternity.[40]

Measurement, "spacing," and the continuity of origins are all questions inscribed in the problem of temporality which explicitly announces itself in the autograph in the Upcott Album. There the youth whose doubles we have been uncovering is tethered within an autobiographical chain of signifiers, measured or bracketed by the dates to which his glance and left foot seem to guide the reader's eye. One is the author's date of birth, the other, presumably, the date on which the autograph was inscribed. These dates by no means remain fixed to these events, however, for their measurements are undercut both by the spacing of the inscription and by its explicit denial of a continuity of origin. Although the most obvious inference to be drawn from the spacing of the design is the startling incongruity between the chronological old age (sixty-nine years) to be reckoned from the two dates and the youthful exuberance of the body stretched between them, the text to the right reads, "Born 28 Novr 1757 in London & has died several times since." The testimony of multiple deaths and the multiple rebirths it implies undermine the privilege of the given birth date. If the original point of the inscription is rather the name "William Blake," we are to infer that it has itself often crossed the threshold between life and death through its very figuration in this autograph; if instead we want to see the youth as the point of origin, then the same could be said of its repetition by iconographic displacement into the larger vortex of the illuminated poems toward which it gestures. The date on which the signature was inscribed could therefore be read as both a birthday and a date of death, for the polarities of birth and death, or the margin between them, can be taken as tropes for the movement of the inscription itself.

Given Blake's insistence on a bounding line that is "distinct, sharp and wirey," one is inclined to begin by asking how such a line figures as a fatal power in writing and inscription. As we have seen from our brief discussion of certain plates in *The Book of Urizen*, the flowing line can be an evil in the form of a fallen notion of time that is based on linear continuity and causality, especially as it takes on reflexive, enclosing, cyclic patterns in compulsive repetition. We have also seen how the line can be viewed as negative, tracing the absence of the form that its determining order seems to signify. Charged with these values, the line that shapes an inscription exemplifies the Biblical dictum that "the letter kineth." The signature is perhaps the paradigm for such a statement, since it not only seems to begin with a break from the authorial presence on which its authenticity has to rest, but, in flowing with energy from the inscribing hand, simultaneously traces its absence. Severed from the living origin, every signature is an epitaph commemorating its writer to its reader, even the simple "X" of the illiterate that recalls the criss-crossed eyes of dead or unconscious cartoon characters.[41]

The design of Blake's autograph is more complex than the flowing continuity of the framing line around it, but, as suggested earlier, its curling progress reflects the shaping of both letters and picture as they unfold under the movement of the reading eye that traces and retraces their relationships. As we have already seen from the iconographic role of the tendrils in *Urizen*, for instance, the flowing line itself can be displaced into a series of visual tropes in the illuminated poetry that can be understood to inform the signifying relations of text and body. Let us consider some examples of their fatal emblematic thrust downward, on the one hand, and redemptive upward thrust, on the other.

In the lyric from *Songs of Experience* entitled "A Poison Tree," for instance, the lines that define the tree, as Erdman has pointed out,[42] grow out of a flourish of the "y" of "My" in the last line of the poem, the line which announces the death of the body at the bottom of the page. The branches of the tree ultimately bend downward to encapsulate the victim in a style typical of what Blake calls "The Tree of Mystery" (cf., for instance, *The Four Zoas* 7:212). In another song from *Experience* entitled "The Garden of Love," the text has gone underground beneath the black hole of an open grave, giving the uncanny impression that the mourners are both burying their desires and reading the hollow inscription of their energies in the negative space or absence of the text below them. Its verses, however, are not only embellished by interlinear worms to emphasize the fear of death and corruption by which they have inscribed their former sensual joys into the grave. The title of these verses is also interlaced with roots that, far from promising flowers, could even be said to have sprouted the mournfully mystified readership of "priests in black gowns" who kneel above ground. If the act of inscription can transcend itself upward into a body, as suggested by the frontispiece to *Songs of Innocence*, it can displace itself in the other direction into a text that is the grave of the body. In both poems from *Experience*, of course, text and design generate one another in a fatal circle of signification and interpretation.

The binding power of inscription as a mystified vegetative power, exemplified in these lyrics and elaborated in the later poetry in the drama between Albion and Vala (cf. Vala, or Nature, binding Albion in her net on Plate 40/45 of *Jerusalem*) can be opposed by its vital liberating energy as exhibited in the border designs of the "Introduction" to *Songs of Innocence* and to "The School Boy" from *Songs of Experience*. In the former, the upward twining of vines defines eight scenes according to a convention of border design in stained glass windows called "The Tree of Jesse."[43] In the latter, the differential play of vine and human body that produces the same twining border suggests the literal metamorphosis of the convention into a concrete embodiment of its historical and prophetic implications. Not only is the tree a trope for the linking of human generations in history but also for their upward climb toward prophetic fulfillment in the birth of Jesus, whose family tree they are[44] and who is the redeeming body of the written word, according to tradition.

To take just one more example of such contaries, let us briefly compare the title page of *Europe* with Plate 6 from *Urizen*. In the former the initial "E" of "Europe" is magnified by repetition in the great curling folds of the serpent who fills the rest of the page. Although this serpent curls upward, his tongue trumpeting prophecy like the voice of the title in anticipation of the "furious circles" of rebellious energy in which the demon Orc rises against Urizen's oppression (5:15–16), his force in the turnings of the text is captured in a cyclic futility ("Thought chang'd the infinite to a serpent," 10:16) characteristic of the fallen temporal order of history. The struggle between Orc and Urizen this records is displaced to a closer analogy with the written text in Plate 6 of *Urizen*, where bodies wrapped in serpents plummet to the bottom of the page. The fall alluded to in the text identifies Satan, Urizen, the serpent, knowledge, and finally its writings in the traditional associations with serpent as emblem. Displaced so close to the written text, this emblem seems more remote from the Logos, although the outstretched arms of the middle figure are supposed to allude to Christ's resurrection and reversal of the fall.

Clearly, the act of inscription can be implicated in emblematic contraries that could be said to provide "positive" and "negative" readings of the movement of the autograph. The signature may be an epitaph, on the one hand, a downward displacement into absence and death traced by the downward movement of its framing line, or this same line may be the shroud just thrown off by the resurrected body of the youth who leaps upward like the figure of the resurrected Christ in the frontispiece to *Night Thoughts*. But as we have already said, the inscription remains open. It is a pattern of spaces rather than a completed circle, a succession of supplementary flourishes in a rhythm of breaks and renewed starts which is repeated at least six times (at "one who . . .," the figure of the youth, "Born . . .," "& has died . . .," the figure of the youth again, and the latter date). Each start is a vital thrust that erases itself and has to be renewed by the next in a broken line of repetition and difference which can only accumulate in an excess of signifiers rather than a unified synthesis or bodily whole.

It could be argued that what gives unity, or a body, or clothing to the autograph is, in fact, the weaving movement of the reading eye playing back and forth with emblematic contraries: "the primal patterns of perception are structured around the image of the human form; every act of consciousness, then, approximates or 'clothes' the human form divine."[45] However, the garment is always the reader's, and "unity is the cloke of folly,"[46] for, as the text says on Plate 15 of *Jerusalem*, "Reasonings like vast serpents / Infold around my limbs, bruising my minute articulation" (15:12–13). Perhaps the closest approximation of the predicament of the autograph can be found in an emblem which is neither positive nor negative, dead nor alive, but at the brink of the grave and the "gates of paradise," namely, the worm.

The worm should immediately come to mind in looking at the autograph, for the sixty-odd years of the artistic career commemorated there happen to fit the familiar trope from the poetry by which man is described as a "worm of sixty winters" (*Jerusalem* 34:57). But although Blake seems to have found the worm a peculiarly expressive emblem of man's mortal career, identifying it with both the embryo in the womb (*Urizen* 19–20) and the old man, the worm is perhaps most provocatively imaged as a threshold figure who sits at death's door in Plate 16 of *For the Sexes* (fig. 5) as an emblem of writing. Anne Mellor identifies

FIGURES 5.5 and 5.6. *For Children: The Gates of Paradise*, plate 15, "Death's Door"; and *For the Sexes: The Gates of Paradise*, plate 16, "I have said to the Worm . . ." Courtesy of The Library of Congress, Rosenwald Collection.

the stick this figure holds as the traveller's staff,[47] but it seems more exact to call it a stylus, for it is held in writing position at the lower tip, not grasped at the top like a walking stick (cf. the traveller's staff in Plate 15 [fig. 5]). That the system of differences in which the self is always displaced and the name figured should be a system of writing is not opposed to the emblem of the weaving worm to which the text of Plate 16 (fig. 6) alludes, for the written text often figures in metaphors of warp and woof in both early and late Blake. But here the inscription at the gate seems to urge the traveller to halt and reflect on his readership:

> The Door of Death I open found
> And the Worm Weaving in the Ground
> Thou'rt my Mother from the Womb
> Wife Sister Daughter to the Tomb
> Weaving to Dreams the Sexual Strife
> And weeping over the Web of Life. (*For the Sexes*, 15–16)

At such a threshold, man meets a riddle in the textuality of his own identity that figures his destiny from embryo to old age in dreamlike doublings.

The "Predicament" of the Autograph: "William Blake"

NOTES

1. Jacob Bronowski, *William Blake, 1757–1827: A Man Without a Mask* (London: Secker & Warburg, 1947), p. 6. As Martin Nurmi points out in his book *William Blake* (Kent, Ohio: Kent State University Press, 1976), p. 34, this image of Blake, which he shares, is much older, occurring in a well-known letter from Samuel Palmer to Gilchrist, Blake's first major biographer, written August 23, 1855.

2. David V. Erdman, *The Illuminated Blake* (Garden City, N.Y.: Anchor Books, 1974), p. 12. Allusions to the commentary on the plates reproduced in this edition will henceforward be indicated by the abbreviation *Illum. Blake.* Readers interested in Blake's art may also want to consult W. J. T. Mitchell's recent book, *Blake's Composite Art: A Study of the Illuminated Poetry* (Princeton, N.J.: Princeton University Press, 1978).

3. *Illum. Blake*, p. 12.

4. Northrop Frye's epochal work on Blake necessarily overstated the unity of his vision to redeem Blake studies from the long-standing tradition that his poetry was incoherent.

5. J. Hillis Miller, "Ariadne's Thread: Repetition and the Narrative Line," *Critical Inquiry* 3 (1975): 57–77.

6. Walter Benjamin, "The Work of Art in the Age of Mechanical Reproduction," in *Illuminations*, ed. Hannah Arendt, trans. Harry Zohn (New York: Schocken, 1969), p. 224. It seems telling that Erdman, whose first book made important discoveries about Blake's historical and political context, should move from there to the arts of book-making and engraving.

7. Benjamin, "The Work of Art," p. 224.

8. *Illum. Blake*, pp. 15–16.

9. Morris Eaves, "Blake and the Artistic Machine: An Essay in Decorum and Technology," *PMLA* 92 (1977): 903–27.

10. Eaves gives helpful guides to the difference in techniques and mentions the nickname, but the entire background of the moment is unfolded by S. Foster Damon in his commentary in *Blake's Grave: William Blake's Illustrations for Robert Blair's "The Grave"* (Providence, R.I.: Brown University Press, 1963). The irony of the whole controversy is, of course, that Schiavonetti wasn't assassinating illusionism but putting it there.

11. *Illum. Blake*, p. 13.

12. The quotation is from an early version of the poem "I asked a thief to steal me a peach" and is grafted on here to protect my readership against idealizing angels, as Varley idealized Blake. Varley couldn't have appreciated Blake's irony when he noted next to one of the heads he sketched that he "drew her to get her out of the way," so he could get a better look at the vision behind her.

13. Especially in the interlinear designs to *The Marriage of Heaven and Hell*, beautifully annotated by Erdman together with Tom Dargan and Marlene Deverall-Van Meter in "Reading the Illuminations in *The Marriage of Heaven and Hell*," *William Blake: Studies in Honor of Sir Geoffrey Keynes*, ed. Morton Paley and Michael Phillips (London: Oxford University Press, 1973), pp. 162–207.

14. I have combined my translation of this passage from Jacques Derrida's *De la Grammatologie* (Paris: Editions de Minuit, 1967), p. 136, with that of Gayatri Spivak, *Of Grammatology* (Baltimore: Johns Hopkins University Press, 1976), p. 89. Of course, no translation is adequate.

15. William Blake, *The Poetry and Prose of William Blake*, ed. David V. Erdman with a commentary by Harold Bloom (Garden City, N.Y.: Doubleday & Co., 1970), p. 638. Hereafter references to this edition will be abbreviated *Blake*.

16. *Blake*, p. 540.

17. *Blake*, p. 630.

18. *Blake*, p. 632.

19. *Blake*, p. 634.

20. William Blake, *The Letters of William Blake, Together with a Life by Frederick Tatham*, ed. Archibald Russell (London: Methuen & Co., 1906), p. 222.

21. The repetition of this expression is especially telling in Blake's *Visions of the Daughters of Albion*.

22. *Letters*, pp. 90–91.

23. Northrop Frye, *Fearful Symmetry: A Study of William Blake* (Princeton, N.J.: Princeton University Press, 1947), pp. 254–59.

24. Harold Bloom, *Blake's Apocalypse: A Study in Poetic Argument* (Ithaca, N.Y.: Cornell University Press, 1963), p. 164.

25. Robert E. Simmons, "*Urizen*: the Symmetry of Fear," *Blake's Visionary Forms Dramatic*, ed. David V. Erdman and John E. Grant (Princeton, N.J.: Princeton University Press, 1970), pp. 146–73.

26. Anne Mellor, *Blake's Human Form Divine* (Berkeley: University of California Press, 1974), pp. 88 ff.

27. Morris Eaves, "The Title Page of *The Book of Urizen*," *William Blake: Studies in Honor of Sir Geoffrey Keynes*, pp. 225–30.

28. *Blake*, p. 662.

29. *Illum. Blake*, p. 192.

30. Mollyanne Marks, "Structure and Irony in Blake's *Book of Urizen*," *SEL* 15 (1975): 579–90.

31. Bloom, *Blake's Apocalypse*, pp. 169–70.

32. William Blake, *Songs of Innocence and Experience*, ed. with an introduction by Geoffrey Keynes (London: Oxford University Press in cooperation with the Trianon Press, Paris, 1970), commentary to Plate 3, showing detail.

33. Eaves, "The Title Page of *The Book of Urizen*," p. 228.

34. Ibid., p. 230.

35. Julia Kristeva, *La Revolution du Langage Poétique: l'avant-garde à la fin du XIXᵉ siecle, Lautréamont et Mallarmé* (Paris: Editions du Seuil, 1974), "La 'chora' sémiotique: ordonnancement des pulsions," pp. 22–29. " 'Energetic' charges and at the same time 'psychological' marks, the pulsations articulate that which we call a chora: a non-expressive totality constituted by these pulsations and their stasis in a motility as animated as it is regulated." I am indebted to a lecture by Jean-Claude Bonne at Hobart College in 1976 on the border repetitions in medieval manuscripts for showing how this notion might be transferred from poems to pictures, and to Grant Holly for first calling my attention to the phenomena of the "B's" and "W's". Max Yeh has since suggested to me that there are signatures even in the material process of engraving because of the V-shaped grooves produced on the surface of the plate and the metal curlicues discarded as a result.

36. Mellor, *Blake's Human Form Divine*, p. 93.

37. Simmons, "*Urizen*: the Symmetry of Fear," p. 149.

38. *Illum. Blake*, p. 195.

39. Cf. the treatment of "la brisure" or hinge in *De la Grammatologie*, p. 96ff., as well as Blake's defining verses on "vortex" in *Milton* (15:21–46). Given the latter, I am rather freely giving the notion of "text" cosmic dimensions.

40. The transformations in the acid bath of the etching process could also be said to allude to the old alchemical notion of the human form as the signature of God, as in Boehme's *De Signatura Rerum*. This allusion should in itself "ironize" the figures who iconographically double the youth in the autograph, if the self-parodic identification of the author with Jehovah and Urizen has not already done so. It is telling that Kathleen Raine bewails Urizenic impulses in Blake for following Swedenborg's notion of correspondences, which she traces to the alchemical signature, in *Blake and Tradition*, Vol. I. (Princeton, N.J.: Princeton University Press, 1968), p. 4.

41. Miller, "Ariadne's Thread," p. 70.

42. *Illum. Blake*, p. 91.

43. Anthony Blunt, *The Art of William Blake* (New York: Columbia University Press, 1959), p. 45.

44. *Isa.* 11, "quoted" by Paul in *Rom.* 15:12.

45. Mellor, *Blake's Human Form Divine*, p. 222.

46. *Blake*, "On Homer's Poetry," p. 267.

47. Mellor, *Blake's Human Form Divine*, p. 84.

48. *Blake*, p. 266. In his article, "The Figure of the Garment in *The Four Zoas, Milton*, and *Jerusalem*," Morton Paley calls attention to a letter from Blake to Linnell (Aug. 1, 1826), in which he refers to his body as "being only bones and sinews, all strings and bobbins like a weaver's loom" (*Letters*, p. 218). Paley's essay is included in *Blake's Sublime Allegory*, ed. Stuart Curran and Joseph Wittreich, Jr. (Madison: Wisconsin University Press, 1973), pp. 119–40.

SIX

"LES RELAIS DU VERBE":
PERSE'S RETICULAR RHETORIC
Richard A. Laden

SEMIOTIC CRITICISM has expended no little effort to show that texts often talk about several things at the same time. A text may have literal and symbolic meanings, or the contesting trains of thought found in jokes; but recent studies of poetry have extended the investigation of complex isotopy or pluri-isotopy—terms launched by Greimas[1]—to semiological isotopies, connecting different sets not of classemes but of nuclear semes. Thus in Mallarmé's "Salut" François Rastier discovers three sememic fields which let us read the poem as at once about a banquet, a sailing ship, and writing.[2] Modern criticism has pointedly distinguished such polysemy from the Text of Kristeva, Sollers, or the later Barthes. Claude Chabrol writes: "Let there be no mistake . . . a *plural* text is not merely a multiplicity of isotopies, even if these escape hierarchical orderings, nor can an undecidability of codes be reduced to ambiguity or polysemy."[3] Much of Derrida's *La Dissémination* is concerned with this issue of a textual process beyond (yet also within) semantics. By fostering a dialogue between ideas of modern criticism and a poem upon which they can focus—a poem that can, Procrustean host, accommodate them, the accommodation being a return of focus or reversal of scope—I hope to show that the distinction is not so clear-cut: that the recognition of multiple semiological isotopies lifts the ex-communication that a structural semantics has pronounced upon the referent, which in turn nibbles away at the concept of isotopy and hence at the very possibility of a "structural" or "scientific" analysis of discourse. At the same time, the recognition of multiple semiological isotopies with their "sememic fields" inserts the text as enunciation into the entire praxis of its civilization, with its store of sememic fields, codes, and prior texts, beckoning toward the *significance* of the plural text. The poem here in question (interpellated/interpolated) is *Vents* I, 1, the first canto of the long work by Saint-John Perse.

Fly-leaf/*Feuille volante*:

separate and connected, the text as swarm, articulated with the article

. . .

Saint-John Perse's *Vents* I, 1

C'étaient de très grands vents sur toutes faces de ce monde,
De très grands vents en liesse par le monde, qui n'avaient d'aire ni de gite,
Qui n'avaient garde ni mesure, et nous laissaient, hommes de paille,
En l'an de paille sur leur erre . . . Ah! oui, de très grands vents sur toutes faces de vivants!

Flairant la pourpre, le cilice, flairant l'ivoire et le tesson, flairant le monde entier des choses,
Et qui couraient à leur office sur nos plus grands versets d'athlètes, de poètes,
C'étaient de très grands vents en quête sur toutes pistes de ce monde,
Sur toutes choses périssables, sur toutes choses saisissables, parmi le monde entier des choses . . .

Et d'éventer l'usure et la sécheresse au coeur des hommes investis,
Voici qu'ils produisaient ce goût de paille et d'aromates, sur toutes places de nos villes,
Comme au soulèvement des grandes dalles publiques. Et le coeur nous levait
Aux bouches mortes des Offices. Et le dieu refluait des grands ouvrages de l'esprit

Car tout un siècle s'ebruitait dans la sécheresse de sa paille, parmi d'étranges désinences: à bout de cosses, de siliques, à bout de choses frémissantes,
Comme un grand arbre sous ses hardes et ses haillons de l'autre hiver, portant livrée de l'année morte;
Comme un grand arbre tressaillant dans ses crécelles de bois mort et ses corolles de terre cuite—
Très grand arbre mendiant qui a fripé son patrimoine, face brûlée d'amour et de violence où le désir encore va chanter.

"O toi, désir, qui vas chanter . . ." Et ne voilà-t-il pas déjà toute ma page elle-même bruissante,
Comme ce grand arbre de magie sous sa pouillerie d'hiver: vain de son lot d'icônes, de fétiches,
Berçant dépouilles et spectres de locustes; léguant, liant au vent du ciel filiales d'ailes et d'essaims, lais et relais du plus haut verbe—

Richard A. Laden

Ha! très grand arbre du langage peuplé d'oracles, de maximes et murmurant murmure d'aveugle-né dans les quinconces du savoir . . .

In what semantics would call a metalinguistic isotopy or isotopy of enunciation, the poem addresses itself to multiple isotopy and to enunciation
as the code of production of meaning (with its modal sequences *vouloir-
savoir-pouvoir-faire*) in a cultural praxis; as the theory of itself—of its
signifiance—it participates in that "general semiotics" (Chabrol) or
"semanalysis" (Kristeva) that modern criticism is elaborating.[4]

If we examine that moment in Greimas's theorization at which the
concept of isotopy arises (*SS*, pp. 98ff.), we find it summoned up as a
totality, the closure of discourse, designed to supplant (/supplement)
another totality, the "stored semantic universe." Where discourse is no
longer the communication of a total Meaning, where it fractures into
pluri-isotopy and oblique definition, the "univers sémantique" and the
world of things behind it threaten to emerge from their repression. Rastier's analysis of "Salut" reads in each isotopy virtually all the words of
the poem, establishing in each case a quasi-continuity of meaning. Yet as
Vents I, 1 will show, an isotopy can be as selective as Saussure's ana-
grams, so that some but not all the lexemes of the poem may be read
according to it.

The major example Greimas uses to illustrate isotopy and textual
closure is Freud's horse-dealer joke. His position echoes what Riffaterre
says about the nonreferentiality of literary language: the text provides
sufficient information for its decoding, rendering superfluous detailed
knowledge about the referents of the words used.[5] In order to decode, to
fit a term into an isotopy, we pick out its relevant characteristics. Here,
we need not know how far away Pressburg is; the joke determines its
value as "a distant place," and the horse dealer is presumably stressing a
virtue of the horse. This presentation of the horse constitutes one isotopy
—"the whole elusive sequence simply amounts to an oblique definition of
a horse"—and to fit this allusive definition into the isotopy we must select
the relevant characteristic of the horse: we search in the "paradigm of
the characteristics of a horse and find "speed." That is, to establish the
isotopy of the closed text we are free to consider, following Greimas's
example, the words not just as sememes, dictionary definitions, but also
as what Greimas terms an "actant semene" with a "paradigm of characteristics," a repertory of predicates that returns the term to the combina-
torial play of cultural codes. This presumption of experience makes
possible what Jonathan Culler has called "interpretive competence," and
the above argument resembles one part of his discussion of Greimas.[6]
Like solving a riddle, establishing an isotopy requires dealing with
oblique definitions that open the closed text to the plurality of the cultural grid(s), the "stored semantic universe" which isotopy as a *textual*

grid should put in parentheses. Beyond a return to interpretive competence, the illimitation of the sememe suggests a different theory of meaning, in which polysemy becomes merely a point of departure for meanings as itinerary or syntax, through a net of associations looser than an
interpretive grid—J.-J. Goux's "previously inconceivable conception of
the network, of a polynodal, non-representative form of organization; the
conception of the text."[7]

In the name of a single symbolic meaning we can slam shut Pan-
dora's box, reduce the play of the text by ignoring the "paradigm of
characteristics" of obliquely defined terms. For instance, Greimas's reading of "Nerval's evocation of the place 'où le pampre à la rose s'allie,' "
which "can be understood by dealing with this definition on the symbolic
level to which it belongs, such that its allusive quality is hypostasized as
the 'uniqueness' in time and space of an event otherwise unidentified"
(SS, p. 91). Riffaterre's reading of Wordsworth's "Yew Trees" illustrates
this principle. (Still, we must know the "tree code" or "snake code," the
"commonplace associations" of literary language [SS, p. 238] upon
which Riffaterre founds the symbol, and which are somehow different
from the "commonplace concepts about things" [SS, p. 235] of what
Riffaterre calls "cognitive language.") In a semiological isotopy, on the
other hand, the basic "paradigm of characteristics" is needed to construct
the "sememic field" of a term. A sememic field cannot be limited to the
pertinent words (rather, meanings: sememes) appearing in the poem;
the entire code is conveyed, relayed, by the words actually occurring. In
Vents I, 1 one isotopy reads a part of the poem that includes several
oblique definitions. Associated with an image obliquely suggested (to
use a traditional vocabulary) is a word—a key term in the sememic field
of the semiological isotopy—that, in a completely different meaning, is a
significant term in another semiological isotopy. This pun upon a word
metonymically present, although not occurring in the poem, suggests the
complex network of isotopies that may be created by the industrious
reader. How does one limit "sememic fields," how does one keep them
from extending their boundaries and overlapping each other beyond the
ability of the most meticulous cadastre to delimit them? The difficulties
of avoiding entanglements increase if the isotopies are themselves ana-
grammatic, interspaced and entangled, if they are no longer commanded
by the single symbolic meaning that unfolds itself linearly and con-
tinuously—the touchstone, for Riffaterre, of the "literariness" of the text.
"A one-to-one referentiality would not suffice per se to turn a faithful
account of reality into a literary text—. . . to endow a recording of reality
with literariness. But what actually happens [in a passage of "Yew
Trees"] is that adjectives and participles all spring from one word . . .
they . . . repeat the same meaning through a modulation from code to

code" (*IDP*, p. 234). Without this unity of signification patriarchally begetting its metaphors, the text becomes, at its literal extreme, a set of marks for the *production* of meanings. Given the play of allusion (displacement) and the richness of experience, the text points, beyond any pragmatics, any sedimentation of codes, toward the world of Reference, of things, that is differentiated by Pythagoras, quantum physics, or Freud's "scientific psychology." It is this codification mythically imposed upon the world, permitting the interplay of reference out of which the possibility of meaning and enunciation arises, that *Vents* I, 1, by its proliferation of references, in a sense deconstructs.

I shall first offer, beginning with a summary, a gloss of the poem from which the main isotopies may be extracted. Any such summary is necessarily arbitrary in that it consists of a selection of terms made before a principle of selection has been announced. Its sketchiness should be regarded not as a contraction of an as yet undefined meaning but rather as a starting point: no seam of symbol yet, just a *faux-fil*. With this caution, let us say that the first poem of *Vents* narrates the renewal of the world. Set in the past of ongoing action (the imperfect), this palingenesis is portrayed in evocations of natural cyclism. It comes in the actions of great winds, "de très grands vents," blowing everywhere, "sur toutes faces de ce monde." The effect of the "vents" is that of the verb "éventer"—"Et d'éventer . . ."—they air and expose, as in a cosmic spring cleaning with its inevitable upheaval. For another epoch is preparing to emerge: "tout un siècle s'ebruitait. . . ." We encounter expressions of disgust—"le coeur nous levait"—beside expressions of "liesse," the insistent celebration of "très grands vents" or the "très grand arbre," the exultation in the "lais et relais du plus haut verbe." The cataclysmic renewal is at once a cataclasm—a break with the past, a destruction of the old—and a propagation of the energy of the world in a new cycle, a new generation.

The first three paragraphs of the poem consist of statements conveying aspects of this narration. We can rewrite these statements as messages a_1, a_2, a_3 . . . , giving the qualifications and actions of the winds; then a statement b expressing the action (interiorized: a reaction) of "nous"; followed by a statement c conveying the action of "le dieu." Here a, b, and c are linked paratactically; as aspects (partial definitions) of a whole, they are explained or set in perspective as detail/overview by the beginning of paragraph 4: $a + b + c$ *car* A, where A ("tout un siecle s'ebruitait . . .") is a "capsule" summary ("cosses") of the event narrated. This event is projected onto the movement present in the description of the tree, which we shall call X: "Comme un grand arbre . . ." states that A $\simeq$ X. The second event (B) announced by the poem is its own creation in an implicit present: "Et ne voilà-t-il pas déjà toute ma page elle-même bruissante." This isotopy of enunciation also projects its movement onto that present in the image of the tree: B $\simeq$ X. We find in addition an anomalous statement (Y) quoting another voice: " 'O toi, désir, qui vas chanter. . . .' " (That Y repeats X links the enunciation of X to that of Y. But Y is quoted, a pre-diction, and the sequence " 'qui vas chanter' "-"ne voilà-t-il pas déjà" can be read as prediction-event. The enunciation of Y would consequently be in a sense prior to itself; as we shall see, this temporal paradox characterizes the entire poem.)

The problems posed by the above telegraphic model of the poem are obvious. The correlation A $\simeq$ X $\simeq$ B recalls the conjunction of isotopies of symbolic discourse.[8] Yet here it is impossible to order the isotopies hierarchically, and the distinction between literal and symbolic must be regarded with suspicion. A symbolic meaning is usually, to use Greimas's labels, noölogical, the image of a founding theology; it is designated by poetic language which literally denotes a more concrete and immediate object. By describing both its creation and a cosmogony in a series of details, the poem blurs the distinction between connotation and denotation, between cosmology and noölogy: it is as much technical as mythical. Furthermore, by linking cosmogony and enunciation the poem vitiates the distinction between the semiotic and the metasemiotic: the signs of renewal the poem reads indicate, by their correlation, the possibility of meaning and enunciation (metaphor, expression-projection of sense: a *pouvoir-dire*). The most serious problem, however, is that when we look at the isotopies that come together, we find that they link events of undetermined content. The assumption of a symbolic meaning is a simplification based on investing words that belong to the "sememic field" of an isotopy with associations derived from frequent encounters with these words in symbolic contexts. On closer inspection, the meaning of the event narrated in each isotopy proves to be a swarm of meanings that fracture and reknit in paradoxical combinations, so that notions such as creation and renewal are relay stations for a shuttling movement of contrary ideas. (In the argument following the gloss, I shall return to these preliminary remarks.)

Taking the proposed structuring of the poem as a symbolic isotopy dominating semiological isotopies—experiences that are images of renewal—also invites difficulties. Expressions like "hommes de paille" have both literal and figurative senses. But other words, such as "gîte," "liesse," or "erre," have meanings that are better described as (1) general; and (2) referring to a specific context of experience: "erre" as momentum or, specifically, the momentum or speed of a ship; "gîte" as a dwelling or resting place, or as referring to the dwelling of an animal, etc. Where a number of these restricted meanings come together and repeat nuclear semes, we find a semiological isotopy (e.g., a ship sailing, an animal roaming) activating a sememic field. As we shall find, the semiological isotopies so produced do not follow the structuring of the poem proposed earlier. Just as nuclear figures dissolve in what Greimas calls the "negative isotopy" of poetry, here the event narrated gives rise to a number of events. These may be its aspects, signs, or images; but the interweaving of semiological isotopies (contexts of experience) redoubles, overflows, and includes the original relation of meaning to event that is the narration, depriving it of its originality.

Let us first take the winds literally and look for words in the poem which bear on the wind, its usual qualities and predicates (Riffaterre's "commonplace associations" of language). The first of these is "aire," in the sense of a direction of the "rose des vents," so that "vents . . . qui n'avaient d'aire" would be the peculiar phenomenon of a wind without direction. Confirming the image is "n'avaient . . . de gîte," taking "gîte" as a modulation of "lit" (the "lit du vent" of *Vents* I, 7). A second strand of meanings arises from the association of "vents" with "éventer." "Eventer" in the sense of exposure to the air is virtually an "enantioseme," a word with contrary meanings: some things are improved by exposure (grain), others suffer. (The poem will generalize this ambivalence.) Although few words apply directly to the wind, in other words of the poem we can readily find chains of associations that contribute to its *signifiance*. These edge the physical image closer and closer to the symbol; except that, as I have suggested, the poem complicates the distinction between symbol and physical phenomenon. For instance, "vents en liesse" seems to jump directly to a personification and to a symbolic statement, yet the expression may be a condensation of several idioms. One speaks of a "brise folle," a fickle wind that keeps changing direction ("qui n'avaient d'aire"); of a "vent fou" (linguistic associations need not maintain decorum; all levels of language participate) like these "très grands vents"; of a "vent de folie," producing the agitation we can see distributed throughout the poem: swirling winds everywhere ("par le monde"), "couraient," "quête," the upheaval of "soulèvement des grandes dalles publiques," the shaking of the "choses frémissantes" and the "arbre tressaillant," the "violence" (and cf. *Vents* II,6: ". . . Et du mal des ardents tout un pays gagné . . ."). To this link "vents"-"folie" we can add other associations. Two that intermingle are "folie"-"joie" ("fou de joie"), which with the image of agitation supports the celebration of "vents en liesse"; and "folie"-"ivresse" or intoxication. Here we might mention the "vin fou," the sparkling wine of the modern advertising slogan. This second link facilitates a whole cluster of images in *Vents*. The "liesse" of the winds is that of the "fêtes du vin" (I,2), the "fêtes du vent" (I,6), and the modulation "vent"/"vin" is used again and again in the poem. Striking images relate the motif of madness and intoxication to the theme of the poet-magus: "Homme infesté du songe, homme gagné par l'infection divine" (III,6), in which the higher spiritual state of poetic intoxication (divine madness) is contrasted to drug-induced hallucinations. Also relevant are "ivre, plus ivre . . . d'avoir renié l'ivresse" (I,3 and I,6), as well as the storm image of II,4: "Ivre d'éthyle et de résine . . .—comme . . . l'homme de langage."

These motifs of intoxication and intensity enter into a positive chain of affiliations, leading to images of celebration and passionate love: "un homme encore épris du vent, comme d'un vin" (IV,6; note "épris . . . vin" modulating the expression "pris de boisson"); the "fêtes du vent" mentioned above, and "La face peinte pour l'amour comme aux fêtes du vin" (I,2); "la face dans le vent" (I,6); "Et mon visage encore est dans le vent. Avec l'avide de sa flamme, avec le rouge de son vin" (II,2). It is in the web or context of these associations that we can read "de très grands vents sur toutes faces de ce monde," ". . . sur toutes faces de vivants," and "face brûlée d'amour et de violence" as condensations and ramifications of common images: wind burns ("le vent brûle"), one "brûle d'amour," we speak of the breath ("souffle") of life; to these elements we may add the rhyme "vents"/"vivants" ("vie" + "vents"), and the notion of the face as light or apparition, a mytheme stemming from the etymology of the word (cf. the Latin *fax*, pl. *faces*, "torch," and the fire imagery of *Vents* as a whole). The eroticization of the winds in the poem is in a sense already present in the configurations of the language (between Derrida's "system of language" and Greimas's "configurations of discourse").[9]

These same motifs have their negative side, which emerges in images of hostility and aggression, poison and venom (recalling Plato's *pharmakon*): the "virulences de l'esprit," "colère," "querelle," and "explosion" (I,3); the "mal des ardents" and the Poet "habité de son mal" (II,6; III,6), the anger of the prophet ("celui qui a morigéné les Rois," I,3); even in such an apparently innocuous image as the "colchique d'or" (I,6), beautiful but treacherously poisonous. In I,1 this aspect—less a group of semes than a group of semantic nodes or relays, a region of a larger network—occurs in the wilderness of winds "qui n'avaient garde ni mesure," with resonances of "ne pas prendre garde" and "n'avoir cure," as well as in imagery of decay and destruction. The violent reaction to a toxin or infection (cf. III,5), "le prurit de l'âme") is ambivalent; here it is manifested with the negative tone dominant in nauseating odors ("ce goût de paille et d'aromates") and in the phrase "Et le coeur nous levait/Aux bouches mortes. . . ."

What this fragment or tangent to a commentary proposes, beneath its deliberate lack of rigor, is a way of reading poetry. Although this conception of reading will, I hope, become clearer with further examples, we may sketch certain of its principles now:

(1) As the mention of the "colchique d'or" illustrates, reference enters into the production of meaning. A sememe is not just a dictionary definition (what dictionary?) but has a full "paradigm of characteristics" or associations attested by an encyclopedic dictionary, library of *usuels*, and the entire web of language in which the lexeme figures. No distinction is made between "cognitive" language and "literary" langue.

(2) The reader's production of meaning involves the (re-)construction of a network of associations, as in the analysis of a dream. These associations use displacements of various kinds: (a) Synonymic, as in "gîte" → "lit" or "brise folle" → "vent fou." (b) Phonic or homonymic, as in "vent" → "vin" or "vie" + "vents" → "vivants." We shall later consider more striking examples, such as "vents" → "vans" or "livrée" → "l'ivraie" → "ivre" → "l'autre hiver" anagrammatically (with another word, "livre," missing but conspicuous by its absence).[10] (c) Syntagmatic concatenations (*scies*), as in the wordgame of rapidly constructing strings such as "château d'eau, eau-de-vie, vie de chien, chien de fusil . . ."; here, as in "brise folle"/"vent fou" → fou de joie" → "joie de vivre," etc. (d) The etymological displacements familiar to readers of Perse.[11] (e) Semiological links belonging to a "sememic field" or code of discourse, as in "vents" → "aire." (f) Classematic dispersal, as when the semes of a word such as "folie," which is subjacent to *Vents* I,1 although it does not actually appear in it (it will appear more directly in other cantos), are paragrammatically distributed throughout the poem in the images of agitation we have mentioned and in images of a special spiritual state we shall examine later. (The components of dream and error—"aberrations" —appear prominently in I,3; but apart from the spiritual values of "icônes" and "fétiches," the "aberrations" in I,1 are principally physical.) Such a dispersal is composed of two operations: a shift, hyperonymic and then hyponymic, from whole (madness) to part (aspects of agitation), and from part to new whole (aspects of agitation to images of movement, searching, things shaking, etc.). (g) Semantic codes— mythemes, themes, motifs—that also support the associations of the web of language woven around the words of the poem. These include literary and social myths, such as the image of the poet as prophet, visionary, or shaman, and the theme of visionary madness or blindness ("aveugle-né"). (h) Contagion and semantic investment that foster associations, as happens in the normal procedure of semantic extraction, where one looks at words of a text that qualify the terms of an initial axis, then at all those modifiers occurring in conjunction with terms of the first cull, etc.[12] Here, rather than positing an initial axis, we start anywhere. The

eros associated with the wind in the tree image, the "désir qui va chanter," turns up later in the phallic verticality of the man standing in the
wind, the eroticization of the wind ("épris du vent") and of the face
("peinte pour l'amour," "dans le vent, avec l'avide de sa flamme, avec le
rouge de son vin"). In other words, by contagion and investment the
poem constructs its own symbolic objects and possibilities of substitution. This form of displacement resembles (f) and (g). It differs from
the first in that it operates on a larger scale, with elements of a vision
rather than semes of a sememe: a word carries the resonance of its
other contexts, even if it is not normally related to them in fixed expressions or "sememic fields" (again cf. Greimas's "configurations of discourse" and Derrida's "system of language"). This form of displacement also operates at a greater distance than (f). It differs from (g), as
it does from (e), in that the symbolic objects so created are not the
direct offspring of codes existing outside the text but are formed within
it.

(3) As for other principles of this reading, we may note that these
links involve the "commonplace associations" invoked by Riffaterre, although they are of greater variety. Riffaterre's somewhat confusing
assertion that "everything in the text happens at the level of the signifier.
The signified is completely subordinate to it"[13] might apply if we include the signified as also a signifier. In contrast to the linear chain of
signification that Riffaterre discovers, the above analysis develops a network. A sense of this unfolding construction inspires a number of the key
images of the poem having connections to a metalinguistic isotopy. Some
of these are images of ramification: the "arbre du langage," the "ramures" of lightning (I,6), and the "treille" and "arbre capillaire" of the
rivers (II,4), which recurs later in the "entraille femelle" (II,5). Other
aspects of the network appear in the swarm imagery running throughout
the poem: the "essaims" (I,1) (cf. those discussed by Derrida in "La
Double Séance" and *La Dissémination*) or the "mêlée d'ailes et de ronces"
(II,6); the rigging of the ship (I,6) or circus tent (I,3); the "mailles"
(II,3), the "filet du dieu d'en bas" (III,5)—an elegant image of the
unconscious—and "tresse" of the poet's "chant" (VI,5). Worth remem-
bering here is one of the first images of *Pluies*: "l'Idée nue comme un
rétiaire. . . ." The expansion of the network is the *propagation*, the system
of relays, so prominent in the poem: e.g., "propageant sur tous les sables
la salicorne du désir" (I,3).[14] It turns up elsewhere, for instance, in the
"Enlèvement de clôtures, de bornes" (I,6), as does also the condensation
(overdetermination) that creates the nexus of the image, "sur toutes
landes de merveille où s'assemblent les fables" (I,3).

(4) The associations that constitute the network resemble to a degree the operations of what Kristeva has labelled "signifying differen-

tials"; like these quanta of sound and meaning, the units involved in my discussion do not separate signifier and signified. (Derrida: "we must speak of the indissoluble union of the signifier and the concept signified," *Diss.*, p. 113.) They permit meaning to arise from what is often referred to somewhat mysteriously as a "logic of the signifier."

(5) In the network developed, isotopies are single arcs of meaning, connecting nodes or points of departure for the larger production of meaning. A pluri-isotopic reading is therefore of necessity a reduction of the text, substituting a part for the whole. Yet the text is not purely the "nonrepresentative form of organisation" that Goux defines; representation and referentiality are inscribed in the text, included in the network's production of meaning.

(6) In the kind of reading suggested, the poem is, where possible, opened to its literary and social context and to the universe of language in which it is situated. This principle is in accord with the notion of intertextuality set forth by Bakhtin and Kristeva. *Vents* I,1, as part of the larger poem *Vents*, provides a specially privileged illustration of the relation of a text to its context. We shall look later at myths and texts assimilated and transformed by the poem.

(7) The proposed reading includes but exceeds the semantic decoding described by Greimas. He explains that reading poetry is no different from the normal decoding of speech but for the factor of negative isotopy: semantic contexts are accumulated, and the receiver reconstructs from these the semantic hierarchy (*taxinomie*) of the sender. A knowledge of this hierarchy permits us to see the text as produced by the play of a basic set of semiotic constraints. While a semantic hierarchy can be found in *Vents* I,1 (the fundamental axis of which is Life versus Death), it is simply one orientation of the text, one component of its deep structure. In the kind of reading I have proposed, semantic contents of words are not fixed. Dictionary definitions are completed by their position within a network, by their connections to other words through sound and meaning in various contexts. Among other factors in Perse's work, signs are systematically perceived as enantiosemes (the same word meaning opposite things), which facilitates such formulas as "Ivre, plus ivre, disais-tu, d'avoir renié l'ivresse" (I,3). By extension, this term covers complexes of concepts in which an idea carries within it its opposite notion: a phenomenon studied most notably by Derrida in "La Pharmacie de Platon" (*La Dissémination*). Perse's poem flaunts its ambiguities: "A Poete, ô bilingue, entre toutes choses bisaiguës . . . homme parlant dans l'équivoque!" (II,6).

(8) In this reading the reader makes meaning. The text furnishes a grid from which to start, a grid already of considerable complexity. Meaning is made by the poet, first as reader and scribe of an unwritten

or partially written text, then as scribe and reader of his written text. Reading involves juggling several criteria: among them, a principle of parsimony which likes the shortest itineraries best and invites us to stick to the text; indices of frequency of occurrence; the power of a nexus perceived, the number of links it makes. "Meanings" themselves are not hermeneutic, but itineraries through the hypertext developed around and within the text.

For a glance at several kinds of itineraries, let us pick up our prematurely interrupted commentary and return to the literal image of the wind. A "vent" is also an odor—I am thinking not of flatulence, but of Littré's definition, "odeur qu'une bête laisse dans les lieux où elle a passé." One uses "flairer" to speak of sniffing the wind or a scent; "éventer" also has this sense (Littré: "flairer les émanations qu'apporte le vent"). Here we have a mini-"semenic field" beginning a code of experience that is a semiological isotopy. The sniffing winds of the poem reverse subject and object of this experience; also, in addition to something being exposed to the winds, the winds expose something. The wind transmits odors; here the transmission, normally passive, is rendered active, divided into the inhaling of "flairant" and the exhaling of "produisaient." The idea of transmission reappears in the tree image: "léguant, liant au vent du ciel," with the sense of *legare*, "send as a messenger." The poem uses what we might call a transformational grammar of experience: the winds— agents, motive forces, transmitters, the "heroes" of a mythical narration —carry odors that are signs, knowledge ("avoir *vent* de quelque chose," "*éventer* un complot"), and carry "ailes et essaims" (the subcontexts of which we shall return to later). Again, simple linguistic associations facilitate a movement from the literal to the symbolic.

These codes of experience involve the assembly of elements that are interconnected in the poem but not all disposed as a linear narration.[15] For example, the conjunction of "très grands vents" and "paille" immediately evokes the image of the wind scattering straw. Here we have images of force, then images of things shaking in the wind: "paille" is linked to the "choses frémissantes," compared in turn to a tree shaking in the wind, followed by images of things flying off into the wind. The image of things flying upward is reinforced by the presence of "soulèvement" and "levait." This interaction of wind and straw draws upon several semantic components of the poem. One is the *linear* motion (of the wind), which can be seen in "couraient" with a destination ("à leur office"); in the "erre" of a ship coasting, moving past us and away ("nous laissaient"); in the association of wind with a huge plane surface, a "face" of the world that is an ocean or plain across which the wind sweeps; in the linearity of "pistes" and transmission or *enchaînement* ("léguant, liant . . . filiales . . . lais et relais"). Another is a *chaotic* motion (of scattering straw, "ailes," etc.) that appears in the above-mentioned images of winds *without* direction, of agitation (we might add "crécelles" to those already listed), of "erre" suggesting "errer," and the search ("quête") everywhere. The two components of motion come together in the image of the swarm ("essaims") moving off. (There is here a "reading" of Baudelaire's clouds in "Le Voyage," of Lautreamont's starlings, as well as a "preview" of Derrida's Mallarmé and Sollers.) The swarm image is homologous to the implicit image of scattering straw. We find a center—tree, central square ("places"), "nous," central depot of civilization ("Offices," the Uffizi Gallery)—balanced against the circumference, the plurality of "par le monde." The shift into symbol is precipitated by an explicit symbolic investment of the "paille" motif: "nous, hommes de paille" or "hommes investis . . . paille," linking straw to a civilization and "En l'an de paille" to an era. All phrases have a metalinguistic dimension; an "homme de paille" is a figurehead, an empty symbol, as are the leaders symbolically "invested," while a year is a figure in a temporal code ("Tu te révéleras, chiffre perdu!" III,6). The symbolic charge increases with the religious overtones of "l'an de paille" (cf. "l'an de grâce," "l'an de Dieu"); while the era ("ère") appears also in "aire," "erre," and "tout un siècle." In other words, one narration—a semiological isotopy of winds sweeping in, lifting up and scattering straw, moving off—is correlated to the disruption of the "monde entier des choses," an image again manifesting the balanced centrifugal and centripetal forces referred to earlier (plurality of "choses"/"entier"). The visions are homologous: there is an explosion of straw, similar to things flying off the tree (an ejaculation of seeds, etc.), to the dispersal of markers in I,3, to the explicit explosions of the circus tent in I,3, of the ship in I,6, of the atom bomb (obliquely defined) in III,2 and III,3. This homology creates a free symbolic interchange: it becomes impossible to say what is a symbol of what.[16]

To see a least common denominator in all of these images deprives them all of symbolic content except by arbitrary and momentary (by context) investment. It reduces each of them to the same set of semantic marks (components, as I have termed them), a hieroglyph with the displacements that create a writing. We can treat each image as a symbol, but without establishing any symbolic hierarchy—each image inscribes the others. What we have then is a non-hierarchical symbolism that does not arrest the play of the poem's *signifiance*. This infinite interplay of homologous images recalls the épistémè of signification that Michel Foucault ascribes to the Renaissance.[17] We shall return to its implications later; for the moment, let us note that these "relais du plus haut verbe," in a *jeu de relais* that is also a paper chase or *jeu de piste* ("qui couraient . . . sur toutes pistes"), undermine the Logos, empty it of theological content. We have in Perse's work not "Dieu" but "le dieu," everywhere, lodging like a vacuous mobile mana in the "whole world of things," in the entire intertext of "rites" (I,2) and "fétiches" (I,1), created not by it but by the play of differences that is writing. The mentality is finally less that of Foucault's Renaissance than that of a "primitive" or "archaic" mind obeying the logic of the signifier.

To resume our commentary, however, let us assume the symbolic stance (the verticality) that is used by the poem (as an axis: *axis mundi*). To the literal isotopy of blowing wind, the poem joins an isotopy of winds as transcendent forces: (1) in the leitmotif "(très) grand(es)," "plus haut," . . . ; (2) in the motif of totality ("toutes faces," "toutes pistes," . . .) present in the plural forms and in the occurrence of items in pairs, often followed by a general term; also in the image of winds not confined to a single direction (roaming everywhere, "par le monde"); (3) in the image of unstoppable winds without resting place ("gîte," or "aire" as aery) or limit ("ni mesure"); (4) in the winds' heedlessness of man ("qui n'avaient garde"), their wildness ("ni mesure"); (5) in the image of a moral destination or function ("office") with religious overtones. This religious dimension continues within the tree simile, in "vent du ciel." The winds, transcendent and proverbially "insaisissables" (cf. the expression of impossibility, "lier le vent"), sweep through the mortal world of things "saisissables" and "périssables." The civilization is represented, as indicated earlier, by its centers, leaders, symbols, and monuments: "hommes investis," "places," "grandes dalles publiques," "Offices," "grands ouvrages de l'esprit," "icônes," and "fétiches." It also appears as a range or mixture of possibilities: "pourpre"/ "cilice" and "ivoire"/"tesson." The semantic axis of this isotopy is Life versus Death—the "vivants" on the one hand, the "hommes de paille" and images of death or decay on the other.[18]

The action of the winds is that of inspection ("flairant"), exposure ("éventer"), and transmission of signs ("produisaient" in its etymological sense). Thus, among general upheaval ("soulèvement des grandes dalles publiques"), there is an heroic quest ("quête"), in which an inner reality is made manifest: a reality first negative, in the "coeur" of "l'usure et la sécheresse," later positive. This transcendent force that brings forth, that produces, that expresses, enables the emergence of a new age— "tout un siècle s'ébruitait," in the sense of "se répandre dans le public" (Littré). Its ubiquitous quest is that of desire, of the life instinct itself. Here we may anticipate the wording of the theme in *Amers* 4.2: "Desir . . . O toi . . . ta quête est la plus vaste." But the transcendent production or expression is that present in the tree image, "où le desir encore va chanter," and concomitantly in the poem, "toute ma page elle-même bruissante." One subcontext (semiological isotopy)

Richard A. Laden

suggests that the life instinct is an "animal" instinct: the sememic field includes "aire" (as aery or territory), "gîte," "erre" evoking the "erres" of the stag (the stag that leaves his tracks elsewhere in *Vents*, in the "ramures" of I,6, the "menées" of I,5, etc., that has several relevant associations in myth); "couraient" as hunting, "pistes" as tracks, "éventer" and "flairant" as an animal sniffing, and "vents" as the scents of animals. Another subcontext links this search to the "hommes de paille" and "hommes investis" taken literally as straw guys: like that of Guy Fawkes" Day (prominent in Eliot's poem—see n. 18), the quest fits into the rites and symbols of agricultural mythology (we shall take up this aspect later).

We must nevertheless bear in mind that the ultimate validity of the opposition Life versus Death as a critical tool is undercut by the cyclism implicit in the poem and by the historiography of Part III of *Vents*. The most apparently unequivocal negative image is linked to a complex of positive images. For instance, the symbolic image "hommes investis," which is negatively connoted in "hommes de paille," is related to the "icône" or "fétiche," also to the images of the poet-magus, and in general to the ambivalence of vision, of the "songe," as both aberration and departure, life and death, truth and error. Like any *mark* of civilization (of life), the "hommes de paille" act as relays, motivating their ambiguous role in the calendar ceremonies of folklore. The expulsion of the straw guy recalls notably that of the *pharmakos*, of the kings who were also sacrificial victims. For this reason our symbolic hierarchy should be regarded as initial or superficial, except that these convenient terms wrongly imply an absolute origin or dimension of depth in what is a function of one's point of entry into the network of the text.

Provisionally, therefore, the quest is a cull: the transcendent force stimulates life, rejects death. Here the rejection occurs in "nous laissaient, hommes de paille" and in "le dieu refluait des grands ouvrages de l'esprit"; it is echoed by the nausea of "Et le coeur nous levait / Aux bouches mortes. . . ." A closer look at the semiological isotopies connected with death and decay will help to clarify the functioning of reference and oblique definition. A point that is overdetermined may or may not in turn determine its connections sufficiently; in the third paragraph of the poem the connections (images) are underdetermined, evoked obliquely. Among the agglutinated images of decay is the phrase "ce goût de paille et d'aromates."[19] Despite its usually positive connotations, "aromates" is negative here by association with "paille." This value is perhaps elucidated (a) by a passage in *Exil* VI—"celui, soudain, pour qui s'exhale toute l'haleine incurable de ce monde dans le relent des grands silos et entrepôts à denrées coloniales"; (b) by images of mummified Egyptian "bêtes de paille" in I,4 and the "fade exhalaison" there;

(c) by the odor of stored grain or hay that must be aired ("éventer").
We read the phrase in conjunction with "soulèvement des grandes dalles
publiques." "Dalles" evokes "dalles funéraires," and the tomb image
gains strength with the "bouches mortes" following. This image mixes
(like an enantioseme) two seemingly contrary elements, dryness ("la
sechéresse au coeur des hommes investis") and rot, as also in I,4. The
isotopy makes dead symbols—literally, embalmed corpses—of the
"hommes investis": cf. "hommes de paille" here and the "bêtes de paille
dans leurs jarres" (I,4). "Grandes dalles publiques" suggests both "la
voie publique" and a common grave or ossuary, as in a phrase of *Exile*
VI: "sous la ville, en lieu d'ossuaires et d'égouts." This last connection is
also possible here, with elements of the sememic field of a sewer: the
odor, "refluait," the "villes." In antiquity some sewers were covered over
with stone slabs ("grandes dalles"), particularly the *cloaca maxima* of
the Roman Forum ("places"). With the images of lifting up a slab,
noxious odors, and nausea, we can read "le coeur nous levait" as disgust
("dégoût"), suggesting, together with the following "bouches mortes,"
"bouches d'égout."

Other subcontexts can be perceived in this paragraph. We can read
"usure" as usury, "place(s)" as the financial center, and attribute the
collapse of a civilization to politico-economic factors. We can then bring
in the historical context of the poem (the end of World War II) or read
the historiography of Part III (e.g., "les hommes d'échange et de
négoce," III,2) as elaborating the enantioseme that is greed, the search
for force, and desire itself. In another subcontext, "bouches mortes des
Offices" metaphorically designates the arches of the Uffizi Gallery, perhaps the three huge archways on the main floor of the Arno facade. With
the noxious odors, "le dieu refluait des grands ouvrages de l'esprit" might
recall the periodic flooding of Florence. The paragraph would then have
a rather deep and obscure connection to the archetypal flood image—
used negatively here, but used positively later with the alluvial "lais et
relais du plus haut verbe." The image of the god withdrawing is, of
course, a common religious image of death.[20] Alternatively, we can take
"Offices" with "le dieu" as religious services in Cathedrals ("grands
ouvrages de l'esprit"); the "goût de paille et d'aromates" might evoke the
odor of incense (cf. n. 19), the "bouches mortes" those of priests inton-
ing the liturgy; and we could interpret the disgust as directed at an empty
form, a rite abandoned by the god—images which anticipate the
"Sérapéum" of I,4. If we chose not to reconstruct the references and read
only a symbolic least common denominator, we lose a great deal: the
secondary interconnections of the images, the structural homology and
contextual links that make possible metaphor and metonymy—expression itself.

The first part of the poem balances these images of death against signs of life: "liesse," "vivants," "Ah! oui . . ." and particularly the Pindaric theme of celebration ("couraient," "pistes," "nos plus grands versets d'athlètes, de poètes"). This semantic axis interacts with categories previously referred to as center versus periphery and centrifugal versus centripetal; it generates images of renewal as an emergence of the new from the envelope of the old. The isotopies of the poem are contexts in which the separation can take place, images of natural cyclism. One of these is the image of seeds in the seed pods waving at the tips of plants: the new "siècle," "dans la sécheresse de sa paille," in the tips or endings ("désinences," "bout") that are "cosses," "siliques," "choses fremissantes."[21] The passage concerning the tree continues the vegetation imagery. We shall try to disentangle the ramifications of its meanings, including those that have roots reaching back into the beginning of the poem.

The "grand arbre" is literally an old, tall, dry tree in winter ("de l'autre hiver"), standing in a grove ("quinconces"). Its appearance in winter symbolizes the dead age ("portant livrée de l'année morte"). The repetition of the death semes in "bois mort" strengthens the symbol, as opposed to the "bois mort" one gathers. "Hardes," "haillons," and "qui a fripé son patrimoine" are, in what Riffaterre would call clothing-code, the twisted dead leaves left on the tree ("'fripé" as "froissé" and suggesting "fripes," "fripier"), ragged remnants of the mantle of green. The color and the association between leaves and petals help determine "corolles de terre cuite"; any positive associations of "corolles" are erased by the parallelism "crécelles de bois mort" = "corolles de terre cuite." The death motif continues in "dépouilles," "spectres," and "léguant," while the poverty motif of "hardes" and "haillons" recurs in "pouillerie" and in the image of the beggar, the "mendiant" who has squandered his heritage ("qui a fripé son patrimoine") and who perhaps wanders, as in the Middle Ages, with his "crécelles." This humble condition, this servitude ("portant livrée") hides a different inner identity, the life force that will find expression. The image of a squandering desire refers obliquely to the parable of the prodigal son, if we compare "mendiant qui a fripé son patrimoine" to a passage in *Exil* III: "force errante sur mon seuil, ô mendiante dans nos voies et sur les traces du Prodigue." It also has mythic associations in a hermeneutic code—the wandering beggar who is actually a prince, prophet, angel, or god. The "quête" of the first part of the poem thus has its parallel here. "Face brûlée d'amour et de violence" is desire as an enantioseme, eros and thanatos: it shows the tree "consumed" with desire, i.e., both burnt out and destroyed by passion, and burning with passion.

The dead tree comes to life in the wind, its face like the "faces de vivants." A tremor and rustle of imminence herald the emergence of the new: motion, like the "choses frémissantes," in "tressaillant" and "berçant"; noise and the susurrus of the wind from the beginning of the poem (34 [s], 13 [z], 6 [ʃ], 2 [ʒ] even before the fourth paragraph), that occur here in a phono-semantic field compromising "s'ébruitait," "crécelles," "chanter," "bruissante," "lais," "verbe," "langage," "maximes" (as the longest plain-chant notes), "essaims," and murmurant murmure." This literal image of the tree shaking with the wind merges with another literal image of swarms ("essaims") of winged seeds ("siliques," "ailes") flying off into the wind. In this isotopy we read "corolles" as envelopes of seeds, the curious shape justifying "étranges désinences . . . icônes . . . fétiches." This sense is reinforced by a passage in *Vents* II,4: "parmi le million de fruits de cuir et d'amadou, d'amandes monstrueuses et de coques de bois dur vidant leurs fèves minces et leurs lentilles rondes, comme menuaille de fétiches." "Mendiant," accordingly, is read as "fruit sec." In this isotopy a key enantioseme is "vain," conveying both pride and emptiness. The seeds fly off in an act of generation (thus "filiales"), while the seed casings are left empty (dead "dépouilles et spectres").

Woven in with this isotopy is a related semiological isotopy of threshing and winnowing. "Vents" and "aire" evoke the "vans" and "aire" of primitive agriculture.[22] The enantiosemic "n'avaient d'aire"/"sur leur erre" is like the contradictory attribution to the winds of no direction and a moral direction: it suggests a global threshing floor. Perse elsewhere uses this image of winnowing for a violent destruction of the old era.[23] "Nous laissaient, hommes de paille" then gains the association of straw left on the threshing floor after the passage of gigantic flails (the winds), which send the spikes of the future flying off. The "hommes de paille" as straw guys recall the mythological dimension of traditional agriculture: the straw guy made at the end of the harvest or the last sheaf tied into such a shape,[24] symbolizing the "année morte" and occasionally carried into the village and exposed to the jibes of the inhabitants, like the "hommes investis . . . sur toutes places de nos villes." The isotopy is actually a fusion of threshing and winnowing.[25] In "paille" the poem includes the glumes or chaff; various dictionaries equate "(petite) paille" and "balle." The winds ("vans") separate the new ("le bon grain") from the tree's chaff of the dead year, the "livrée"—read "l'ivraie"—"de l'année morte." The "dépouilles et spectres de locustes" in this isotopy are the empty glumes of the spikelets left behind, according to Littré's definition: "locuste: terme de botanique. Epillet de certaines plantes graminées." To complete this code we detour through another isotopy. As the seeds move off in the wind or the grain in the winnowing-fan, the tree is left behind, "murmurant murmure d'aveugle-né dans les quinconces du savoir." These patterns of dots ("quinconces") bearing information ("savoir") evoke the Braille characters which the blind man ("aveugle-né") slowly deciphers, mumbling to himself ("murmurant murmure").[26] In the astonishing pun to which I alluded in my introduction, the "Braille" that the tree is left with becomes the "braille" of the empty grain hulls (Littré [1881], s.v. "braille": "balle du blé, séparee du grain"). From this emergence of the grain we can understand the "liesse" of the winds as its etymon: the joy of fertility and the celebration honoring the goddess Laetitia, rejoicing in the arrival of wheat in Rome.

Another isotopy of renewal is obtained by taking "locustes" as insects, *Locusta migratoria*, embodying the voracious search that is desire. Locusts also rise from apparent death: they develop in metamorphoses, casting off the old skin, and ultimately emerge as the adult insect. The isotopy includes this final molt: the adult insect is an "imago" or "image," putting "icônes" and "fétiches" in the sememic field. The triumphant completion of the "insecte parfait" justifies the pride of "vain de son lot. . . ." The dead "dépouilles" (Littré: "la peau rejetée par les serpents et les insectes lors de leur mue") preserve the shape of the living insect, whence "spectres." The key enantioseme here is "berçant": the tree lays the dead to rest (Littré: "bercer, endormir") but is also the cradle of the new. The living are sent off, just as locusts migrate ("ailes" and "essaims") in search of a better land when "sécheresse" has caused overcrowding. The "essaims" are explicitly the "filiales" we see here: "essaim: colonie d'abeilles sortant de la ruchemère pour aller chercher une autre habitation" (Littré). In the cycle of generation, the grain/seeds/insects are bequeathed to the wind ("léguant"), a new "patrimoine": sent as messengers, as noted above,[27] and delegated to found a new civilization. "Liant," suggesting an "enchaînement," stresses the continuity of life. "Lais et relais" supports the idea in several ways: (1) the image of tidemarks evokes a sequence; (2) "lais" suggests saplings left to regenerate a forest after timber is cut; (3) "relais" carries the meaning of "prendre le relais." Phonically, "relais" is the repetition "re-lais," while the alliterative [l] and the [ã] tie the passage together ("léguant, liant," etc.). The "lais et relais" also designate the new land, the alluvial soil prominent in the fertility cults of Osiris and later.[28]

This tree that symbolizes the endless renewal of life is the archaic *axis mundi*: World Tree, Tree of Life, and Tree of Knowledge are united in the iconography of the poem. We can read "icônes" and "fétiches" as the beliefs (symbols, traditions) of the past era, but there actually is a tree hung with religious images and bearing terra-cotta flowers ("corolles de terre cuite"): the Mexican tree of life decorated with pottery. Similarly, we have read "hardes" and "haillons" in other isotopies, but there is a tree adorned with rags that offers "oracles," that rustles in the slightest breeze: the *Ficus religiosa* or Indian tree of life.[29] The rags which "are symbolic of wounds and gashes in the soul"[30] suggest the destruction of the past, of the tree's fabric of the cosmos.[31] Other trees of life were decked with *oscilla* ("icônes," "fétiches"), and their rustling was oracular.[32] This "grand arbre" is syncretic, as are some mythic trees: it represents the "árbol de vida . . . florida" (cf. "corolles") and "el de muerte (o de la ciencia . . .) seco y con señales de fuego" (cf. "face brûlée"). In its references the poem here exploits the traditional association of trees of life with death and regeneration, with both rites of fertility and rites for the dead.[33] The Nordic Yule was both, and the Christmas of today combines this tradition with the Near Eastern one. Among other trees, the bedecked "grand arbre" evokes a Christmas tree and the Christian tradition in which the tree of life is the cross of Christ.[34] The connection, which might seem farfetched, is made by a tree in *Pluies* VI: "Moi je portais l'éponge et le fiel aux blessures d'un vieil arbre chargé des chaînes de la terre." The "crécelles" in this context recall their use during Holy Week: perhaps a Christian version of the noisemaker which announces the presence of the (sky) god ("vent du ciel") among the celebrants.[35]

The proliferation and underdetermination of the references are essential to the poem. They necessitate a syncretism that is, like the homologous series, at least common denominator, so that every reference can be considered an image of every other or of the whole series. All traditions come together in this tree, which is an image of the "siècle," the world, "langage" and "savoir," just as all things come together in the "monde entier des choses," and all isotopies and networks of associations come together in the poem. In its use of myth the poem "reads" a "text" that we might call the archaic mentality. This mentality appears in certain motifs which go deeper than the folklore of the harvest: one is the perception of a cosmic center or axis, and we can add this tree that joins ("liant") earth to heaven to the images of centers listed earlier. Another characteristic is the "sacralization of the *strange* object [respect] sacré à l'égard d'un objet *étrange*],"[36] seen here in the "étranges désinences," in the "locustes" as a prodigy of nature, and in the interpretation of great natural phenomena in general (mighty winds, a huge tree) as signs of a higher spiritual order ("arbre de magie"). Archaic rites of regeneration or spiritual initiation are an image of the original cosmogony: they imitate the primordial chaos of the *illud tempus* (in the orgy, etc.) from which creation emerged. We can see this "text" in the wildness of the winds, the agitation and upheaval they cause, the chaotic motion of the quest. In that the poem is an ejaculation of signs—sending out, in chaotic proliferation, words and images free to develop webs of associations among themselves—it is a triple imitation. As *énoncé* it "imitates" the archaic mentality, the rites and symbols that imitate the actions of the *illud tempus*; and as *énonciation* the poem imitates its content as *énoncé*. It is this imitation which *Vents* I,2 makes explicit: a program that becomes an implicit deconstruction of that (rite or symbol: signification of a sundered, ambiguous "origin") which it purports to repeat—"Et de tels rites furent favorables. J'en userai. Faveur du dieu sur mon poème."

Before examining the metalinguistic (and metasemiotic) isotopy of the poem, let us note what is perhaps its grandest "imitation" of an archaic text: the paragram of Biblical Creation. In Genesis the spirit of God—literally, the wind of God, *ruac'h elohim*—hovered over the face of the waters (*al-p'nai hamayim*). The verb used (*m'rac'hefeth*) means "hovered like an eagle." Here we find transcendent winds "sur toutes faces de ce monde," with water implicit in the image of a ship ("couraient . . . sur leur erre"), images of omnipresence, and "aire" as the aery of a bird (cf. *Exil* VII, "sur son aire l'aigle . . ."). In the Bible Creation occurs through acts of separation: light from darkness, heaven from earth, dry land from ocean (cf. "lais et relais"), day from night. In this poem antithesis ("pourpre"/"cilice," "ivoire"/"tesson," "vivants"/"morte") and acts of separation (threshing, winnowing, molting, seeds flying off, etc.) also mark a cosmogony. Finally, the "plus haut verbe" recalls the beginning of the Gospel of Saint John: "Au commencement était le Verbe."

This creation becomes, in the metalinguistic isotopy of the poem, a praise of poetic creation. As with the sacred trees mentioned above, the susurrus of the wind becomes oracular and poetic speech in this isotopy. The prophetic tree—magus, "arbre de magie"—is an "arbre du langage," center of the branching possibilities of language: a less symbolic hierarchy or semantic taxonomy than starting point of *signifiance*. Plant tips are word endings, "désinences"; the agitation of the world is a state of speech, a traditional image attested by the name of the poplar or *peuplier*, here suggested by the tree "peuplé." The tree's effort of generation is comparable to the poem taking shape on the "page bruissante"; its inner "désir" is a poetic impulse that will "sing" ("va chanter"). The tree, filled with images ("icônes"), transmits them (as adult locusts, imagoes or imagines), as does too the poet's page swarming with images and sequences of signs ("liant," "lais et relais" as tidemarks). This "chant" of desire is that of the "plus haut verbe." (Before turning to the implications of this formulation, let us read the isotopy through to its ambiguous conclusion.) The "arbre du langage," "aveugle-né dans les quinconces du savoir," is here too an enantioseme. On the one hand, left behind with its empty seed-casings and shells of locusts, it symbolizes the blindness of the old age, its "savoir" mere superstition ("icônes," "fétiches") or sterile complexity ("quinconces"). Its "murmure" is what *Vents* I,3 calls a "murmure de sécheresse," contrasting it to a "murmure et chant d'hommes vivants." Yet in another subcontext, the blind man reads prophetic signs ("oracles," "maximes"); with the "murmure" of the man reading Braille, the isotopy superimposes the prophetic tree in a sacred grove (like the oak at Dodona) on the traditional image of the blind prophet (cf. the end of I,3), who is closed to this life but attuned to a higher existence. The motif of blindness conveys as well the obscurity of the future, like the wandering of the "quête": the blindness of desire, not desire of a subject for an object, but desire, Lacanian "discours de l'Autre," for a transcendence that is always elsewhere, always absent. If life is wandering, the consciousness of life is witnessing the wandering of signs, straying beyond any code: "beaucoup de signes en voyage, beaucoup de graines en voyage" (*Anabase* X). The poet's accession to language—his experience of the world as text—necessarily involves the "imitation" I have alluded to. For psychoanalysis, "language implies that being is not just a copula but a return, a desire to return."[37] The poet therefore wanders *in* language and is surrounded by swarming signs, in a movement that is a return to a mythical archaic time: "voici que j'ai dessein d'errer parmi les plus vieilles couches du langage . . ." (Neiges IV). The tree "dans les quinconces du savoir" conveys the image of the observing eye surrounded by signs, each sign itself possessing a center and periphery or ramifications.[38] One wanders in the "quinconces" as in a maze; a passage in *Vents* III,3 states as much, given the homology between "quinconces" and a checkerboard: "Nous y trouvons nos tables et calculs pour les égarements nouveaux. Et c'est Midi déjà sur l'échiquier des sciences, au pur dédale de l'erreur illuminé comme un sanctuaire." Transmitting the signs he reads, the poet sends his poem off into the unknown—"Et nos poèmes encore s'en iront sur la route des hommes . . ." (IV,6)—with the ironic musing, "Et nos grands thèmes de nativité seront-ils discutés chez les doctes?"

Learned or not, the commentary predicted by the poem takes its place as the catechumen or "Ecoutant" beside the "maître" (I,2). What falls into the toils (*rets*) of the poem, if it is not to fuse with the poem, is an abridgment of itself: not the entire web of language that I began to spin around the "vents," but a pluri-isotopic reading, which despite its ramifications, subcontexts, and ambiguities, greatly limits the text, simplifying the interactions and cross-references possible among the constituents of its isotopies. For practical reasons it becomes, to use Barthes's term, "readable." But if this polysemy be taken, depending on our orientation, as either a coalescence of or starting point for a network of associations, the distinction between such a pluri-isotopic text and the infinitely plural text blurs, with isotopies furnishing the guts of the textual machine. Although this multifariousness appears implicitly in the "monde entier des choses," it extends beneath the surface of the text, beneath plurivariance and pluri-isotopy; and if prolonged, our commen-

Richard A. Laden

tary of the enunciation reaches a place that is not thematic ("thèmes de nativité") nor prescribed by the poem.

Let us return to the enunciation as sketched in what I have called the metalinguistic isotopy, where it, as Greimas says, "can be formulated as an utterance [enoncé] of a particular type . . . called the speech event [énonciation] because it includes another utterance as its object-actant."[39] This is the isotopy that identifies the poetic act with the quest of desire, that assimilates in Pindaric fashion the "athlètes" and "poètes," and portrays the poet as an "athlete" in the general sense of someone who struggles for a cause. Thus in certain utterances so far neglected in our commentary—the "Ah! oui . . ." and the exclamation point, for instance—the performative value of the utterance outweighs its information, or the act of quotation or anaphora counts more than the substance of the quotation. The struggle or search is that of the man standing in the wind. Having experienced these winds of renewal, this generation, the poet can write—generate his poem—and transform the "tu" of experience (the winds as interlocutor, for the "très grand cri de l'homme dans le vent" of I,6) into the third person of the narration ("C'étaient de très grands vents . . .") or into quotation: from "O toi, désir . . ." to " 'O toi, désir. . . .' " This is the symbolic project of the poem: to turn the infinite plurality of the "monde entier des choses," like the swarm, into a code, a movement of generation. From the chaos of the swarm or the wandering of the search, it posits the insects or seeds or winnowed grain as symbols of cosmic renewal, as it also posits the poet-observer, the central eye/I who is the subject of this pageant. The poet is in this respect reminiscent of Dante in Sollers's presentation,[40] who having lived the experience he narrates, having understood the nature and coherence of signs, founds the possibility of his writing upon this coherence. The union of actor and author permits us to imagine a modal sequence of the speech event. Its *vouloir* is here "désir," the "face brûlée d'amour et de violence," a blind "murmure" or "quête." Its *savoir* is semiosis, the association of a thing with a signifier, its perception of a symbolic relationship that is also a reading of an earlier text: "Et les textes sont donnés sur la terre sigillée. Et cela est bien vrai, j'en atteste le vrai" (II,6). The rôle of the poet is to translate what he knows ("son occupation parmi nous: mis en clair des messages" III,6). The poem is made possible—and here is the *pouvoir* of the speech event—by the coherence of signs, of subcontexts or isotopies that are homologous, allowing the metaphoric exchange or translation that is the expression of a meaning. Here, the experience of language—the simultaneous convergence and dispersal of isotopies, the proliferation of references that come together to overdetermine meanings—is homologous to the convergence and dispersal of the "monde entier des choses." The expression—the text—is the poet's "chant": the *faire* of the speech event, the interweaving of isotopies in the textual grid from which the reader must in turn make meaning. *Vents* IV,5: " 'Et à la tresse de son chant vous tresserez le geste qu'il n'achève. . . .' "

To appreciate the consequences of this modal sequence, we must return to Greimas's statement regarding the speech event and restore what was initially omitted: "Either the speech event is a non-linguistic performative act, in which case it lies outside the purview of semiotics, or else it is in some way or other present in the text—as an implicit presupposition, for instance—in which case the speech event can be formulated. . . ." What is in question here is the "présupposé implicite," the *savoir* and *pouvoir* of the speech event: a logical linking that is the construction of a sign, a semiotic act. Yet it is not, despite what Greimas says, an "utterance of a particular type," an "utterance called the speech event because it includes another utterance as its object-actant," for such an "utterance called the speech event" is what we have called the metalinguistic isotopy or isotopy of enunciation. This isotopy sutures the developing poem to the prior utterances by analogy or sign ("ne voilà-t-il pas déjà"); but there is a logically anterior speaking subject who sees signification or analogy as possible: a situation presupposed or implied by the weaving of the "monde entier des choses" into homologous isotopies. And beneath this subject there is another virtual or absent center: that of what Derrida calls the "system of language," of the connections which provide the materials of meaning.

Such an underlying condition of enunciation seems to place the poem in the symbolic category of a typology of discourse, by a convergence of isotopies recalling Dante and Foucault's description of the Renaissance épistémè. Yet this symbolic unity, this origin, is subverted by the poem, along with the unity of the subject observing. Despite the "lais et relais du plus haut verbe," in the poem there is no symbolic relationship in which all the signs of the world are the images of a single higher (divine) truth or presence. If seeds or insects are signs of renewal, renewal is not a goal but a quest, a movement toward some kind of truth or transcendence that is assumed but never attained: the un(ful)fillable *manque* that is desire. For the poem to be symbolic, we would have to imagine a God (as He appears in the work of another modern poet, Jean Grosjean) who is not the fixity of a Logos but (always already) separation from Himself and movement toward Himself, who is, like any sign, a mixture of opacity and transparency; a deferment/difference or archi-trace out of Derrida. The endless quest, the un(ful)fillable *manque—tonneau des Danaïdes*—is a decentering, or rather, a de-termination of symbolism. We can see this best in IV,2. The search there continues westward, always "Plus loin! plus loin!" But the revelation of the "face nouvelle" is always beyond, losing itself in the emptiness of the ocean. ". . . Et au-delà, et au-delà, qu'est-il rien d'autre que toi-même—qu'est-il rien d'autre que d'humain?" Instead of the symbolic term, the transcendence, we find only the sign, the movement-toward, the writing that is desire. But without a symbolic term the movement-toward becomes a "return, a desire to return" (Safouan, see n. 36), a search for a unity mysteriously lost: "'Tu te révéleras! chiffre nouveau'" (III,3) becomes "'Tu te révéleras, chiffre perdu!'" (III,6). The unified self dissolves into the "monde entier des choses," for the movement-toward of symbols of transcendence is equated to the movement that underlies desire and creates it out of a play of memory-traces. "Mais si tout m'est connu, vivre n'est-il que revoir?/. . . Et tout nous est reconnaissance. Et toujours, ô mémoire, vous nous devancerez, en toutes terres nouvelles où nous n'avions encore vécu./Dans l'adobe, et le plâtre, et la tuile, couleur de corne ou de muscade, une même transe tient sa veille, qui toujours nous précède; et les signes qu'aux murs retrace l'ombre remuée des feuilles en tous lieux, nous les avions déjà tracés" IV,2).

For these reasons *Vents* is less a poem of symbol than of symbolization, of desire as a creation of signs that are symbolically invested. The tree displays the process, emitting signs of the "plus haut verbe" that are the construction, the "chant" of desire. In its proliferation of contexts, in its manifold references to traditional symbols and beliefs, the poem illustrates the possibility of mythifying anything in the "monde entier des choses."[41] What authorizes the mythification is not a theological center or logos, but a language within that makes possible the symbolic substitutions of traditional cults. By the imitation I have described, the poem is not syncretically religious but offers rather a religion of religion. With respect to an origin, the poem suggests instead what amounts to an endless regression: the illimitation of the homologous series, the search which is a *fuite en avant* ("Plus loin! plus loin!") toward a transcendence which always takes the form of signs anticipating itself. (The divine manifestation is never a presence, always a sign—"chiffre perdu" or "nouveau"—or else an opaque mask: "Plus d'un masque s'accroît au front des hauts calcaires éblouis de présence" [II,6].) But the signs also constitute an (infinite) regression: signs of signs of signs, imitation of an imitation of an imitation. "Tout nous est reconnaissance . . . une meme transe tient sa veille qui toujours nous précède. . . ." What constitutes the "origin" is not a presence but a difference, an interaction: the *frayage* or writing of the body that is here evoked by the image of the man standing in the wind: the image of desire. In this endless and un-original movement we can see the underlying principle of what I have called the "temporal paradox" of the poem: the desire that leads to desire, the quest that culminates in a quest, the enunciation that precedes itself. What precedes us in our search is simply the world, and the possibility, created by language, of perceiving it as writing. The swarm image ("essaims") of the poem suggests not (or not only) that we see the physical images as symbols of life, subsuming the isotopies of the poem in an opposition of sememe-actants Life versus Death; but rather, that we see Existence (Life and Death) as a context realizing the play of marks that is writing. If writing is a net, the components of this play are the nexus, point of condensation of marks, the intensity that is a multiple approach to the Same—symbolically, the omnipresent signs of transcendence— and the divergence or set of marks (of references) present in any object, in the multiplicity of its associations (displacements) or codes within which it figures. "Existence" is thus formed from the convergence of eros and the dispersal of thanatos. "Life" is the search leading outward in all directions, the net expanding and weakening as it expands "dans de plus larges mailles, et plus lâches . . ." (II,3: image of the lassitude of the South), to the exhaustion of its movement: ". . . Et l'homme en mer vient à mourir. S'arrête un soir de rapporter sa course" (IV,2).

The status of the symbol in *Vents* I,1 may help guide us through the genotext or deep structure of the poem. In view of what I have proposed so far, the genotext should be construed not as a formula but as a three-dimensional network, consisting of possibilities of interaction among various planes of connections. Let us now consider these various planes.

(1) A symbolic plane, involving (a) a semantic hierarchy dominated by the opposition Life versus Death, doubled (as a *doublure* or inner lining) by its mirror image; and (b) what we might consider domains of experience or sememic fields, especially when these involve interactions between man, nature, and the divine: e.g., nature and the divine in the tree of life, man and nature in agricultural imagery, etc.

(2) Aspects of the network as propositional sequences, establishing an alternation of convergence and divergence—energy of a point gradually increasing, leading to an explosion; movement outward, dispersal; a new gathering, and repetition of the cycle (such as the oscillations of certain stellar phenomena)—or, as linear motion (a one-dimensional projection of the cycle), an explosion and departure; a movement exhausting itself or trailing off into a suspension; a new intensification of an approached point; and a new generation and departure. These sequences form the motion inherent in the various contexts of imagery of the poem; these either convey the whole cycle or a stage of it.

(3) A modal sequence *vouloir-savoir-pouvoir-faire* applied to the

Richard A. Laden

preceding movement, either to the whole or to a stage of its progression. Interiorized, action becomes the emotional progression that culminates in the "chant."

(4) A pragmatics, in which the objects that are images of the movement participate in various cultural codes in addition to the inherent motion just indicated. This pragmatics includes actional sequences which support the narrative aspect of the poem. The interaction of this pragmatics and the propositional sequences referred to in (2) produces what Greimas calls "configurations of discourse" and "figurative sequences" (*SNT*, p. 172).

(5) A hermeneutic code of enunciation, in which an image is progressively "unfolded" by the poem, which approaches a symbolically-invested aspect of the image as an inner mystery. (The presentation of the "grand arbre" is an example.)

(6) The intertext of the poem. We have mentioned certain earlier texts "read" by *Vents* I,1—Eliot's "The Hollow Men," the Bible, images of romantic and symbolist poetry, images of *Les Chants de Maldoror*, various archaic myths and customs of folklore. We can add further examples: the Vergil of the *Georgics* or the "Pollo" ("Adspice venturo laetantur ut omnia saeclo . . ."), or certain Greek lyrics, particularly the Pindaric odes. In addition to their vocabulary or style (and the traditional style of the French *version latine*), such texts offer the poem their semantic content and their propositional or narrative sequences.

(7) Principles of linguistic association such as I have set forth at the beginning in relation to the network of language around the poem: phonic links, syntagmatic links, synonymic and homonymic shifts, etc.

(8) Principles of poetic flow. The meaning of this vague term may be clarified by examples. One principle is mimetic: the first two paragraphs convey the sweep of the winds, using long lines, a series of shorter phrases linked by repetition of words and assonance, and relatively short phrases that prolong themselves in suspension points. The effect is a wave-like movement that crests and then trails off into the distance. The third paragraph initially continues the broad narrative sweep, but interrupts the movement in the third line with the end of the sentence; the next sentence breaks awkwardly in the middle, and the result is a group of short phrases that hang in the air, imitating the image of upheaval and disruption to form a mimetic contrast with the energy of the sweeping movement that went before. If the break after "levait" constitutes a pivot, the longer sentence ending the paragraph comes as a kind of countermotion, reinforcing the image of "refluait." This mimesis again symbolically sutures the speech event to the context of the utterance. It may be seen again in the "vertical" presentation of the tree as a

repeated axis with ramifications of imagery. We may examine another aspect of poetic flow by reading the poem linearly, taking it as not merely representational but cinematographic, as a series of shots, each with a certain breadth of vision. In the beginning of the poem there is an interaction between the semantic content on the one hand, and the convergent-divergent movement as a form of poetic flow (beyond the inherent motion of the imagery mentioned above). We can take the long first line as a long shot or overview; the shorter phrase following, with its repetition, would be a closer look at the same subject, a medium shot; next, the details, aspects of the subject, would correspond to a still closer focus; the following "nous" would represent a center, the object of the preceding convergence of focus; then the repetition of "Baille," "paille," with the longer second phrase seeming an expansion of the first (semantically, "an" expands "hommes"), and the movement then resuming, trailing off into suspension points as if the camera were pulling back in a long shot and fade-out. The convergence-divergence of the movement would then support the meaning, confirming the idea of a worthless center that is rejected, left behind in the movement-away of the "erre." The worthless center is a negative or failed center: the center without the normal intensity of convergence, the center that does not generate or explode or disseminate. Yet in another isotopy (threshing and winnowing), the center *is* present in "nous, hommes de paille"; it is symbolically charged, but hidden or implicit—the grain, the emergence of which underpins the poem later.

These structural principles create connections that probably have varying degrees of "depth." The figure of the network clearly dominates them, as a genotext that projects itself onto the phenotext or surface structure; and the kinds of connections I have suggested are perhaps realizations of the network at intermediate levels below the surface structure of the text. The above list should be taken as an hypothesis sketching lines of further research. Yet it is clear from it that given the multifarious infrastructure of the text, any purely semantic reading, like any critical reading confined to a single plane or cross-section of *signifiance*, must arbitrarily limit the object of its inquiry in order to preserve its closure as a science.

Nevertheless, we may envisage here, among directions of further research, a defense of semantics that would bring into sharper focus the polarization we might label Greimas versus Derrida or polysemy versus dissemination. At issue is the sememe: if the sememe is limited, then meanings are stable and a semantic taxonomy is possible. Greimas's semantics would then be structural, although less in the modern sense than as an eighteenth-century sort of tabulation or hierarchy, participating in that classical épistéme Foucault describes. For Derrida, however, a meaning is not closed and unitary, but the locus of production of differences: what he calls the "same that is not identical . . . the medium in which opposites oppose each other" (*Diss.*, p. 145). In this way I have tried to speak of the referent—which may be a thing, an arbitrarily delimited idea, or the graphic and phonic substance of a word—as a nexus of a net, a relay of propagation. Greimas would perhaps counter by introducing true temporal and spatial dimensions into what should be an atemporal and aspatial net, so that rather than propagating an original divergence, a sememe would complicate itself in context by adding, in a second stage, semes that are outside its essence—auxiliary quantities or information not intrinsic to the definition of a word—or else by uniting itself to its opposite or to related sememes through the relay of a lexeme. From a Derridean perspective, the distinction between inside and outside, upon which hangs the closure of the sememe as a dictionary item, uses metaphysical categories that no longer pertain, since they are produced by the same movement of *différance* that simultaneously creates and dissolves the sememe in its play of differences. A critical judgment cannot decide (*krinein*, cut), cannot be certain. My description of meaning as an itinerary should be correlated to this view that "the syntactic composition or decomposition of the sign vitiates the distinction between inside and outside" (*Diss.*, p. 250).

To the fusion of signifier and signified (I have referred to the *pharmakon sign*, hoping to indicate by this expression that we must speak of the *indissoluble* union of a signifier and a signified concept," *Diss.*, p. 113) Greimas would oppose the separation of a lexeme and the several sememes (related or antithetical) to which it corresponds. Yet what for Derrida is a system of language that exceeds semantics[42] exists for Greimas, albeit as a secondary set of connections, of "configurations of discourse" linking already constituted sememes. Addressing himself to the question of the "éventail" or "blanc" in Mallarmé, Greimas would not see even in articulation and spacing a "non-sense" (*Diss.*, p. 284). While this "blanc" might also differ for him from the "polysemic series," he could invoke another isotopy, metalinguistic or more accurately metasemiotic, into which the "plus" or "surcroît" would fit. It would represent what he calls a "relational seme" not included in the semic content of the words it links. We can best grasp what separates Derrida's dissemination from Greimas's polysemy if we reread together with "La Double Séance" the brief section on the heterogeneity of discourse and the "manifestation of relations" in *Sémantique structurale* (pp. 39–41).

The preceding approach to Perse's "essaims" and "relais du plus haut verbe" has explored this difference not as a gulf but as an articulation: both joint and separation. It has been encessary to weave back and forth between the two, in addition to proceeding straight down avenues of meaning, in this deconstruction of the textual surface, this at least partial (re)construction of the web which could not be constructed if it did not already exist. As Saint-John Perse's poem projects the network from its deep structure onto its surface structure, I have here, by an approach that mimes its subject at the risk of entangling itself in its arguments, tried to expand and unfold the text so that we see not the contours of the poem but the poem enmeshed in a way of reading poetry. Perhaps a traditional criticism will deem this reticulum ridiculous, finding in it no net gain; but perhaps others interested in ties between critical theory and critical practice may see in it a *rets* of hope.

NOTES

1. A. J. Greimas, *Sémantique structurale* (Paris: Larousse, 1966), hereafter *SS*. All translations of this and other French texts are my own, unless otherwise indicated.

2. François Rastier, "Systématique des isotopies," in *Essais de sémiotique poétique*, ed. A. J. Greimas (Paris: Larousse, 1972), pp. 80–106.

3. Claude Chabrol, *Sémiotique narrative et textuelle* (Paris: Larousse, 1973), p. 28. Hereafter abbreviated *SNT*.

4. The poem is a text in Kristeva's sense: "Let us designate as a *text* any linguistic practice in which the operations of the genotext appear in laminar form in the phenotext, so that the phenotext serves as a projection of a genotext and invites the reader to reconstruct from it the entire signifying process. The concept of the text, although particularly applicable to that so-called modern literature that rejects the classical canon of representation, need not exclude certain older texts characterized by a less deliberate or systematic transposition of the genotext into the phenotext." ("Quelques problèmes de sémiotique littéraire à propos d'un texte de Mallarmé: 'Un Coup de dés,'" in *Essais de sémiotique poétique*, p. 216.)

5. See, for instance, Michael Riffaterre, "L'Explication des faits littéraires," in *L'Enseignement de la littérature*, ed. Doubrovsky and Todorov (Paris: Plon, 1971), p. 348f.; and Riffaterre, "Interpretation and Descriptive Poetry: A reading of Wordsworth's 'Yew-Trees'" (hereafter *IDP*), *New Literary History* 4, no. 2 (1973): 229–47.

6. Jonathan Culler, *Structuralist Poetics* (Ithaca, N.Y.: Cornell University Press, 1975).

7. Jean-Joseph Goux, "Numismatique II," *Tel Quel*, no. 36 (Winter 1969), p. 59; I was reminded of this article, quite different from the present one, by Derrida's quotation of this passage in *La Dissémination*.

8. See the typology of discourses proposed by Sorin Alexandrescu in "Le Discours étrange," *SNT*, p. 94.

9. Derrida, *La Dissémination* (Paris: Larousse, 1973), p. 149 (hereafter *Diss.*); Greimas, "Les Actants, les acteurs et les figures," *SNT*, p. 170.

10. The network of language I am describing here is, in fact, according to Roger Little, at the origin of the poem. To the possible surprise of those who find Perse's work more noteworthy for the preciosity of a *bien-dire* than for Joycean wordplay, Little informs us that "Each page of the *brouillon* is pain-

stakingly worked over so that finally it is studded with blocks of words growing out of each other, linked by short connecting lines of words. . . . Thus one might find the following words grouped (with others we can only imagine) before they are chosen to take their place in 'Exil', III:

ressac	aile	aigle	grève
l'accès	aire	angles	glaive
	tire-d'aile	aigres	
		naître	

The substitutions are based on senses as well as sounds" (Roger Little, *Saint-John Perse* [London: Athlone Press, 1973], p. 112). Little speaks of the "extraordinary network" of the draft and informs us that "the later manipulation and reduction of what Perse considers to be his real poetry is for him inferior donkey-work, necessary only to satisfy the demands of publishers and friends who recognise that the reader will expect a single line of printed text." I regret that other preoccupations of this present article preclude dealing with the phonic aspect of the network except in certain cases where it has semantic value; but the reader can easily glimpse such modulations as "aire" ("ère")-"ailes"-"filiales," "cilice" ("haire"-"hère")-"siliques," etc.

11. See Pierre-M. van Rutten, *Le Langage poétique de Saint-John Perse* (The Hague: Mouton, 1975), pp. 103–7.

12. The model is Greimas's reworking of Yücel's study of Bernanos in the last chapter of *Sémantique structurale*.

13. Riffaterre, "L'Explication des faits litteraires," p. 346.

14. A propagation, by what we might spell as markottage, in "lais et relais": a dissemination that follows the play of the Latin *pro-pango*, driving outward while driving in the nail, the mark to be surpassed (the relay); a forward to a work of which it is itself a moment; a desire, the relay of which is today the *page*.

15. Rastier, "Systématique des isotopies," p. 82: "An isotopy is defined syntagmatically but not syntactically; it is not structured. . . ."

16. Cf. Derrida on Mallarmé (*Diss.*, p. 290): "Tout devenant métaphorique, il n'y a plus de sens propre et donc plus de métaphore. Tout devenant métonymique, la partie étant chaque fois plus grande que le tout, le tout plus petit que la partie, comment arrêter une métonymie ou une synecdoque? Comment arrêter les *marges* d'une rhétorique?"

17. Michel Foucault, *Les Mots et les choses* (Paris: Gallimard, 1966), esp. pp. 32–59.

18. One of the texts "read" by the poem is T. S. Eliot's "The Hollow Men." With respect to the "hommes de paille," we should note Perse's translation of part of this poem, printed in *Commerce* in 1924 (reprinted in the Pléiade edition of Perse's work, p. 465); it begins, "Nous sommes les hommes sans substance, nous sommes les homme faits de paille. . . ."

19. Cf. "ce parfum d'humus et de benjoin," *Pluies* VIII.

20. In a Christian context, cf. Leon Bloy: "Quand vient la minute, l'insaisissable point qu'on nomme la mort, c'est toujours Jésus qui se retire." The choice of "refluait" to describe the departure of the godhead recalls images of the water of life, the sea as the origin of creation, etc., such as the mention in *Vents* I,5 of the Babylonian god Ea, god of the abyss and progenitor of civilization. In connection with the "ouvrages de l'esprit" from which the godhead withdraws, we might note the association with the title of the first section of

La Bruyere's *Caractères*, suggesting the moralist looking at his society.

21. Cf. III,2: "agiter le futur dans ses cosses de fer."

22. "Van" and "vent" have the same root, and the number of forms showing alternation between "vent-" and "vann-" continues the close relationship between the two: "vannage" or "ventage," "vannure" or "venture," "vannelle" or "ventelle," etc.

23. "Vannez, vannez, à bout de caps . . . ," he wrote in *Pluies* V: "Et qu'on évente. . . ."

24. James Frazer, *The New Golden Bough*, abridged from the original and revised by T. H. Gaster (New York: Criterion Books, 1959), pp. 249–70 and 404–44 passim; see also Mircea Eliade, *Patterns in Comparative Religion*, trans. Rosemary Sheed (1958; rpt. ed., New York: World, 1971), pp. 340–41.

25. The winds as threshing flails separate the "balle" from the "tiges" or "paille," whereas the winnowing-fan separates the wheat from the chaff, the heavier wheat remaining in the basket while the lighter fragments of the "balle" are blown away. The winds as "vans" could carry away the grain in the basket, the straw having been left on the threshing floor; but the winds as "vents" carry away the chaff and leave the grain.

26. This image was pointed out by Arthur Knodel, *Saint-John Perse* (Edinburgh: Edinburgh University Press, 1966), p. 107.

27. Gaffiot *(legare)* notes A. Gellius, *verba ad aliquem legare*; cf. "léguant . . . plus haut verbe."

28. Littré, S. V. "lais": "alluvion, ce que la mer ou une rivière donne d'accroissement à un terrain. . . . On dit fort souvent au lieu de lais simplement, les lais et relais de la mer." The Larousse adds "et qui est mis en culture."

29. See E. O. James, *The Tree of Life, Numen* supplements, no. 11 (Leiden: E. J. Brill, 1966), p. 24.

30. Cirlot, *A Dictionary of Symbols*, trans. Jack Sage (New York: Philosophical Library, 1972), s.v. "Rags and Tatters."

31. James, *The Tree of Life*, p. 159.

32. Mentioned by Vergil. Some related sacred trees: trees with hanging images of Helene "Dendritis," Artemis, Charila, or Erigone, the Chinese *k'ung sang*, the Norse Yggdrasil, the *Ficus ruminalis* of the Roman Forum, the Mayan tree of the Palenque slabs, the trees of Mohenjo-Daro, the sacred oak of Dodona. See Eliade, James, and also L. R. Farnell, *The Cults of the Greek States* (Oxford: Clarendon Press, 1909), esp. v. 5.

33. The tree of the Dionysiac cult was connected with the death and regeneration of Dionysos. The Mexican tree-of-life pottery has a related symbolism; this sometimes Christianized representation of Mother Nature and her creatures is usually made as censers or candelabra, especially for the Mexican Day of the Dead. Despite the occasionally macabre accoutrements of such festivals, they are actually fertility rites. Many celebrations united harvest rites or fertility rites and funerary elements. See Francis Toor, *A Treasury of Mexican Folkways* (New York: Crown Publishers, 1947), passim; Eliade, *Comparative Religion*, pp. 350–352.

34. Cf. Ambrose, *De Isaac*, 5, 43, quoted by Eliade, in *Myths, Dreams, and Mysteries*, trans. Philip Mairet (New York: Harper, 1967), p. 67.

35. Cf. the Australian bullroarer or the rhombos of Greek mysteries.

36. Mircea Eliade, *Forgerons et Alchimistes* (Paris: Flammarion, 1956), p. 26.

37. Moustafa Safouan, *Le Structuralisme en psychanalyse* (Paris: Seuil, 1968), p. 41.

38. The tree in the "quinconces du savoir" exemplifies a figure commonly used by Perse for isolated seekers after knowledge. Cf. the "Algébriste au noeud [X] de ses chevaux de frise" in *Vents* III,4, or certain "Princes de l'exil" in *Exil* VI. Significant for the present dsecription of language as a network or web is the image of the spider in *Vents* III,4: "le Contemplateur nocturne, à bout de fil, comme l'épeire fasciée."

39. *Essais de sémiotique poétique*, p. 20.

40. Philippe Sollers, "Dante et la traversée de l'écriture," in *Logiques* (Paris: Seuil, 1968), pp. 44–77.

41. Jean-Marie Le Sidaner has written of "the operation of taking stock of and decentering myths which, in view of Perse's position as a poet writing within the Western tradition, suggests an attempt to deconstruct or rather fragment the linear unity of the Logos"; he speaks too of Perse's "lecture deconstructive des mythes" ("Saint-John Perse, à rejouer," *Sud* 12 [Spring 1974]: 106, 107).

42. Derrida speaks of "the system of the language," of "associative forces," of "hidden forces of attraction." One wonders whether this nineteenth-century scientific metaphor is inevitable. (The present essay is not exempt from it.) Denis Guenoun raised an important issue when he accused Kristeva of using certain terms as "scientific hocus-pocus" ("A Propos de l'analyse structurale des recits," *Linguistique et Littérature*, spec. no. of *La Nouvelle Critique*, Cluny Colloquium of April 1968, p. 69).

SEVEN

ABYSMAL INFLUENCE:
BAUDELAIRE, COLERIDGE, DE QUINCEY,
PIRANESI, WORDSWORTH
Arden Reed

Devant vos profondeurs j'ai pâli bien souvent
Comme sur un abîme ou sur une fournaise,
Effrayantes Babels que rêvait Piranèse.
        Hugo, "Les mages"

CRITICISM has always been concerned with delineating traditions, with tracing antecedents. In writing the history of Modernism, for example, critics inevitably refer to the influence of the nineteenth-century French *symbolistes* on poets like Eliot. The *symboliste* movement is said to begin with Baudelaire, and Baudelaire in turn is ultimately influenced by some of Coleridge's speculations. (This already raises the question of where to stop: with Coleridge? with Schelling, Schiller, or the Schlegels? with Plotinus? with Plato?) While no one has shown that Baudelaire ever actually read Coleridge, it is not difficult to establish filiations between them, one via De Quincey, another via Poe (and Poe's reference to *The Night-Side of Nature* by one Catherine Crowe).[1]

What literary histories like this one presuppose is of course the notion of influence. More specifically, they presuppose a certain kind of influence, the kind critics have examined most often, namely, the unidirectional influence of an earlier writer on a later one. (One might contrast, say, the influence of reading one text on the reading of another, a variety that is not historically bounded. How is one's sense of Browning altered by having read Kafka, for instance?)[2] The job of literary history so understood is to write a genealogy, to draw a family tree, in short, to trace a line of influence. But it may not always be possible to trace a line. There may be times when that line gets hopelessly tangled in a labyrinth or lost in an abyss.[3] The instance of Coleridge and Baudelaire that I have mentioned is an example, for the rhetoric of history or cause and effect will account for some textual relationships between these poets but not all of them. To characterize the remainder it will be necessary to supplement the notion of cause and effect with the "notion" of involuntary and uncontrollable repetition, and with something like a rhetoric of the uncanny.

If one wanted to do a *Quellenforschung* of this relationship one would probably begin with the *Confessions of an English Opium Eater*, since Baudelaire translated it in the *Paradis artificiels*. And one would no doubt concentrate on the solitary mention of Coleridge in De Quincey's text, the passage in which Coleridge tells De Quincey the story of Piranesi. But just where one is confidently following the line of influence, the text itself inscribes a labyrinth, doubling and redoubling the line, folding it over and in on itself:

> Many years ago, when I was looking over Piranesi's *Antiquities of Rome*, Mr Coleridge, who was standing by, described to me a set of plates by that artist, called his *Dreams*, and which record the scenery of his own visions during the delirium of a fever. Some of them (I describe only from memory of Mr Coleridge's account) represented vast Gothic halls: on the floor of which stood all sorts of engines and machinery, wheels, cables, pulleys, levers, catapults, etc. etc. expressive of enormous power put forth and resistance overcome. Creeping along the sides of the walls, you perceived a staircase; and upon it, groping his way upwards, was Piranesi himself: follow the stairs a little further, and you perceive it come to a sudden abrupt termination, without any balustrade, and allowing no step onwards to him who had reached the extremity, except into the depths below. Whatever is to become of poor Piranesi, you suppose, at least, that his labours must in some way terminate here. But raise your eyes, and behold a second flight of stairs still higher: on which again Piranesi is perceived, by this time standing on the very brink of the abyss. Again elevate your eye, and a still more aerial flight of stairs is beheld; and again is poor Piranesi busy on his aspiring labours: and so on, until the unfinished stairs and Piranesi both are lost in the upper gloom of the hall.—With the same power of endless growth and self-reproduction did my architecture proceed in dreams. In the early stage of my malady, the splendours of my dreams were indeed chiefly architectural: and I beheld such pomp of cities and palaces as was never yet beheld by the waking eye, unless in the clouds.[4]

A further problem arises when one turns to the *Paradis artificiels* to check Baudelaire's version of the story, for although he translates the lines immediately preceding and following, Baudelaire quite skips over Coleridge's account of Piranesi. This omission or suppression has con-

FIGURE 7.1. G.-B. Piranesi, *Carcere* VII (second state)

tinued to puzzle critics, for the text is surely no less interesting than the surrounding passages that Baudelaire did choose to translate.[5] Another look at De Quincey's text may suggest some reasons for Baudelaire's decision.

De Quincey is looking over Piranesi's famous engravings of Roman antiquity—the equivalent of our glossy coffee table books—when the irrepressible babbler Coleridge intrudes from the sidelines ("standing by") to tell a story. This interruption disrupts De Quincey's quiet perusal in several ways. Coleridge shifts the context from history (*Rome*) to fiction (*Dreams*) (and so it could be said breaking the line of influence from classical antiquity), from the present engravings to a missing set of engravings, and from a visual artifact to a verbal one. Moreover, the story itself concerns disorientation, the delirium of Piranesi's fever. Despite these jarring dislocations, however, Coleridge easily gets De Quincey involved in the narrative. At first De Quincey simply retells Coleridge's story, keeping himself clear of it, but very soon he introduces the second person (and the "you" refers to both De Quincey and the reader of the *Confessions* as they simultaneously receive Coleridge's story); he moves the story up from past to present ("you perceived"/ "you perceive"); he even becomes anxious about the character's fate ("What ever is to become of poor Piranesi. . ."). The status of this narrative with respect to emitter and receiver has fast become unexpectedly unstable, complicating efforts to trace a simple line of influence. De Quincey repeats Coleridge's story to the reader, that is, a repetition of Coleridge repeating Piranesi's story to De Quincey, which is in turn a repetition of Piranesi repeating Piranesi's story to himself.

Or is it? Coleridge's "account" turns out to be no accurate description of Piranesi (if it were even possible to translate a picture accurately into language), but rather a creative misreading of the engravings, adding another fold to the line. First of all, Coleridge calls the etchings *"Dreams"* (a word De Quincey picks up), when Piranesi's actual title was *Carceri d'Invenzione* (*Imaginary Prisons*). While the plates contain numerous figures who seem to be related only by their common plight, Coleridge reads them all as the same person. He also condenses all sixteen plates into one, so that even if De Quincey had them in front of him he could not turn to any one engraving to compare it with Coleridge's account. Most importantly, however, Coleridge identifies the figure in the engravings as the engraver himself, making the story into a parable of the artist: "groping his way upwards was Piranesi himself." Coleridge's narrative thus renders the plates ironic, or rather, compounds the ironies. What the *Carceri* represent to Coleridge is the artist imprisoned in his own design—Piranesi as Daedalus.[6]

What is the nature of an artist's prison? Although Coleridge's account is short, the building he is sketching has infinite dimensions. That is, the description stops but it never ends, leaving off with "unfinished stairs." If the prison is infinite, the topmost visible stair is still a kind of bottom stair, with the "real" top nowhere in sight. In fact, words like "top" and "bottom" lose their meaning, and "Piranesi" could as well be descending into hell as rising into heaven. The word "gloom" hints at that, offering no increase in clarity or illumination such as one normally expects to accompany great ascents.[7] This labyrinthian structure is thus a kind of abyss. In fact, it literally contains an abyss—if anything can be said to "contain" that figure—for "Piranesi" stands "on the very brink of the abyss." More accurately, there is not just one abyss in this text but a potentially infinite number, one at the end of every step. As infinity stretches out in all directions before him, how is the prisoner to know the inside of his prison from the outside? As will become evident, the connection between the texts of Coleridge and Baudelaire is not any bridge over this abyss but is, paradoxically, the abyss itself, the "place" where, despite all the distance between them, Coleridge and Baudelaire come together, for in the abyss near and far are indistinguishable. If etymologically "influence" means a flowing in, the process may not be as benign as it might sound, for it involves, at least in this case, an endless emptying out into the abyss.

This text that "contains" an abyss (*abîme*) is itself a *mise en abîme*, that is, a text composed by doubling and redoubling itself within itself. The labyrinth is not a single structure but one that proliferates itself (*s'abîmer*) endlessly in Piranesi's engraving, and through a series as one engraving repeats itself in another, interrupted by the abyss between plates. It is this self-duplicating power that imprisons the artist: his creations become self-creating and swallow him up. Exactly like Coleridge, Baudelaire reads the story as an ironic parable of creativity. "[D]epuis longtemps [long since]," he says, significantly failing to situate a precise beginning, De Quincey "n'évoque plus les images, mais . . . les images s'offrent à lui, spontanément, despotiquement" (429) ["has ceased to call forth images, and now the images are presenting themselves to him, spontaneously, despotically" (134)].[8] It will become clear that Coleridge's insight into Piranesi and Baudelaire's insight into De Quincey result from their sensing the situation to be uncannily familiar.

So potent is the repetition in the *Carceri* that it cannot be contained within the frame of the engravings (or within the frame of Coleridge's narrative), but moves on to engender a like multiplication in De Quincey: "With the same power of endless growth and self-reproduction did my architecture proceed in dreams." As though he were supplementing "Piranesi" De Quincey takes up—or is compelled to take up—the narrative just where Coleridge leaves off. When "the unfinished stairs and Piranesi both are lost in the upper gloom of the hall" De Quincey extends "Piranesi's" upward trek into the clouds, clouds whose form, like the engravings, are "chiefly architectural." (De Quincey's ascent is of course simultaneously a descent. He introduces the Piranesi anecdote in the first place to exemplify the effect of opium on his dreams, and he describes this dream experience as a fall: "I seemed every night to descend, not metaphorically, but literally to descend, into chasms and sunless abysses, depths below depths, from which it seemed hopeless that I could ever reascend. Nor did I, by waking, feel that I *had* re-ascended" [103].) By projecting his image onto the *Carceri* De Quincey in a sense appropriates Piranesi's construction, but only at the price of being himself imprisoned in it.

As Coleridge's text relates to De Quincey's, so De Quincey's relates —more or less—to Baudelaire's; in other words, the Piranesian imagery exceeds all the authors who wind through it. "—Hélas!" says Baudelaire, "tout est abîme,—action, désir, rêve, / Parole! [Alas, everything is an abyss—action, desire, dream, speech!]." The reason that Baudelaire omits the story of Piranesi, leaving a gap if not an abyss in his adaptation of the *Confessions*, has to do, I think, with the oblique way in which these texts interact. Just as Coleridge provides no simple translation of Piranesi, so Baudelaire does not exactly repeat De Quincey. Although the Piranesi story does not directly figure into the *Paradis artificiels* it does not disappear but gets displaced, leaving its traces elsewhere in Baude-laire. The lacuna in the translation is filled (or, perhaps, "abyssed") by a proliferation of Baudelairean images similar to those De Quincey re-marked. The missing paragraph of the *Confessions* turns out to be the absent center of a nexus of Baudelaire texts that it generates. The center, in other words, is itself an abyss. Like Coleridge's inaccuracies, Baude-laire's omission is curiously faithful to Piranesi. The only way to remain faithful to a Piranesian text, it seems, is by violating it.

I now turn to a rather detailed account of some of these Baudelaire texts, my purpose being not so much to show how a phrase from Cole-ridge eventually works its way into a poem of Baudelaire's as to reveal how Baudelaire necessarily redoubles the doubling image of "Piranesi" in his prison. It is less a case of one writer passing on an image to another than of all three writers enmeshed in a figure from which they cannot escape. The closest Baudelaire comes to telling Coleridge's story is to translate it into his own idiom. Without any mention of Piranesi Baude-laire writes, rather abruptly, "D'étonnantes et monstrueuses architectures se dressaient dans son cerveau, semblables à ces constructions mouvantes que l'oeil du poète aperçoit dans les nuages colorés par le soleil couchant" (428) ["Monstrous, stunning architectures rose in his brain, like those shifting structures that the poet's eye perceives in clouds colored by the setting sun" (133)]. If De Quincey perceives his own dream architecture in Coleridge's story, Baudelaire thinks of the anecdote in terms of a poet. The addition of a sunset to De Quincey's scene is not gratuitous, for by doing so Baudelaire in fact shifts the reference from the *Confessions* to one of his own essays. He has in mind a text written some three years before the *Paradis artificiels*, a rebuttal to the "professeurs-jurés" who had denigrated what they called decadent literature.

Ce soleil qui, il y a quelques heures, ecrasait toutes choses de sa lumière droite et blanche, va bientôt inonder l'horizon occidental de couleurs variées. Dans les jeux de ce soleil agonisant, certains esprits poétiques trouveront des délices nouvelles; ils y découvriront des colonnades éblouissantes, des cascades de métal fondu, des paradis de feu, une splendeur triste, la volupté du regret, toutes les magies du rêve, tous les souvenirs de l'opium.[9]

[The sun which, some hours ago, was shattering everything with its harsh white light, will soon be flooding the western horizon with multifarious colours. In the restless sport of this dying sun certain poetic spirits will discover new delights—dazzling colonnades, cascades of molten metal, fiery paradises, melancholy splendours, the sensuous pleasures of regret, all the magic of dreams, all the memories of opium.][10]

The decadent literature Baudelaire here defends is specifically that of Poe; hence, this description draws Poe into the abyss as well. One could, it seems, articulate the abyss joining Coleridge and Baudelaire by starting with Poe (the abysmal whirlpool in "MS. Found in a Bottle" for example, or "A Descent into the Maelström") as well as with De Quincey. But while Baudelaire seems to cast De Quincey as a kind of Poe figure, similarly caught up in an opiated cloud vision, it could equally well be said that Baudelaire imagines Poe in terms of the De Quincey who listens to Coleridge's story of the *Carceri*, since Baudelaire had a close familiarity with the *Confessions* by the time he wrote this Poe essay. But Baudelaire's portrayal of the "littérature de décadence" describes his own work better than it does either Poe's or De Quincey's. The setting sun drowning the sky with color is found in the *crépusculaire* poems; the colonnades and cascades belong to the imagery of "Rêve parisien"; the setting sun itself figures the dandy in *Le peintre de la vie moderne.*

In the *Paradis artificiels* where one might rightly expect Baudelaire to translate Coleridge's story he does not; conversely, one would less expect to find passages from that story figuring directly in Baudelaire's poetry. But that is exactly what happens. Absent from the *Paradis artificiels*, the story of the Carceri reconstitutes itself and spirals through the *Fleurs du mal* and the *Spleen de Paris*. The endless profusion of staircases appears first, perhaps, in the very early poem "Sur *Le Tasse en prison* d'Eugène Delacroix" (1844). Already Baudelaire depicts an intoxicated poet regarding "l'escalier de vertige où s'abîme son âme [the vertiginous staircase where his soul is swallowed up]," a staircase that forms a *mise en abîme* of the poet's own situation. The same staircase winds through "Rêve parisien," where the speaker calls himself "architecte de mes féeries [architect of my fantasies]." Further, "L'irrémédiable" pictures a "damné descendant sans lampe, / Au bord d'un gouffre [damned man descending without a light, on the brink of the pit]," recalling De Quincey's "standing on the very brink of the abyss." At the brink he comes upon Piranesi's stairs: "un gouffre dont l'odeur / Trahit l'humide profondeur, / D'éternels escaliers sans rampe [a pit whose odor betrays the humid depths of endless stairs without balustrades]." But perhaps the most Piranesian of Baudelaire's poems is the sonnet "Obession," which takes up the theme of painting, of an artist trapped in his own designs: ". . . les ténèbres sont elles-mêmes des toiles / Où vivent, jaillissant de mon oeil par milliers, / Des êtres disparus aux regards familiers [the shadows themselves are canvasses where live, leaping from my eye by thousands, vanished beings with familiar looks]."[11]

The Piranesian imagery I have followed in Baudelaire occurs in Coleridge as well; indeed, as I have indicated, the narration of the *Carceri* can itself be considered a Coleridgean text. Compare, further, the Piranesian abyss in "Kubla Khan," "where Alph, the sacred river, ran / Through caverns measureless to man / Down to a sunless sea . . . that deep romantic chasm," to De Quincey's descent "into chasms and sunless abysses." It could be shown, although not within the scope of this essay, that Baudelaire did know the "Ancient Mariner" and that he interprets the blessing scene in that poem in terms of Piranesi. The "irremediable" descends "endless staircases without balustrades" to encounter the slimy ("visqueux") and phosphorescent watersnakes that flash through the waters around the Mariner's ship. The key poem in this context, however, is "Constancy to an Ideal Object," Coleridge's version of "Obsession." "And art thou nothing?" the speaker asks his absent lover in the closing stanza of the poem.

> Such thou art, as when
> The woodman winding westward up the glen
> At wintry dawn, where o'er the sheep-track's maze
> The viewless snow-mist weaves a glist'ning haze,
> Sees full before him, gliding without tread,
> An image with a glory round its head;
> The enamoured rustic worships its fair hues,
> Nor knows he makes the shadow, he pursues![12]

Here, once again, is the solitary on an endless and hopeless journey through a nebulous labyrinth ("snow-mist . . . maze"), ironically propelled by his own painting upon the shadows. This simile implicates De

Quincey as much as Baudelaire, for it refers to the "Spectre of the Brocken," about which De Quincey likewise wrote. In fact, as Hillis Miller suggests, De Quincey's text on the Spectre forms a kind of repetition of the Piranesi story since both exemplify the frightening multiplication of the self within the self.[13] In face of the phenomenon of doubling on the Brocken, Coleridge and De Quincey double each other. And so, from De Quincey to Baudelaire to Coleridge the staircase thus winds back to De Quincey. In sum, Baudelaire's characterization of De Quincey's images as "despotic" thus applies to his own and to Coleridge's images as well. The artist repeats a figure, but the figure has already been repeating itself, and so inscribing the artist who would inscribe it in his text.

Why is it that the story of Piranesi should articulate such powerful textual energies, compulsively reappearing in so many seemingly unrelated places? What is the nature of its abysmal influence? Assuming for the moment that such questions are apposite or answerable, one could begin by recalling that Piranesi's engravings form a kind of mirror in which Coleridge, Baudelaire, and De Quincey all recognize themselves. But why should that be the case? The context of the story in the *Confessions* may once again offer a hint. De Quincey has been attempting to explain his opium dreams psychologically, in terms of what would today be called hypnagogic visions. Under the influence of opium, he theorizes, one regains the child's power of imagination, the "power of painting, as it were, upon the darkness, all sorts of phantoms," a "command over apparitions" comparable to that of "a Roman centurion over his soldiers" (102). After some commentary on these visions De Quincey proposes an illustration, and here the Roman reappears, bringing with him Piranesi and Coleridge.

De Quincey's story of hypnagogic visions sounds, like so many of these stories, weirdly familiar. It sounds, in fact, very much like what Freud calls the "omnipotence of thought."[14] Perhaps Freud can provide a fuller psychological explanation of these texts than the one De Quincey proposes. The "omnipotence of thought" is the belief that one has only to desire something for that desire to be fulfilled in reality, and it is characteristic, Freud says, of an earlier stage of development, the childhood either of the individual or the race. Nevertheless, even the grown-up retains "certain residues and traces" of the primitive stage through which he has passed.[15] When those traces are "reactivated"—as when De Quincey listens to Coleridge's account of the *Carceri*—the individual experiences the uncanny. In his essay on "The Uncanny" Freud could as easily have used the texts I have cited as Hoffmann's "Sandman" or the "Ring of Polycrates," for they likewise exhibit characteristic traits of the uncanny: the omnipotence of thought, the strange that is yet familiar, the differing repetitions, the repetition compulsion so strong that it can overpower the pleasure principle.

But as many recent commentators point out, Freud's investigation likewise fails to establish the cause of the uncanny. The hierarchies he proposes get subverted, the evidence he musters gives rise to doubts, in short, his hypotheses cannot sustain themselves. The movement of Freud's essay parallels that of De Quincey's, for in each case the inquiry after the cause of the uncanny results only in redoubling uncanny effects. De Quincey's speculations about childhood visions lead to the anecdote of Piranesi, and Freud's scientific text that was to explain the uncanny in literature turns into a kind of (theoretical) fiction, perhaps a twentieth-century version of the story of Piranesi.[16] The most striking moment is a tale that serves as a paradigm of the entire essay, the story of Freud's getting lost as he wanders the deserted streets of an *Italian* (N.B.) town, a labyrinth that is "strange to me" but whose character "could not long remain in doubt."[17] If, as all of these texts suggest, one cannot discover the origin of the uncanny, it is because of the repetition involved. The story of Piranesi, for instance, is always already in progress, even before anyone begins to *re*count, for it is the story of repetition itself, and repetition only occurs when the beginning is already presupposed.

Freud envies the artist's ability to paint phantoms on the darkness, and he privileges art as the only area left in the grown-up world in which the omnipotence of thought still functions.[18] In his view, the artist is free to evoke or dismiss the uncanny. But if Freud's essay implicitly reads De Quincey, Baudelaire, and Coleridge, their texts in turn read his essay and demystify the Freudian image of the artist. If the artist alone retains the power of magic, they would reply, he alone is cursed by it, for the very extent of his power renders him, like Midas, powerless.

De Quincey's account of his architectural dreams is incomplete as I have cited it. I have reserved the end of the paragraph on Piranesi until now in part because the closing usefully demonstrates the complexity of the literary historical questions that have arisen. After telling the reader that the pomp of his dream cities had never been equalled "unless in the clouds," De Quincey offers an example of cloud architecture from Wordsworth's "Solitary."

From a great modern poet I cite part of a passage which describes, as an appearance actually beheld in the clouds, what in many of its circumstances I saw frequently in sleep:

> The appearance, instanteously disclosed,
> Was of a mighty city—boldly say
> A wilderness of building, sinking far

And self-withdrawn into a wondrous depth,
Far sinking into splendour—without end!
Fabric it seem'd of diamond, and of gold,
With alabaster domes, and silver spires,
And blazing terrace upon terrace, high
Uplifted; here, serene pavilions bright
In avenues disposed; there towers begirt
With battlements that on their restless fronts
Bore stars—illumination of all gems!
By earthly nature had the effect been wrought
Upon the dark materials of the storm
Now pacified: on them, and on the coves,
And mountain-steeps and summits, whereunto
The vapours had receded,—taking there
Their station under a cerulean sky, etc. etc. (106–7)

It is easy to see why at this point in his story De Quincey should think of the passage from *The Excursion* (II, 834–51), for Wordsworth's construction seems to repeat "Piranesi's." Like De Quincey the Solitary explicitly locates the source of the vision in a projecting imagination. The scene wrought by the mind contains all the familiar—or uncanny— elements: the multiplication "without end" of "terrace upon terrace," the resulting vertiginous disorientation of clouds "sinking" upwards "into a wondrous depth," the corresponding syntactic inversions "sinking far"/ "Far sinking," and so on. For all the Piranesian features of this text, however, it hardly resembles Piranesi's *Dreams* or what De Quincey saw in sleep. De Quincey's visions are dark, like the "gloom" in which "Piranesi" is lost at the end of the hall, but the Solitary transforms the "dark materials of the storm" into "serene pavilions bright." While 'Piranesi's' structure is a prison, the Solitary's is spacious and airy. In other words, De Quincey is mastered by his images while the Solitary, no idle cloud gazer, masters his; he even "pacifies" the storm. Thus De Quincey fears his imagination will make him a Midas, "for, as Midas turned all things to gold, that yet baffled his hopes and defrauded his human desires, so whatsoever things capable of being visually repre- sented I did but think of in the darkness, immediately shaped themselves into phantoms of the eye. . ." (103). The Solitary, by contrast, takes on the role of Midas, turning the "materials of the storm" into diamonds and gold, and does so not simply willingly but with bravura: "boldly say." Taken on its own the *Excursion* passage is dazzling, but set against the background of Baudelaire's and De Quincey's texts, it becomes quite phenomenal that Wordsworth's narrator never yields to the terror of vision.

What distinguishes Wordsworth's imaginative situation from the other writers' so that he can carry off this virtuoso performance? How does the Solitary negotiate "that profound abyss" (II, 373), the valley he inhabits? The vision continues on for another twenty-four lines past De Quincey's citation, but then it ends abruptly in mid-line, as the language loses all its strength:

> —"I have been dead," I cried,
> "And now I live! Oh! wherefore *do* I live?"
> And with that pang I prayed to be no more!"— (875–7)

In other words, the vision was available only when the speaker was in some imaginative sense detached from earthly existence. (The "time" of this vision is likewise divorced from that of the rest of Book II. As with the apostrophe to the Imagination in the sixth Book of *The Prelude*, the Solitary experiences this vision at the moment of narrating it, and the vision disrupts the story he has been recounting: "—But I forget our Charge, as utterly / I forgot him . . ." [878–9].) The return to life, and to the tale of the "Old Man," seems to necessitate the loss of vision, which is why the Solitary expresses the desire to "be no more." This attempt to situate oneself imaginatively beyond human life is a common one in Wordsworth, as in the cancelled stanza of the "Immortality Ode," where he pictures himself already in the grave.[19]

It is the inscription of "death" that marks Wordsworth's text as different from those of Coleridge, Baudelaire, or De Quincey. According to De Quincey's hypothesis, the imaginative act involves a two-part process: first, the painting of visions on the darkness, which is expansive and liberating, but second the inevitable return of those visions to plague and imprison the artist. (The disarticulation of before and after that occurs in the uncanny renders suspect De Quincey's essentially temporal scheme. It may well be that the childhood phase of freedom is a golden age that originates only after the fact in the prisoner's desire. Perhaps De Quincey's imagination has always been a kind of prison.) For Wordsworth's Solitary there is no question of escape by an imaginative return to childhood or by dreams. His vision is "beyond" anything available to either the waking or the dreaming subject (832–33). If the Solitary is free, it is rather because he is "dead," and hence detached from the self. This is crucial because as Coleridge, Baudelaire, and De Quincey all discover, *any* self will necessarily get trapped in the labyrinth. (But is the narrator any longer the Solitary? is he a "he" at all?) To be dead is to be one with one's spectral double, to be nothing other than the process of doubling itself. In this context it is worth noting that the voice of the vision never realizes it is dead, but discovers its own death only *après coup*, only after the vision. In fact, the loss of vision is inseparable from the discovery of death, for that realization reconstitutes the self as that which is conscious of having been dead. Alone among the artists in the labyrinth, then, Wordsworth seems to have the creative freedom Freud desires, but like the others, he too pays a price Freud does not bargain for.

If the narrator in this passage is "dead," it is necessary to amend my earlier remarks about his mastery, for there is no longer any question of a subject either controlling or being controlled. If there is no subject, it is impossible to read the lines "By earthly nature had the effect been wrought / Upon the dark materials of the storm" as the projection of the subject's imagination upon objects, the way Coleridge seems to treat the "*stranger*" in "Frost at Midnight," for instance. The Solitary's vision is "unimaginable" in that sense (852). "By *earthly* nature" must then be read literally, as referring to the earth itself, the place where the subject has already been "Rolled round in earth's diurnal course, / With rocks, and stones, and trees" ("A Slumber did my Spirit Seal"). Further, this earth cannot be separated from the sky, for the vision welds together "Clouds of all tincture [sky], rocks [earth] and sapphire sky [the two conjoined], / Confused, commingled, mutually inflamed, / Molten together . . ." (854–56).[20] What "wrought the effect" is hence indistinguishable from what the effect was wrought upon: "self-with [-] drawn"—not drawn by a detached self. If the subject is absent from this passage, so are any stable objects: nature is culture ("a wilderness of buildings"), water ("Clouds, mists, streams") is fire ("blazing," "inflammed"), the dissolution of form ("Confused, commingled . . . / Molten together") is the creation of form ("composing thus, / Each lost in each, that marvellous array / Of temple, palace, citadel . . ."), etc. Nor, finally, does the text leave the opposition life/death intact, as I may have implied. The Solitary's condition is not death so much as it is Death-in-Life, a "condition" so sublime that life itself is seen in retrospect to be a Life-in-Death.

By explicitly associating the Piranesi anecdote with Wordsworth's poetry De Quincey suggests the possibility of reading Coleridge's story about the engravings as an allegory of literature—a hint I have taken up throughout this essay as I traced the journey of Piranesi not through his plates but through the texts of De Quincey, Baudelaire, Coleridge, and Wordsworth.[21] Wordsworth likewise associates the labyrinth with language, for some one hundred lines before the passage cited in the *Confessions* he had identified the elements of the scene, "The mist, the shadows, light of golden suns . . .," as "A language not unwelcome to sick hearts / And Idle spirits . . ." (713–17). His vision can thus be seen as a manipulation of (or by) these linguistic signs.

Baudelaire is no exception to this allegorizing tendency, and one of his poetic labyrinths is particularly relevant here. He refers to the Piranesian structure in "Rêve parisien" as a "*Babel* d'escaliers."[22] This image makes one pause to ask whether Piranesi did not have the Tower of Babel in mind all along in his design of a tower with spiral staircases extending infinitely into the sky, and represented in the universal language of pictures. De Quincey would thus come after Babel. For him the Tower is already destroyed, leaving a multiplicity of languages in its wake. The fragments of the Tower scattered or disseminated everywhere are the texts I have followed, each text resembling a broken piece of a holograph, still retaining a multidimensional image of the original. The abyss, in other words, becomes all the more abysmal in its dispersal. The "phantoms" that De Quincey "painted upon the darkness" are thus linguistic constructions which represent not so much the omnipotence of thought as the omnipotence of texts. The terror comes less from encountering a projection of the self than from being haunted by one's language.[23]

In the story of Piranesi the line of influence is abyssed into a labyrinth, inweaving those who weave it. Let me in closing reiterate three points at which causal explanations fail to account adequately for the Piranesian relationships among Coleridge, De Quincey, Baudelaire, and Wordsworth.

(1) The beginning, the narrative of Piranesi's engravings, has no true beginning because it is itself already the story of the story of endless redoublings. Having no identifiable origin, that story could, in principle, begin anywhere. But each beginning is also different, because there is always a curious slippage between the various retellings of the story.

(2) As has perhaps already occurred to the reader, there is no way to determine the author of the Piranesi story, even in the strict sense of that term. Although De Quincey says that his knowledge of the engravings comes solely from Coleridge's account, it is impossible to tell whether the narrative as he prints it is an accurate report of Coleridge's words, or whether his memory worked further displacements on Coleridge's displaced story of displacement. All of my references to "Coleridge's narrative" must therefore be taken figuratively. How can one draw a line of influence from father to son if no paternity can be established, if all the prisoners in the labyrinth are sons?

(3) De Quincey introduces "Coleridge's" account as if to describe the genesis of his own architectural dreams, but there is no indication that De Quincey was in fact influenced by that account. Despite the similarities, his reveries may well have begun long before Coleridge ever mentioned Piranesi to him. As he says, "the splendours of my dreams were *indeed* chiefly architectural"—the "indeed" hinting more at uncanny coincidence than at cause.[24] But how is one to write a literary history of these intertwinings, a history that moves beyond the comfort-

ing stability of a straightforward genealogy like "Coleridge influenced
De Quincey who in turn influenced Baudelaire," and the reassuring
categories of cause and effect? Where is the Ariadne who will lead us out
of Piranesi's labyrinth?

As a figure for influence, the abyss or the labyrinth resists easy
categorization. The interminable, twisted repetitions create a sense of
vertiginous monotony (as Baudelaire calls it) that unhinges the dimensions of time as well as space.[25] If every step is like every other, how can
the Piranesian traveller tell how long he has been moving, or how far he
has come or gone? His dizziness turns the Tower of Babel upside down
or inside out, so that it becomes an abyss from which there is no escap-
ing. As De Quincey stands listening to Coleridge's story he finds that he
is already inside it, imbedded in a narrative that is new and yet familiar.

But if there is no being outside Piranesi's figure, so conversely the
inside of his prison may be paradoxically spacious. The closed, private
space of his phantoms is so open and transparent that De Quincey,
Baudelaire, and Coleridge all see themselves within it. (It is not accidental that Piranesi drew on a public image, the baroque stage sets of
Venetian opera houses, to represent his most personal visions.) The
prison is liberating in that while it haunts these artists it likewise releases
astounding energies. The figure I have been tracing, the figure that has
ensnared me, is thus at once a vast gothic prison and a palace of airy
pavilions and alabaster domes.

NOTES

1. See for example Henri Peyre: "Baudelaire lui-même devait . . . quelque
chose à diverses déclarations de Poe, lui-même familier avec quelques affirm-
ations de Coleridge . . ." (Qu'est-ce que le symbolisme? [Paris: Presses universitaires de France, 1974], p. 51). Or René Wellek: "Coleridge was the main
source . . . for Poe, and thus indirectly for the French symbolists" (A History
of Modern Criticism: 1750–1950 [New Haven: Yale University Press, 1955],
vol. II, p. 157). M. H. Abrams criticizes the Coleridge/Baudelaire filiation,
however, in "Coleridge, Baudelaire, and Modernist Poetics" in Immanente
Ästhetische: Ästhetische Reflexion, ed. Wolfgang Iser (Munich: W. Fink,
1966), pp. 113–38, as does Margery Sabin in English Romanticism and the
French Tradition (Cambridge: Harvard University Press, 1976), pp. 181–234.

2. For examples of unidirectional studies of influence, see the theoretical
summaries of J. T. Shaw, "Literary Indebtedness and Comparative Literature
Studies," in Comparative Literature: Method and Perspective, ed. H. Frenz
and N. A. Stallknecht (Carbondale: Southern Illinois University Press, 1971),
or Ulrich Weisstein, Comparative Literature and Literary Theory (Blooming-
ton: Indiana University Press, 1973). Two notable exceptions are Ihab
Hassan, "The Problem of Influence in Literary History," Journal of Aesthetics
and Art Criticism 14 (1955): 66–76, and Claudio Guillén, "The Aesthetics of
Literary Influence," in Literature as System (Princeton, N.J.: Princeton Uni-

versity Press, 1971). By narrowing the question of influence to "father/son" relations, Harold Bloom and Leslie Brisman made an advance on most earlier influence studies by showing that the relation of sons to fathers may, perhaps must, be ungracious and subversive—"ce qui ne revient pas au père." Nevertheless, by treating the influence of Milton on the Romantics, say, or of Emerson on Stevens, Bloom and Brisman accede to the fundamental critical assumption that influence is a one-way street. By contrast, Jorge Luis Borges, like T. S. Eliot in "Tradition and the Individual Talent," makes a decisive break with all of these critics by shifting the emphasis from writer to reader and asking how we will read *Don Quixote* if it was written by Pierre Meynard? But Borges's approach does not exhaust the varieties of influence even by generalizing that concept to include influence on the reader, for, although he reverses its direction, he still describes a line.

3. On "lines" of narrative and the labyrinth see J. Hillis Miller, "Ariadne's Thread: Repetition and the Narrative Line," *Critical Inquiry* 3 (1976): 57–77.

4. *Confessions of an English Opium Eater* (Baltimore: Penguin, 1971), pp. 105–6. Future references will be to this edition and will be incorporated in the text.

5. See Henri Focillon: "Baudelaire n'a pas cru devoir conserver ce passage dans son adaptation, ce qui est assez surprennant de la part de l'auteur des *Curiosités esthétiques*" (*G.-B. Piranesi* [Paris: Librarie Renouard, 1918], p. 302). See also Luzius Keller: "D'autant plus grande est notre surprise de voir le traducteur passe sous silence la page étonnante de De Quincey, comme si l'image de l'escalier piranesien n'était pas digne de figurer dans sa traduction" (*Piranesi et les romantiques français* [Paris: J. Corti, 1966], p. 201). The word "digne" arouses suspicion, for what writer was less concerned to uphold traditional standards of literary decorum than Baudelaire?

6. Baudelaire is sensitive to the mythological implications of Coleridge's account, and four or five pages after the Piranesi story he applies the same myth to De Quincey: "la manière subtile, ingénieuse, par laquelle l'infortuné sort du labyrinthe enchanté . . . ," "Un mangeur d'opium," in *Oeuvres complètes*, ed. Y.-G. Le Dantec and Claude Pichois (Paris: Gallimard, 1961), p. 436. Further references to this edition will be given in the text.

7. With reference to De Quincey's visions, Baudelaire makes this confusion in directions explicit. He pictures De Quncey "montant à des *hauteurs* inconnues et s'enfonçant dans d'immenses *profondeurs* . . ." (p. 428, my italics) ["rising to unknown heights and plunging to enormous depths," *Artificial Paradise*, trans. Ellen Fox (New York: Herder, 1971), p. 133]. Further references to this translation, which I have modified slightly throughout, will be given in the text.

On "the danger of [the artist] ascend[ing] beyond his own limits into a place from which he can no longer descend," an ascent that is in fact "an upward fall," see Paul de Man, "Ludwig Binswanger and the Sublimation of the Self," in *Blindness and Insight* (New York: Oxford University Press, 1971), pp. 46–50.

8. One might object that the control Baudelaire refers to is that which opium exercises over the opium eater, but opium, "eloquent opium" as De Quincey calls it, is itself an ironic kind of inspiraton, whose control manifests itself in the production of images, whether visual or verbal.

9. "Notes nouvelles sur Edgar Poe," in *L'art romantique*, ed. Henri Lemaitre (Paris: Garnier, 1962), p. 620.

10. "Further Notes on Edgar Poe," in *The Painter of Modern Life and Other Essays*, ed. and trans. Jonathan Mayne (New York: Phaidon, 1965), p. 94.

11. Compare "Je suis comme un peintre qu'un Dieu moqueur / Condamne à peindre, hélas! sur les ténèbres. . . [I am like a painter whom a mocking God condemns to paint—alas—on the shadows]" ("Les ténèbres"). Among other examples, one could cite "Le port": "l'architecture mobile des nuages [the moving architecture of clouds] and "Le voyage," which recalls De Quincey's rhetorical construction. De Quincey: "I beheld such pomp of cities and palaces as was never yet beheld by the waking eye, unless in the clouds." Baudelaire: "Les plus riches cités, les plus grands paysages, / Jamais ne contenaient l'attrait mystérieux / De ce que le hasard fait avec les nuages [The wealthiest cities, the greatest landscapes never held the mysterious attraction of chance playing with the clouds]." Indeed, Keller calls the "architecture" of the *Fleurs du mal* Piranesian as a whole (*Piranesi et les romantiques français*, p. 202). Beyond Baudelaire, to confine the range to nineteenth-century French literature simply, Keller finds Piranesian echoes extending backwards and forwards to Balzac, Gautier, Hugo, Mallarmé, Musset.

12. See Coleridge's depiction of the abyss in "Limbo" and "Ne Plus Ultra."

13. *The Disappearance of God* (Cambridge, Mass.: Harvard University Press, 1963), p. 68.

14. The principle references, all to the *Standard Edition*, ed. James Strachey (London: Hogarth Press, 1955), are in "Notes upon a Case of Obsessional *Neurosis*," 10:233–5; *Totem and Taboo*, 13:85–90; and "The Uncanny," 17:238–41, 247–48.

For another perspective on the question of repetition in the context of art work, see Walter Benjamin, "The Work of Art in the Age of Mechanical Reproduction," in *Illuminations*, ed. Hannah Arendt, trans. Harry Zohn (New York: Schocken, 1969), pp. 217–51. All of the texts I cite belong to this "Age of Mechanical Reproduction"; in fact, Benjamin mentions engraving as an early form of such dissemination (p. 219).

15. 17:240. Compare De Quincey: ". . . of this, at least, I feel assured, that there is no such thing as *forgetting* possible to the mind . . . the inscription remains for ever . . ." (p. 104).

16. See Hélène Cixous, "La fiction et ses fantômes. Une lecteur de l'*Unheimliche* de Freud," *Poétique* 10 (1972): 199–216.

17. Freud, 17:237.

18. Freud, 18:90.

19. I am indebted for this insight to Earl R. Wasserman.

Space does not permit me to bring into play the repeated stories of death and burials in Book II that form the context for the passage De Quincey cites, but it should be noted that the Solitary's "death" is a displacement or a doubling of the Old Man's death, narrated both before and after the vision. On the Solitary as a figure of death, see Geoffrey Hartman, *Wordsworth's Poetry, 1787–1814* (New Haven: Yale University Press, 1964), p. 307. But the *Excursion* passage is not a case of "death by vision" as Hartman suggests (p. 309); if anything, as I shall show, it is one of vision by death.

20. These lines reflect the etymology of "cloud": "Middle English *cloud*, hill, mass of earth, cloud, Old English *clūd*, rock, hill" (*The American Heritage Dictionary of the English Language* [1969], s.v. "cloud").

21. See also De Quincey's comparison of his dream phantoms to "writings in sympathetic ink" (103).

22. An interesting slip in Baudelaire's translation of the *Confessions* reveals an appropriate confusion between architectural and linguistic constructions. When De Quincey speaks of "friezes of never-ending stories drawn from times before Oedipus or Priam" Baudelaire translates "d'interminables bâtiments [interminable buildings]" (426). ("interminable buildings"). (The error is noted by Fox, *Artificial Paradise*, p. 131 n.)

23. Freud lkewise builds (and destroys) a Tower of Babel with the polylinguistic dictionary that opens the essay on the uncanny. This Tower is perhaps a displacement of Hoffmann's tower that Freud mentions a few pages later. (Cixous reads Hoffmann as Freud's double ["La fiction et ses fantômes," p. 211].)

24. Coincidence similarly displaces cause in the De Quincey/Wordsworth relationship. Although De Quincey considers the writing of *The Excursion* and his own dreams to have occurred independently of each other, Wordsworth is uncannily able to describe "what . . . I saw frequently in sleep." The sentence following the passage I have cited sums up the dilemma. "The sublime circumstance—'battlements that on their *restless* fronts bore stars,'—might have been copied from my architectural dreams, for it often occurred" (De Quincey's italics). (This is the only point in Wordsworth's passage that resembles De Quincey, the only "restlessness" in a vision that dismantles the opposition between stasis and motion.) One is confronted with the hard (or soft) fact that circumstances Wordsworth portrays "often occurred" in De Quincey's dreams without any explanation of how this came to be. In place of a genuine cause De Quincey can only offer the fiction of a "might have been."

Some eighteen years later, in his *Tait's Magazine* essay on Wordsworth, De Quincey recalls a similar coincidence. He tells how the sight of a familiar landscape was altered by a fortuitous interpenetration of mist and sunlight so that the scene was "absolutely transfigured, it was seen under lights and mighty shadows that made it no less marvellous to the eye than that memorable creation amongst the clouds and azure sky, which is described by the Solitary in 'The Excursion.'" "Wordsworth," in *Recollections of the Lakes and the Lake Poets*, ed. David Wright (Baltimore: Penguin, 1970), p. 165, n. 1.

25. De Quincey: "Space swelled, and was amplified to an extent of unutterable infinity. This, however, did not disturb me so much as the vast expansions of time . . ." (103–4.). For the whole question of the artist in the labyrinth see Richard Macksey, "The Artist in the Labyrinth: Design or *Dasein*," *MLN* 77 (1962): 239–56.

NOTES ON CONTRIBUTORS

MICHAEL FRIED is professor of humanities and history of art at The Johns Hopkins University. Starting in the late 1960s with his work on Manet, he has been developing an account of a central problematic in French painting between the middle of the eighteenth century and the advent of Impressionism. Recently he completed *Absorption and Theatricality: Painting and Beholder in the Age of Diderot* (University of California Press); the essay on Courbet in this issue will form part of a longer study of that painter.

PHILIPPE LACOUE-LABARTHE, who teaches philosophy at the University of Strasbourg, has written on Freud, Nietzsche, Heidegger, and German Romanticism. He recently translated Hölderlin's version of Sophocles' *Antigone* into French and collaborated on its production by the Théâtre National de Strasbourg.

RICHARD A. LADEN teaches French literature at the University of Minnesota. His article on la Comtesse de Sigur appeared in *MLN*, and he is currently working on a mongraph about metanarrative texts constructed like jokes, particularly Louis Forton's *La Bande des Pieds Nickelés*. Another article on Saint-John Perse and his translations of the poetry of Denis Rigal have also been published.

Notes on Contributors

ARDEN REED teaches English and comparative literature at Wayne State University. He has written on Kant's and Nietzsche's theories of art and is completing a book on figurative language in Coleridge and Baudelaire, of which his present essay in *Glyph* forms the "Interchapter."

PEGGY MEYER SHERRY has written on Kleist translation, on literary criticism in the GDR, and on the early Brecht. She has taught in the comparative literature program at Hobart and William Smith Colleges in Geneva, New York and is now a lecturer in German and comparative literature at the University of California, Riverside.

HENRY SUSSMAN teaches in the comparative literature program at SUNY-Buffalo. His first book, *Franz Kafka: Geometrician of Metaphor*, will be published in 1978 by Coda Press.

SAMUEL WEBER teaches in the Humanities Center of The Johns Hopkins University. His *Unwrapping Balzac* will be published by the University of Toronto Press.